Straight Talk about AD/HD

William K. Wilkinson, a Galway-based educational psychologist, operates an independent practice specialising in the assessment and treatment of learning and behavioural problems. Specific areas of interest are AD/HD and dyslexia. A graduate of Northern Arizona University and San Diego State University, he completed his doctoral work at John Hopkins University, Baltimore, MD, USA.

Straight Talk about AD/HD

A Guide to Attention Deficit/Hyperactivity
Disorder for Irish Parents and Professionals

William K. Wilkinson

The Collins Press

Published in 2003 by
The Collins Press
West Link Park,
Doughcloyne,
Wilton,
Cork

British Library Cataloguing in Publication data.

Printed in the Ireland by ColourBooks Ltd

Typesetting by The Collins Press

ISBN: 1-903464-32-3

TABLE OF CONTENTS

For Mary –
for everything

PREFACE

In most families, parents can identify one child who is more difficult to manage compared to his or her siblings. Why? How is it
that children show such different behaviour patterns when reared
in similar environments – same parents doing the same thing in
the same house?

Teachers can usually identify one or two children in each class
who are 'difficult'. Despite their best teaching practice, this small
minority of children will behave in a perturbing fashion – they
will not complete school work, do not seem to be listening during
instruction, are easily distracted, may be out of their seat often,
and generally require a great deal of teacher attention. Why is this
so if the setting for each child is relatively similar? The most common response to this question is that all children are different –
some have more 'challenging personalities' while others behave
within normal limits. These 'hard to manage' children usually
struggle at school, frequently test adult limits, and require more
adult attention compared to other children. Closer inspection
may show long-standing inattention, impulsivity, and overactivity. For these children, it is reasonable to suspect Attention
Deficit/Hyperactivity Disorder (AD/HD), also known as
Attention Deficit Disorder, and sometimes referred to as
Hyperkinetic Disorder (depending on which side of the Atlantic
one lives). Attention Deficit (AD) and Hyperactivity (HD) are two
problems in one, which explains the forbidding term and the
backslash – Attention Deficit (AD)/Hyperactivity (HD).

The interest AD/HD evokes is remarkable. I doubt that all
other childhood difficulties combined have generated the prolonged and intensive scrutiny given AD/HD. The amount of
research pertaining to it appears to be more numerous of late and
of far greater quantity compared with other learning and behaviour difficulties. Also, the media have taken the AD/HD topic to
task as noted by the large number of articles in the popular press

(mainly in the United States but on the rise in Europe). Why the fascination?

Despite all the interest, scholarly and otherwise, AD/HD remains an elusive disorder. Recently, an expert panel found that there was no clear cause of AD/HD, no test to identify it, and no clear guidelines for treatment. In other words, it was concluded that little is known about the what, why, or how to assist those with AD/HD. The panel recommended further study of AD/HD. At first glance, this suggestion seems at odds with the ever increasing research and public debate about attention problems and hyperactivity. Yet, that is the nature of the problem–AD/HD defies precise specification. It seems that the more focus given it, the more vague it becomes.

Take the issue of cause. Are children born with AD/HD or do parents make them so? Some view AD/HD as a medical disorder caused by certain neurochemical abnormalities. Yet there are many books which totally disregard medical treatments which purportedly correct AD/HD-type problems. These authors believe that a different parenting approach is what is needed. If this is the case, there is a tacit assumption that parents are major contributors to their child's behaviour and learning problems. Also, some view attention and hyperactivity as largely a symptom of our fast-paced, highly strung culture. Further still, there are some who believe that ADD is really Male Deficit Disorder, since the occurrence of the problem runs nine times greater in boys than girls. This approach ties into cultural factors, in that AD/HD is not so much a disorder as a basic societal problem in the way we perceive and relate to boys.

Perhaps the most controversial issue is that of treatment. A tremendous amount of research shows that the single most effective treatment of AD/HD is psycho-stimulant medication (the most commonly used medication is Ritalin). This medication improves concentration, productivity, and reduces activity and distractibility. All medications have side effects and Ritalin is no different. But it is not just the side effects of Ritalin which create controversy. There are far wider implications about which children should and should not receive medication. Some professionals are quick to diagnose and prescribe medication and when this happens, more appropriate treatments may be overlooked. Another mistake is the failure to detect AD/HD, perhaps because of professional belief that AD/HD does not exist. In these cases, children receive ineffective treatments, while missing out on interventions which could lead to dramatic improvements. There is also the question of responsibility. Some argue that medication takes the ownership of behaviour change out of the hands of children and adults, and places it in a pill.

Finally, there are professional obstacles which hinder services to children with AD/HD. There are professional divides as to which specialties are needed in the assessment of AD/HD. Is psychiatric opinion alone sufficient? Is psychological assessment adequate? What other professions, both medical and otherwise, should be involved in an assessment of AD/HD? There are also differences in procedure, such that certain professional assessments of AD/HD rely entirely on parent report, even though teacher input is essential.

Despite these fundamental difficulties, there are some certain general facts. We know there are children who, despite adequate parenting and not for lack of appropriate stimulation, present with difficult behaviour. In some cases, these children are described as giddy, lack persistence, tire quickly of mental activities, leave tasks unfinished, frequently interrupt others, and are very active. This cluster of behaviour is known as AD/HD. While the cause is not entirely understood, there are clear linkages with certain brain chemicals which control attention and regulate activity and impulse control. The problem behaviours associated with AD/HD can be improved but only after a complete assessment.

This book precedes from these basic principles. Information is packaged so the reader can (a) understand AD/HD in general, and the AD and HD components separately; (b) learn of the many diagnoses which overlap and may supercede AD/HD (c) identify causes and contributing factors, (d) glean the components of an AD/HD assessment, (e) learn of validated treatment programmes, and (f) know of the most prominent issues and controversies.

I wish to make this book concise and readable for an audience who is assumed to have no prior knowledge of AD/HD. Some books on AD/HD provide a new slant on the problem, or focus on a particular controversy. As this is an overview for the novice, it would be inconsistent with the purpose of this book to focus on a particular issue. Being a 'realist' my desire is to cast AD/HD in a 'realistic' perspective, neither exhorting the condition as a panacea, nor downgrading it to the misguided beliefs of a small group of parents. Some children have a bonafide attention deficit and/or are hyperactive, and it is vital that we accept, identify, and treat these problems. The consequences of overlooking AD/HD are enormous. Adults and children may be unnecessarily suffering in the absence of information about AD/HD. Equally frustrating is the amount of misinformation about AD/HD. For example, one of the most common misconceptions is that children 'grow out' of inattention and hyperactivity. It is hoped that the material contained herein will help alleviate misunderstandings and assist those who truly suffer from AD/HD.

By the same token, it is equally deplorable that AD/HD can be promoted as the answer to most childhood problems. In some cases, it seems that an informed public may self-diagnose the condition, and then find it disappointing, after consultation with a prudent clinician, that there is another more significant problem. Subsequently, the consumer may look for validation from a professional who may call anything AD/HD. Inevitably, all parties are satisfied and content. Yet, by not recognising the importance of other relevant conditions, one can recommend treatments for the wrong problem and therefore miss treating the 'right' problem. A balanced and realistic view of AD/HD will assist the reader in making the most informed judgements. That is the major goal of this book.

WILLIAM WILLKINSON
JANUARY 2003

Chapter 1

AN OVERVIEW OF AD/HD

Attention Deficit/Hyperactivity Disorder (AD/HD) is a very
unappealing name, having the unfortunate combination of Deficit
and Disorder. My guess is that most people, upon initial glance,
will take AD/HD to be a highly specialised, technical and medical
topic.

However, AD/HD is an extremely relevant topic at the start of
the millennium. It is a controversial subject and more enigmatic
than the title suggests. When you come to the conclusion of this
book, you will understand that AD/HD relates to most aspects of
life – health, child-rearing, family process, education, culture and
politics. You will also realise that there is no precise definition of
AD/HD, no known cause and great debate about how to intervene.

If any issue in the health professions needs public attention
AD/HD is the one. Learning about AD/HD is important simply
for understanding this common but often misunderstood topic.
But there is more to disseminating information about it. There is
the need to think reflectively about the many issues related to
AD/HD. Some of these issues are fundamental to all our lives.
Take one of the most complex – what causes AD/HD? Are chil-
dren born with AD/HD, or do parents create children with
AD/HD? Is our present Western culture, with its emphasis on
speed and stress, causing AD/HD? Or is AD/HD a biological,

brain-based disorder? If you read between the lines, the more complex issue is what is the basis for children's behaviour?

This is why we need to bring AD/HD to the public forum. It is a topic steeped in our attitudes about behaviour and the larger cultural context in which behaviour occurs. By discussing AD/HD, we can debate, dialogue, and develop an improved understanding of our personal views about these issues.

WHAT'S IN A NAME?

The exact origins of AD/HD are unknown but a reasonable starting point is Phineas Gage. Gage had worked with dynamite circa 1860, when an accidental explosion sent a metre-long tampering rod through the front of his skull. Amazingly he survived, but the accident resulted in significant changes in his personality. Previous to the accident, he was persistent, energetic, and intelligent. Subsequently, he was described as 'irreverent, impatient, obstinate, vacillating, and devising many plans but never finishing them'. Some of these symptoms are related to the modern-day version of AD/HD. It also represents the first indication of the brain areas which relate to planning, control of behaviour and concentration.

In the early twentieth century we learned of Fidgety Phil, made famous in the following poem:

'Let me see if Philip can
Be a little gentleman;
Let me see if he is able
To sit still for once at the table.'
Thus Papa bade Phil behave:
And Mama looked very grave.
But Fidgety Phil,
He won't sit still;
He wriggles,
And giggles,
And then, I declare,

Swings backwards and forwards,
And tilts up his chair,
Just like any rocking horse –
'Philip! I am getting cross!'
See the naughty, restless child
Growing still more rude and wild,
Till his chair falls over quite.
Philip screams with all his might,
Catches at the cloth, but then
That makes matters worse again.
Down upon the ground they fall,
Glasses, plates, knives, forks and all.
How Mama did fret and frown,
When she saw them tumbling down!
And Papa made such a face!
Philip is in sad disgrace ...

This verse was published in a medical journal, *Lancet*, in 1904. Some feel this is the first reported case of AD/HD.

Around this time, medical professionals were noting a theme which described the behaviour of a certain group of children. The children were described as lawless, spiteful and lacking in behaviour control, despite competent parenting and reasonably 'good environments'. Yet, no 'name' for these children was advanced.

In the 1930s, a classic example of scientific 'serendipity' occurred. A physician discovered, by accident, that stimulant medication effectively reduced problems like lack of self-control and inability to concentrate. This finding crystallised the notion that the behaviour difficulties were organic (brain based) and led to the first of many names given AD/HD – Minimal Brain Dysfunction.

In the 1950s new stimulant medications were used and the name Minimal Brain Dysfunction gave way to that of 'Hyperkinetic Syndrome'. Until recently, the term 'Hyperkinetic Syndrome' remained the technical title for AD/HD in Europe.

Thus, the European perspective focused mainly on the hyperactive element (HD) but not the AD component. This is now under review.

In the early 1970s, the American psychiatric classification system introduced the term 'Attention Deficit Disorder' or ADD for short. The syndrome described continued to focus on the hyperactive element.

During the 1980s (and continuing to the present) there was an unprecedented explosion of research and public interest in ADD. The result of this increased scrutiny was the introduction of the term 'Attention Deficit/Hyperactivity Disorder – AD/HD'. The title AD/HD does not normally have a slash between the AD and HD, but I use it as a standard convention to make it clear that AD/HD is really two problems in one title. The AD and HD represent different conditions.

So what's in a name? The term AD/HD is quite revealing. First, its history is deeply rooted in the medical tradition: symptom ▶ diagnosis ▶ cause ▶ treatment. The cause is related to specific brain areas which control attention and goal-directed behaviour (as Phineas Gage's case made clear). The use of medication as a primary treatment method also solidifies AD/HD in the medical domain.

Perhaps a more subtle implication is that the AD/HD name has changed far more frequently when compared with other learning and behavioural problems. Specific learning difficulty (aka dyslexia) is a relatively stable title. So too is depression, autism, epilepsy, vision impairment, etc. To me, this presents a fundamental difficulty with AD/HD – it remains largely an enigma despite the great research and public focus given it.

I do not like the present title and look forward to future revision. Experts now believe that AD is completely separate from HD and we may see the two as separate classifications. I also do not like the terms 'deficit' or 'disorder'. My preference for AD is 'Attention Difficulty, 'Attention Weakness' or 'Inattentiveness'. As for HD, I would rename this 'Over-Activity' or 'Lack of

Behaviour Control'.

AD/HD – An introduction by example

The following case history is used to describe AD/HD. While there are many variations of Steven's profile, his is the 'prototype' situation. The behaviours he displays illustrate the types of concerns parents may report.

Steven is a seven-year-old boy, who, according to his parents, finds academic work difficult. At home, he never initiates school work. When asked to get started on his homework this request is met with resistance (e.g., 'just a minute'.) More often than not, he has left his school materials at school, or lost them altogether. When he eventually starts his homework, he is not fully engaged. He may fidget at the table, or is unable to sit for any length of time. Unless he is constantly supervised, he will fidget, leave the table and complete minimal work.

History shows no significant medical complications (e.g., no hospitalisations, accidents, injuries). Steven was described as a 'demanding' baby who slept little, was very alert and wakeful. He enjoyed Montessori school and no complaints were noted at this time. When he started primary education, his parents were told that Steven was very active and tended to rush through school work. Good ability and learning attainments were reported. A similar disposition was related the following year. Now, midway through his third year at school, Steven's behaviour is becoming a source of concern for his parents and his teacher. His resistance to academic work is the main trouble, but there are other significant issues. For example, he has an older brother, and he increasingly argues with him. He is not inclined to follow through on parent requests (e.g., completing household tasks). His diet is reasonably good, but parents are concerned that Steven cannot fall asleep before 10 pm. No significant marital discord or family problems were mentioned.

> Teacher report is that Steven is easily distracted and often off-task. He may sit for a short period, but when doing so, looks out the window or interrupts other students. He requires a significant amount of teacher supervision, which detracts from the needs of the other students. Socially he is a good mixer and is quite athletic.

Steven's profile seems consistent with AD/HD. However, for one to understand how his behaviour issues relate to AD/HD, one must know of the 'symptoms' which collectively define it.

AD/HD – THE GENERAL 'SYMPTOMS'
Parents and teachers often report the following:

- 'not applying themselves'
- 'not achieving to potential'
- 'not motivated'
- 'can't complete work, always unfinished'
- 'can't concentrate'
- 'giddy'
- 'won't do homework unless continually supervised'
- 'highly distracted'
- 'inconsistent – good one day, bad the next'
- 'cannot remain in seat when required to'
- 'scattered'
- 'not with-it'
- 'never follows through on directions; have to repeat request over and over until the task is done'
- 'attention seeking – asking questions, interrupting, making unnecessary comments'
- 'short attention span, no lasting power'
- 'will only concentrate on activities he/she likes, such as computer games, videos, outdoor activities, etc.'
- 'can't wait turn; needs everything immediately'
- 'chatterbox'

- 'bored easily; needs to change activities often'
- 'demanding'
- 'cannot leave unsupervised in public places, will take off'
- 'doesn't recognise danger (runs across street) or doesn't seem to fear dangerous situations (climb to top of highest tree and swing off top branch)'
- 'often on the go, perpetual motion, difficulty sitting still'

Within this list, two general groups are derived. One relates to AD, the other to HD. The problems are related yet different. Children who are easily distracted, disorganised and inattentive are not necessarily hyperactive. Likewise, over-active and impulsive children are not automatically 'attention deficit'. Sometimes children have elements of both the AD and the HD.

It is the HD or 'hyperactivity' part that people recognise. Everyone is familiar with the term and use it often to describe a child's behaviour at a particular moment (e.g., 'he is really hyper today') or as a general disposition (e.g., 'he is a hyper child ...'). It is assumed that 'hyper' means excessively active, restless, can't sit still, giddy, non-stop talking, can't wait – must have everything immediately, can't play quietly – always making noise, and so on. The specific behaviours associated with the psychiatric definition of AD and HD will be outlined later in this chapter.

For many years, hyperactivity was the foremost element of AD/HD. Not until the 1994 publication of the *DSM-IV* (a manual used most often by American medical and mental health professionals) was there a separate set of symptoms referring to AD. Why the division between AD and HD? During the 1980s it was increasingly clear that children need not be over-active for significant problems to be present. A separate cluster of problems was noted in many children who were not hyperactive, yet were unable to concentrate, were distracted, messy, disorganised, dreamy, forgetful, not appearing to listen when spoken to, and were unable to pay attention to detail. These children were appropriately self-controlled, yet resisted mental work and required constant supervision to complete school assignments. This pattern is now known as Attention Deficit (AD). The inclusion of inattention means that AD/HD is applicable to a far greater range of children relative to HD only. It is also important for the reader to understand that AD/HD does not necessarily mean hyperactive, nor does it imply that children with AD/HD will be disruptive and unable to control behaviour. In fact the AD-only child, as just noted, may be timid, spacey, messy and disorganised. There is no inference that the child is impulsive, rash and overactive.

Think of two AD/HD children in a classroom. The HD child will cause the greater headache for teacher because he is frequently out of his seat, fidgets with everything in sight (pencils, books, clothes), never does what he is supposed to, interrupts and disrupts other students, wants everything now, and commands a tremendous amount of teacher energy.

By contrast, the AD child may not require as much teacher attention, because she will remain in her seat and not disrupt others. However, neither will she get much work done. She may just look at her work, do one or two problems, then stare out the window and 'day-dream'. These are very different patterns but both could be considered AD/HD.

In my experience, I would go a step further and recognise that within either the AD or the HD groups there are further divisions. For example, within the AD group I find that some children can have excellent attention spans, but be 'spacey', forgetful, and disorganised. The HD contains two factors – one hyperactive the other impulsive. Children do not necessarily have both. Sometimes a child is not excessively active but can be extremely impulsive.

ATTENTION DEFICIT (AD)

Consider the following list of difficulties associated with AD:
- difficulty completing academic work; assignments

unfinished; delayed initiation of homework.
- difficulty concentrating.
- needs constant supervision to complete mental work.
- highly distracted.
- inconsistent – good one day, bad the next.
- scattered.
- not with-it (not alert).
- problems following through on directions; have to frequent ly repeat request until the task is done.
- short attention span, no lasting power.
- only concentrates on activities he/she likes, such as computer games, videos, playing with certain toys.
- disorganised, messy.
- forgetful, dreamy, spacey.
- doesn't pay attention to detail, careless; doesn't notice changes in environment.
- doesn't appear to listen when spoken to.

On this list, the items which are inevitably discussed are home-work problems and the enigma that the child will pay attention but only if it involves a preferred activity. In fact, both items are related, since homework is not a preferred activity.

ATTENTION AS A BASIC YET COMPLEX PROCESS

As an undergraduate psychology student, I recall observing what appeared to be extreme loss of attention. As part of a course on mental retardation, my class visited a hospital unit serving pro-foundly retarded children. The children had extreme 'hydro-cephaly' (abnormally swollen head), were confined to hospital beds and were connected to various life support systems. What I recall was a uniformly 'blank' expression, almost as if the children could not respond to external stimulation. There was no 'orient-ing response' as you might observe when you make a noise and an infant directs his/her attention to the sound. Essentially, the children in this unit seemed devoid of physical and mental life.

Attention is one of the most fundamental and complex psychological processes. In fact, it is difficult to disentangle attention from consciousness (e.g., awareness, being). Attention is so basic a mental process that it is akin to breathing. If we stop breathing, we cease to exist. Likewise, if one could imagine not being able to attend, there would be no mental life.

Much investigation in the area of attention is found in the field known as Cognitive Psychology (how we learn and process information). To better understand the importance of attention, it is useful to overview some of the terms and models of thinking which relate to it. Let us begin with a commonly accepted model of information processing.

As the Figure below shows, attention regulates what input comes into the system and how this input is sensed, perceived,

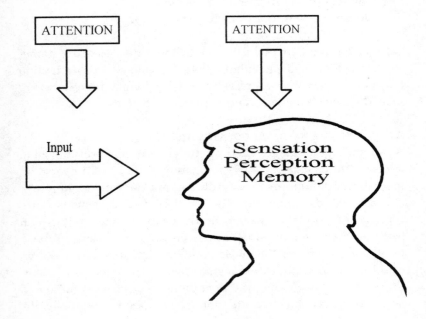

remembered and stored for future use. Adults often note that an inattentive child does not seem to be listening when spoken to. For example, the input given to the child might be, 'please hang up your coat and put your shoes in the wardrobe'. The input is not received because the child was not attending (e.g., attention is directed elsewhere – book, television, etc.). Or, attention may be partial (e.g., child hears put coat away but leaves shoes). If the request is fully registered through the 'ears', success is not guaranteed because attention can falter in the interpretation (perception or thinking phase). The child may put the coat in the closet and the shoes near the coat stand. Again, attention regulates the flow of information, how it is processed, and ultimately how the task is performed.

In the information processing approach, attention has several technical names.

Orienting (alert) attention. This is the general capacity to be ready to perform the task. Readiness is influenced by motivation. If one is motivated, one attends. If one attends one can learn. This seems to be the general theme – students with attention deficits are not always deficit in attention. That is, children find some activities motivating and subsequently are ready to perform these tasks. This baffles many parents and teachers. If the child is so attuned for some tasks, why not others?

Sustained attention. Once attending, it is necessary for attention to continue until the information is fully processed or a task completed. Lack of sustained attention is another way of saying 'short attention span' or 'poor concentration'. It is also the precursor to the problem of 'leaves tasks incomplete' and 'never seems to finish things he/she starts'.

Selective attention. Selective attention refers to one's ability to focus on what matters, and to simultaneously block out (filter) what is not important. For example, if a child is doing homework, what really matters is the work at hand (writing answers to questions). However, many other stimuli need to be filtered out, such as noise and visual input (e.g., posters, books). In addition, one must filter out distracting thoughts – associations, ideas, news – not related to the work at hand. Children with AD/HD often derail their work with a chain of thought unrelated to the task. One observes this when a child is performing a task which requires his or her undivided attention, but the child interrupts the task by making irrelevant (or unnecessary) comments. This is known as 'easily distracted'.

Visual attention. Visual attention simply refers to attention directed to visual input, such as pictures, symbols, puzzles, blocks, video technologies, charts, and other forms of visual stimulation.

Auditory attention. In contrast to visual attention, auditory attention consists of the input received through the 'ears' without visual reinforcement. Examples would be oral conversation, audio tapes, verbal instructions, etc.

In most cases, dividing attention into the basic sense modalities of eyes and ears is not revealing. That is to say, there is no selective deficit in attention for either sensory channel. Children are deficit in both or neither. However, for some children, there is a discrepancy in attention as a function of where the input is received. As an example of auditory attention deficit, a child may be very alert and perceptive in terms of pictures and recall of visual images (e.g., child can recall visual details about past events, places, or people). This child may also notice changes in the environment (e.g., one might make a small change to the child's room and the change will undoubtedly be noted). On the other hand, this same child may be forgetful and not seem to listen when spoken to. Information which is given verbally without visual back-up may be forgotten quickly.

ATTENTION – SOME BASIC INFLUENCES
If attention is a complex concept, it follows that it will be influenced by other concepts (Cherkes-Julkowski et al, 1997). What

follows are a some of the factors which bear upon attention. Realise that attention effects these variables as much as being affected by them – it is a reciprocal cause and effect loop.

Motivation. As noted earlier, motivation can direct attention. How else can one explain the constant comment from adults that the child can 'attend to certain activities, but not others'? Situational variation in attention is believed to be the result of motivation.
A further implication is that if the child 'wished to' he/she could perform the task without difficulty.

There is some merit in this view. Recall a time when you engaged in an act in which you did not want to participate but felt pressured into the situation. For example, someone might suggest a 'computer course' which you do, not because you want to, but at the request of another party. One could predict that your attention will not be maximised because the activity is not self-selected (thereby less rewarding).

However, motivation does not provide the complete answer to attention deficit. Children with AD may be motivated but still experience widely fluctuating attention (frequent shift in activity, disorganised play, etc.). There is also the further need to analyse why the child may be motivated in certain situations and not others. Does the child frequently experience failure regarding tasks in which he or she is perceived as unmotivated (or success when motivated)?

There is an inherent danger in placing too much emphasis on motivation and that the belief is that children are in charge of their own 'system'. If they want to, they can do it. This sentiment is frequently reflected in school reports where the comment is made, 'child will achieve better results when they work harder/try harder/give more effort/apply self'. There is an implicit assumption that children can control their motivation and subsequent effort. This may be true for a large per cent of the population, but it is certainly questionable in the case of children with AD.

Type of Activity. When the comment is made that the child can attend for long periods of time for certain activities but not others, a close inspection of the type of activity is usually revealing. For example, children with AD (and HD) can usually attend better to tasks which are visually or physically stimulating, provide immediate feedback and are novel. On the other hand, attention is said to be very poor for activities involving less visual/physical appeal, little if any feedback, and which are repetitive. The types of tasks which can better sustain attention and those for which AD children are 'at-risk' of loss of attention, are given below:

Activities with better Attention	*At-Risk Activities (less attention)*
Video games (play station, computer, etc.)	Reading
Toy play (lego, toy figures, etc.)	Writing
Physical Activities (outdoor games)	Arithmetic
Television (high action programmes)	Homework
Construction/Assembly (things)	Study

This brief sample is revealing in that children with AD can focus attention far better to activities with certain features. These tend to be self-selected, providing immediate feedback, and are active (or viewing action). For example, children with AD typically enjoy computer-based technology. One reason for this is that computers are visually stimulating, present novel stimuli and can tell the child how he/she is doing immediately after a response is made.

On the other hand, tasks with less novelty, more repetition, less chance for immediate feedback, are the ones most likely to cause trouble for the child with AD. These tasks also involve a high degree of sustained mental effort.

The list of activities which are likely to cause difficulty introduce two other important features – learning difficulty and motivation.

Co-Existing Diagnoses. It is possible that children who have trouble concentrating do so because they experience specific cognitive difficulties (visual processing). Likewise, children who are depressed or anxious can be inattentive but the inattention is due to another problem. There are many such co-existing problems which can be the root of AD and these will be discussed in Chapter 2.

Motivation. Reference has already been made to the importance of motivation. The role of motivation is so integral to AD than it may well be called MD (Motivational Deficit). If children are inattentive and easily distracted regarding sustained mental effort, one could explain the problem not as a biological one (as AD/HD implies) but as one of learning history. What if the child has received far more negative feedback than positive relating to mental work? If mental work is associated with negative outcomes, no wonder a child would avoid it, be distracted, and escape the learning situation as quickly as possible. Learning can take on aversive associations by virtue of past learning history, and such negative associations will obviously reduce motivation and lead to the emergence of AD-type problems. However, the real problem may be learning difficulty, failure to individualise the child's learning programme, unrealistic expectations, lack of positive feedback during learning, etc.

THE ROLE OF DEVELOPMENT IN DETERMINING 'WHAT IS NORMAL ATTENTION'

Knowledge of child development helps determine what is 'excessive' and therefore a potential problem. The determination of a 'problem' is based on how much a child's behaviour deviates from a similar age group. For example, we can use information about child development to determine when a child's attention span is significantly shorter than his or her age group, or when a child's activity level is significantly greater than his/her peers.

Nonetheless, I am continually amazed by the vast disparity in expectations about children's learning and behaviour. When expectations are unduly high, problems may be perceived when in fact the child's behaviour is actually within normal developmental limits. For example, a seven year-old child may bring home two hours of daily school work. The child may tire after 30 minutes of work and find it difficult to continue. The perception is that the child has an 'attention problem', 'lacks effort' and has difficulty 'concentrating'. What if I informed you that twenty minutes of sustained mental effort is the upper limit for a seven-year-old child and that continued mental work beyond this time period is unreasonable for any child this age. Now, the problem takes on an entirely different form. It may not be that the child has an attention problem but that the work demands are unrealistic.

The following Table provides a general overview of changes in attention skill during early childhood.

THE DEVELOPMENT OF NORMAL ATTENTION SPAN

Age	*Attention Span*
0-12 months	Very little sustained attention; may gaze or stare at an object for short period but immediately distracted by novel stimulus (e.g., a person walking into room).
1-2 years	Can concentrate, but must purposely block out other stimuli. For example, if an adult interrupts a toddler who is engaged in a task (e.g., putting rings on a stick), the child may get upset. This is due to inability to switch attention; that is attention is single-channelled and all other stimuli must be ignored in order to focus on the task at hand.
2-3 years	With adult assistance, children can now switch attention from one activity to another (e.g., from play to listening to an adult). However, tasks cannot be completed simultaneously (playing and listening to the adult at the same time).
3-4 years	Attention is still single channel (either toy play or listening to adult), but shifting of focus can be accomplished without adult prompting. That is, children can immediately shift attention to a new

Age	Attention Span
	stimulus (and back to the original one) on their own accord (adult assistance is not required).
4-5 years	Attention is now two-channelled. A child can listen to an adult without interrupting play. Or child can be engaged in task while receiving instructions in how to complete an aspect of the task (whereas before the child would have to stop the activity completely to listen to instructions). Concentration span is short, but group instruction can be initiated. It is no coincidence that primary schooling usually begins when children have at least two-channelled attention skills and can learn in groups.
5-6 years	'Mature' attention formed – all channels (e.g., visual, auditory, tactile, kinesthetic) are co-ordinated. Basic for later multi-sensory experiences, such as talking while driving a car. Can ignore distractions.

The question of how attention develops after the age of six remains largely unexplored. There are a myriad number of factors which influence attention. Michael J. Connor (1997) summarises the situation cogently when he states that attention may be influenced by:

> The nature of the task; the nature of the previous task; the child's particular interest; the child's learning style; the child's ability and experiences; the time of day; the mood of the child, peers, teacher, etc., etc.

Basically, because attention is intertwined with so many other factors it is difficult to know what levels of attention and concentration to expect for school-age children.

Personal experience bears out the complexity of attention because the most repeated theme about AD/HD children's behaviour is that their attention span depends on interest level. Specifically, when they are interested they attend and when they are not interested, they do not attend. Typically, interest diminishes when tasks are imposed on an AD/HD child (e.g., homework) whereas the child can attend for long periods of time on self-initiated tasks (e.g., toy play, television, etc.). While this pattern is probably true to some degree for all individuals, children with AD/HD show an extreme divide, a sort of 'all or none quality' – all play and no mental work.

Also Connor makes note of other critical factors such as previous learning history. If children have any form of learning difficulty it is natural that school, and mental work in general, will be viewed with disdain and reluctance. This attitude may appear on the surface as 'inattention' when in fact the child may have a learning problem.

Also relevant is the nature of instruction and the type of task the child is expected to complete. The challenge for teachers is presenting information in novel, multi-sensory methods, in order to maximise interest and capture children's attention. Likewise, the types of assignments students complete also bears on their motivation.

A final comment about the development of attention is that any child's deviation from age-expected attention span may be detected through standardised assessment procedures. For example, there are computer tests of attention where the child must engage in a monotonous task for a specific period.

HYPERACTIVITY DISORDER (HD)

HD is the second group of problems forming the AD/HD dyad. To introduce HD, a case history told by the child's mother is provided.

---

*The Story of Tom**
'At the age of three, Tom often ran away from school, home and during shopping trips. He once got a train from the west to the east coast.

In primary school, he was considered "disruptive". He had constant battles with teachers and would not complete homework

---

without constant supervision. When unsupervised, he ran off to read comics or go outside.

He remained in formal education until his Junior Certificate year at which time he was expelled. The principal said Tom was "mad". He could not enroll in another secondary school given his poor report. Our marriage was suffering as the result of Tom's behaviour.

Tom enrolled in a small, private school which was able to provide more individual attention. He did well and got good Junior Certificate marks. Unfortunately, the secondary school closed.

We spent lots of time and money bringing Tom to psychologists and psychiatrists. We were told that we did not "set limits", that Tom's father was "laid back" and I was "ultra conservative". We thought Tom might be dyslexic. He wasn't. We tried Tom in another secondary school but he was expelled. He argued with teachers and did not study.

Tom is now 24. Since the age of sixteen, he has had fourteen jobs, the longest of which lasted six months. He is talkative and adamant in his views. He doesn't seem to see another person's view.

He ends up in trouble, losing things, not keeping his word, never finishing things he starts. He crashed his car, fell out of favour with his friends and recently got in a fight which almost landed him prison time. He goes from incident to incident. He is not sleeping well, and he is losing his temper more frequently. What can we do? Everything we try doesn't work.

* Tom's mother wrote the above material. I asked Tom to write his version of his difficulties, and he said he would. However, he failed to deliver on his promise.

I met Tom when he was 24. He was bright and articulate, but frustrated that his relationships were short-lived and his education and career outcomes were much lower than his ability would predict. Early in Tom's life, his parents sensed something different about him. They thought his activity level was excessive and said he was very difficult at homework time. His success in primary school varied, depending on the teacher. In some cases, teachers felt he was productive and focused. Other teachers noted high 'distractibility'.

It was during secondary school that Tom's difficulties became more conspicuous. School reports indicate that he was 'giddy', unco-operative, and his academic attainments declined. Eventually, he was expelled from school for 'disruptive' behaviour. Later, he was expelled from two other secondary schools. Although Tom did not survive the traditional secondary school format, he did quite well in a private secondary school which maintained low student-teacher ratios (as fate had it, the school could not maintain its secondary school programme).

After secondary school until the time I saw Tom, he was employed sixteen times. His impatience, need for novelty, restlessness, and explosiveness led to termination in each of these positions. Given his good facility in oral expression, he was able to 'talk his way into jobs' but just as easily talked himself out of them.

Perhaps the most frustrating experience for Tom and his parents was the lack of assistance given them by the mental health profession. He was 'assessed' by psychologists and psychiatrists but nowhere was reference made to AD/HD. Instead, references were made to attributes like 'energetic', 'precocious' and 'bright'. While these are accurate trait descriptions, they are euphemisms and do not convey the seriousness of the condition.

Just after I met Tom, his problems came to a dangerous climax. He became extremely aggravated during a conversation and was physically abusive to the other party. He was charged with 'assault' and barely escaped spending time in prison.

How could a person like Tom, with good potential and energy, find his life in utter chaos? At 24 years of age, he had experienced one failure after another and there was very little hope. Imagine how Tom must feel, some 22 years after his parents first suspected something was 'different' about him, but not having anyone tell Tom or his parents how or why, or what could be done to help him.

During my meeting with Tom, his parents provided me with previous psychological and psychiatric reports as well as school reports, both primary and secondary. They also wrote a mini 'life-history' for my review. It turns out that Tom's first psychological assessment was at the age of eight. Intelligence tests revealed that he was very bright. The assessing psychologist found that Tom's parents needed to be more 'consistent' in their discipline.

After Tom's behaviour deteriorated in secondary school, he was psychiatrically treated. Again, the recommendation was 'lack of parent-child boundaries' and that 'parents need to set limits'. Suggestions corroborate Thomas Phelan's (1996) view that most mental health practitioners continue to dubiously assert that AD/HD is caused by poor parenting. A more balanced, realistic view is that poor parenting is not the cause of AD/HD; rather, parents react non-optimally to their children's difficult behaviour.

As Tom's situation continued to disimprove, his parents heard of 'dyslexia' and wondered if this might be the problem. Tom was again assessed and the opinion given was that he was not 'classically dyslexic'.

Several years later, Tom's parents heard about AD/HD, and they considered the experience a 'revelation'. They were stunned by how well the problems of AD/HD matched the ones their son had experienced. This rekindled their interest in obtaining a professional evaluation of AD/HD and it was in this context that I met Tom.

Problems Associated with HD

The term 'hyperactive' implies an activity level beyond what is normally expected for a particular age group. Again, one of the key terms is 'normal' expectation. As Betty Robertson (1987) notes:

> Pathological hyperactivity, however, needs to be differentiated from age-appropriate activity levels. It is possible after all, for students to have higher than average activity levels and nonetheless fall within the average or normal range.

Unfortunately, there is no 'precise' test of excessive activity or impulsivity. Further, compared with attention span, less is known about the normal development of activity and impulse control. One would think we would know more about the normal development of impulse control and activity level given the prevailing belief that excessive impulsivity and activity are easily observed. Again, the ultimate 'litmus' test is whether these excesses interfere with learning and social development. If they do, the child is considered 'hyperactive'.

To help distinguish normal from abnormal levels of impulsivity and hyperactivity, three points are developed. These are (a) to provide the behaviours associated with significant impulse problems and overactivity, (b) to follow the course of an AD/HD child's atypical development, and (c) to realise the larger constellation of problems associated with hyperactivity.

HYPERACTIVITY
- Can't stay in seat when required to do so (e.g., at dinner table, in school seat).
- Fidgety, restless, always touching objects, can't keep hands still.
- No end to energy level – always on go, constant activity.
- Excessive climbing, running, jumping, moving, which puts child at greater risk for accidents and injuries (e.g., running into street).
- Frequent vocal output, either talking constantly (e.g.,

questions, comments, ideas, etc.), whistling or making a variety of sounds.

- Can't seem to relax, or be quiet for any significant length of time.
- Difficult to control in open, public contexts, such as supermarkets, or shopping centres.

IMPULSIVITY
- Difficulty controlling impulses, such as blurting out comments.
- Impatient; demands that requests be met without delay.
- Has difficulty waiting in lines or awaiting turn in games or group situations.
- Constantly interrupts others (e.g., when adult on the phone, or during adult conversations).
- Grabs other people's possessions.
- Strong attraction to 'no' objects, such as playing with potentially dangerous objects (e.g., stove, knives, etc).
- Thrill seeker (e.g,. run across street in heavy traffic).

Once again, when children present with the above types of behaviours, and these behaviours impede the child's well-being (e.g., academic difficulties, social problems, threat to child's safety), then the notion of 'hyperactivity disorder' is worth investigating.

THE DEVELOPMENT OF ACTIVITY LEVEL
The atypical development of hyperactive children is another way to discriminate normal from excessive activity level. What follows are developmental periods and associated qualities which may distinguish HD children from non-HD children:

- *0-12 Months.* During the first year of life there are few reliable markers of hyperactivity. Some parents recall issues like inadequate sleep, irritability, feeding problems, rocking in cot, excessive crying, and colic. However, these problems may be confined to infancy with no development of later child behavioural difficulties. Or, if later problems are reported, they may be of a different in kind to that of HD children.

- *12-24 Months*. Towards the end of this age period, there are more reliable behavioural differences between HD and non-HD children. Parents note there is 'something different' about the child. Naps are stopped at an early age, and children are perceived as very demanding (e.g., require constant adult attention). The first signs of heedlessness develop, but this is frequently associated with the 'terrible twos'.

- *3-5 Years*. Now the difference between normal activity and excessive activity is apparent. Parents report severe temper tantrums and difficulty controlling the child in public places. HD children do not respond to discipline techniques that are normally effective with other children, creating a particularly stressful period for parents. At this time, children may start a Play or Montessori school. The more unstructured the environment the less likely teachers will perceive problems. However, the greater the demands a teacher makes for children to remain seated at certain times (e.g., story time) and to play quietly, the more likely the teacher will report concerns. Peer interaction problems also develop, and teachers report the AD/HD child does not share, demands more of classmates, and tends to 'boss' others.

- *5-12 Years*. In primary school, further differences between HD and non-HD children develop. For instance, there is a general expectation that children will remain seated and complete school assignments. It is at this time that the characteristic behaviours mentioned earlier are especially noteworthy. During this period, HD children may sense something is different about themselves, blaming everyone and everything else. Self-worth may diminish. Serious rule

infringements may occur at the later ages in this interval
(e.g., stealing, lying, etc.)

- *Adolescence*. The good news during this period is that over
  activity diminishes. This decrease is understandable.
  Problems like 'excessive climbing and jumping' or 'non-stop
  motion' qualities apply mainly to younger children. In
  adolescence, the primary problems are feelings of
  restlessness and resultant difficulty completing activities
  which are sedate and inactive (e.g., homework, listening to
  school lectures, etc.). This is precisely why HD adolescents
  'hate' school (a comment I often hear from over-active
  teenagers). No wonder! Imagine completing primary school
  when expected behaviours like listening, staying on-task
  and remaining seated are completely antithetical to attention and impulse control problems. By the time HD children
  reach secondary school, they face even more intensive
  learning with a shaky knowledge foundation and ongoing
  HD-type problems. With incredible patience and persistence,
  some adolescents will complete the Leaving Certificate
  examination while others will drop out after the Junior
  Certificate.

  The other predominant feature of HD during the
  teenage years is the sense of despair and hopelessness felt
  by parents and children. At this point, parents may believe
  that nothing can be done, and feel discouraged. Likewise,
  teenagers may question their sanity, especially after
  continually hearing they are 'not applying themselves' and
  'not living up to potential'.
- *Adulthood*. It is now accepted that HD-problems are not
  outgrown. Rather, problems continue to manifest in careers,
  relationships, and in the general task of independent living.
  HD in adults will not be covered in this book.

AD/HD – ELEVEN BASIC ISSUES
1. SOME AD/HD IS PART OF NORMAL, EVERYDAY EXPERIENCE

One shortcoming with the problems noted is that difficulties like short attention span, forgetfulness and giddiness are common problems that most people can relate to. All of us experience some of the behaviours at some time. It is not humanly possible to be 100 per cent attentive to everything we see or hear. Sometimes we do not listen, sometimes our mind wanders and sometimes we make fidgety movements that escape our consciousness. Lapses in concentration, daydreaming and distractibility make us human and differentiate the human experience from that of a machine.

Anyone reading a list of AD/HD-type behaviours can identify with one or more items. We can all relate to inattention because it is such a common experience. Perhaps at this very moment, your attention is 'wandering'. Did you remember to close the back shed? Did a co-worker imply you should be less critical of the boss? Are those hunger pains you feel? Is it time to get a snack? Likewise, most of us experience daily and normal mood changes, moving from sober and serious to fun and 'giddy'. At times, we may be quiet and reflective, at others talkative, 'chatty'. This author certainly knows the meaning of forgetful, and is often described as 'absent-minded'.

That most of us can relate to selected aspects of AD/HD is both a blessing and a bane. It is a blessing because most of us, if we really think about it, can empathise with how our inattention interferes with productivity. Unfortunately the bane is that the commonplace nature of the problems associated with AD/HD make it easy to rationalise these behaviours in ourselves and others.

The ultimate challenge is distinguishing between 'normal' (common experience) and 'abnormal'. The general rule of thumb is that the more excessive the behaviour the more abnormal it is and the more obvious the difficulty. Parents and teachers may find themselves spending an inordinate amount of time managing a child's behaviour and supervising his/her learning compared to other children. As extra energy and time is allocated to managing 'inattentiveness' both adults and child become increasingly frustrated. Attempts to improve the situation are usually unsuccessful. In the end, adults are understandably perplexed because their resources are devoted to the 'problem' child while they may be overlooking the accomplishments of other children in the family or classroom. The child usually senses he/she is 'difficult' but does not know why. Situations like this can continue for many years. In the end, the child's behaviour persists and prevents them from reaching age-expected goals. Hence the great distress and desperation felt by parents and teachers. When these conditions are met, it is natural to think that the behaviours noted are indeed 'abnormal'. These 'abnormalities' are re-stated as a 'deficit' or a 'disorder' for medical/professional purposes.

A brief example to underscore the divide between 'normal' and 'abnormal': Consider the items 'forgetful' and 'loses personal belongings'. All children occasionally forget things; they leave a lunch box at school, misplace a pencil sharpener, or forget to bring home a required assignment. Fine! Nobody is perfect and life continues without great stress.

By contrast, consider a child who forgets or loses things on a daily basis. Jackets are left at school, pencils are never in the pencil case, assignments are not brought home. Parent frustration rises and an element of stress and irritation is introduced. Parents give the child daily reminders to remember the assignments, bring home supplies, and not forget clothing, all to little avail. This is when we think of an 'attention problem'.

2. THE IMPORTANCE OF SITUATIONAL FACTORS TO AD/HD

It is amazing how often parents report that AD/HD difficulties are noted in some situations but not others. One situation which is frequently mentioned is homework. Some parents have told me that they have two different children, a kind of 'Jekyll and Hyde' Syndrome – the good child who has certain non-academic interests and is a joy to be around when school is not in session, and the 'monster' child who avoids, argues, and requires non-stop attention regarding school work.

It is during homework when difficulties come to the fore. Parent and child may have the following discussion:

Parent: Do you have homework tonight?
Child: No.
Parent: Certainly you must have some work to do. This is the third straight night without anything.
Child: I did it in school (parent subsequently finds out that home-work was given but not taken home).
Another variation of this conversation could be:
Parent: Do you have homework tonight?
Child: Yes, I'll do it later.
(Later)
Parent: What about your homework?
Child: Just a minute.
More time elapses. Parent reaches frustration tolerance (e.g., voice tone has significantly increased); child senses parent 'cue' and takes out school bag. Unfortunately, the English and Maths work-books left at school.
Child: My workbooks are at school. I'll do it tomorrow.

When AD/HD children finally begin homework, resistance in the guise of distractibility sets in. The child may do one problem and need a drink of water. A few more seconds and the pencil tip breaks. There seems to be little focused attention to academic work, but great sensitivity to input unrelated to school work (e.g., sounds, sights, an itch, etc.).

One can imagine the difficulties classroom teachers encounter, especially considering that school is precisely the place where undivided attention and sustained concentration are fun-damental to learning and appropriate conduct.

Teachers report that an inattentive child can undermine the

entire classroom process by demanding frequent supervision. Without intense teacher monitoring, the inattentive child may distract other children (e.g., due to boredom and the need for novel stimulation) by talking when it is inappropriate to do so, or by leaving the seat when staying seated is expected. At the very least, the inattentive child will not be overtly disruptive but will not be engaged in school work. Instead, these children can quietly amuse themselves with a number of non-academic pursuits (e.g., scraping the paint off a pencil with fingernail) or stare into space (e.g., daydream).

3. Is AD/HD nature (Biology) or nurture (Environment)?

Are children wired to be inattentive, easily distracted and lack behaviour control? Or, is it something to do with an adverse event (e.g., such as an accident, marriage breakdown, bullying victim, vaccination side-effect, particular food substance, etc.). The answer is both – nature and nurture. The nature part is becoming increasingly evident and is summarised by Russell Barkley (1997):

> Although multiple etiologies (causes) may lead to AD/HD evidence points to neurological and genetic factors as the greatest contributors to this disorder.

This view is supported by parents' reports. For example, when parents recollect their child's temperament as an infant, it is common to hear descriptions like 'demanding', 'wakeful', 'alert', 'very active', 'need for constant stimulation', etc. In other words, within the first six months of life, parents may be witnessing the early emergence of AD/HD.

AD/HD is not a 'here today gone tomorrow' quality. There is a permanence to it, in that the problems manifest early in life and seem to be a fundamental part of the child's 'personality'. Subsequently, AD/HD children have difficulties 'settling' when they begin primary school. It is interesting that one of the diagnostic features of AD/HD is that the age of onset is typically given as four to seven years. This corresponds to the first years of primary school.

However, even if AD/HD is all 'biology', there is still a child to rear. How we manage the child's behaviour is crucial and parent-child interactions are proven to be an important determinant of prognosis. For example, Barkley notes that the more hostile and negative the parent-child interactions, the poorer the prognosis. In many cases, parents need information on how to cope with the many challenging behaviours exhibited by children with AD/HD.

A valuable lesson from the nature and nurture argument as it pertains to AD/HD is understanding that AD/HD is a real problem yet not an excuse for inappropriate behaviour . For example, AD/HD is a bonafide disorder like any other disorder (e.g., dyslexia, autism). Thus, behavioural problems stemming from AD/HD are not intentional but due to the 'biology' of the condition which results in difficulties controlling behaviour, acting responsibly, etc. If one views AD/HD as a legitimate problem, then it is possible to set realistic goals, be more understanding/ tolerant, reduce frustration and promote success.

On the other hand, one should not use the AD/HD label as one of 'forgiveness'. Children and adults with AD/HD require structure, routine, consistency, firmness and immediacy, far more than individuals without AD/HD. In other words, AD/HD is not an excuse for problems, but a 'wake-up' call for action.

Parents' views are often split along these perspectives, depending on gender. Typically, mothers accept AD/HD and make allowances for it. This results in opposition from fathers who view their spouses/partners as too 'tolerant', 'forgiving' and 'easily manipulated'. Fathers on the other hand, over-adhere to the 'it's not an excuse' view and as a result, make no allowances and treat the child as if his/her needs are the same as any other child's. This is inaccurate and can result in great frustration for all family members.

Further, if AD/HD is viewed as an essential part of a child's 'character' or 'style', one could argue that since all children have different 'styles' how can one consider a particular temperament as a 'disorder' while others are not? The key principle is whether the behaviours associated with an AD/HD 'temperament' are excessive and creating problems. If so, then it is neglectful to view the child's behaviour as, 'that's just the way he/she is ... all children are different'. Likewise, children on the other side of the behaviour spectrum, who are extremely passive, inhibited and fearful, could also be considered as having a 'deficit' or a 'disorder' if these behaviours cause significant distress.

People refer to AD/HD as a 'chronic' problem, one which can improve with proper treatment, but never be completely eliminated. There are a number of questions raised about 'how much' improvement can occur and what is 'proper treatment'. Most experts believe that under ideal conditions, AD/HD children can make significant and lasting changes to problem behaviours.

4. AD/HD – EPIDEMIC OR UNHELPFUL LABEL?

There is a fundamental divide in perceptions about AD/HD. On one hand, some see AD/HD as one of the most overlooked and misunderstood of all childhood difficulties (Kewley, 1999). For these individuals, AD/HD symbolises a 'hidden handicap' in that parents, teachers, and professionals have limited (if any) awareness about the condition. Lack of awareness means that children, families and teachers may suffer in silence, when in fact much can be done to alleviate the situation.

One of the main missions of the AD/HD as hidden handicap group is advocating and disseminating information about the problem. This is the most obvious way to reveal it. Yet, in this process, some individuals may develop a blind allegiance to AD/HD. AD comes to represent 'Anything Difficult' so that no matter what the child's problem, it must be AD/HD. A further slant is that medication for AD/HD is the panacea treatment.

Professionals may also fall into either of these camps. I can relate a personal example of the over-zealous AD/HD view at a recent one day seminar on the topic. The bias towards AD/HD was subtle, but present in some of the diagrams. For example, take a look at the Figure below:

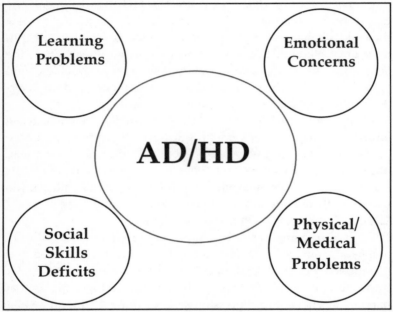

What struck me is that AD/HD was promoted as the cause of all other difficulties. While this may be true in some cases, it is equally true that other problems can cause AD/HD-type difficulties. For example, children experiencing emotional difficulties, such as anxiety and unhappiness, may communicate these feelings through inattentiveness, restlessness and distractibility (the same problems associated with AD/HD). Likewise, children with fundamental learning problems who are taught as if they have normal learning skills will be perceived as unproductive, off-task and disruptive. However, it may be that they are not capable of the work given them. The point is that each of the smaller outside circles could easily occupy the central position, with AD/HD relegated to one of the smaller outside circles. The slant is subtle but it is there.

On the other hand, some do not accept AD/HD as a viable problem. At best, these people feel that AD/HD may occupy a small outside circle in the Figure. At worst, they believe AD/HD does not exist. This is equally aggravating.

AD/HD sceptics make the point that if a person is told their child has AD/HD, there is now a reason to excuse the problem. Difficult behaviours can be attributed to AD/HD, whereby AD/HD becomes reified as a 'biological disorder' and a convenient label for many child behaviours that adults cannot manage. For the sceptics, AD/HD is little more than a meaningless label which offers an excuse for not engaging in the difficult task of changing problem behaviours.

For example, Reid and Maag (1997) make the point that the AD/HD label is one of 'forgiveness'. Instead of interpreting difficult behaviour (e.g., not listening) as intentional and wilful, problem conduct is attributed to a medical/biological disorder. As such, the behaviour is due to AD/HD, and all other causal factors (e.g., parent-child issues, under-stimulating educational environment, etc.) recede in importance. In the end, one can forgive behaviour if it is due to a biological disorder as it's not a child's fault, it is AD/HD. Their point is that no one is responsible for the problem – parent, teacher, child, professional, or society. It is biological destiny.

However, complete scepticism is as much of a mistake as complete blind faith. On many occasions, parents inform me that, despite repeated contact with mental health professionals, their child's situation has disimproved, despite what appears to be an obvious case of 'true' AD/HD. In these situations, parents are usually told that 'the child will be fine. He's a fine healthy boy. Let him be'. In these cases, downgrading or denying AD/HD is a tragic error with serious consequences. For example, it is now known that if AD/HD goes untreated through childhood, the adolescent is at much greater risk for substance abuse, early school leaving, and even criminal conduct.

A prudent and sensible view of AD/HD lies somewhere between these extremes. AD/HD does exist! The prevalence of the condition depends on the diagnostic guidelines employed. Russell Barkley (1997) reviewed fifteen international studies employing relatively strict criteria for determining AD/HD. While prevalence rates vary depending on the country, the range is from 2 to 9.5 per cent. Some children, regardless of culture, and despite skilled parenting and teaching, display temperamental features like distractibility, inattentiveness, impatience, and excessive activity. These are ingrained dispositions which typically come to the fore during the first few years of formal education (although this is not always the case). This is the true meaning of AD/HD.

In sum, a diagnosis of AD/HD simply informs us that a certain number of behavioural difficulties are present and that these difficulties are significantly impairing a child's personal and/or academic development. That is all we know. A diagnosis of AD/HD does not inform about cause, because AD/HD is viewed as 'aetiological' (without cause). That is, there is still no conclusive evidence about the basis of AD/HD, even after extensive review of the available research (Cantwell 1996; Tannock 1998). Therefore, AD/HD is a descriptive 'label'. It gives a thumbnail sketch of a child's learning and behaviour needs. Identifying AD/HD should be viewed as a warning to all involved that the problem is serious and requires commitment on the part of all involved to work towards a solution. It is certainly a mistake to think of AD/HD as an excuse for problem behaviour.

5. AD/HD PROBLEMS ARE VAGUE AND ILL-DEFINED

It is difficult to precisely define terms like 'short attention span', 'disorganised', 'difficulty waiting turn' and 'excessively active'.

Words like 'short', 'difficulty', 'excessive' beg the question of what their referents are. Shorter than what? More excessive than? There is an implicit assumption that attention span is short compared to other children of similar age, much like a child can be shorter than the average height for his/her age. But what if the child's activity level is actually what it should be for similar aged children? We may now have a new problem – people may be expecting too much of the child. Maybe the child is expected to remain seated for a duration which is not appropriate to the child's age.

There is also a circular logic about ascribing a label to a set of behaviours which are presumed to define it. That is, inattention is a core symptom of attention deficit. How are behaviour and diagnosis different? Take the analogy of a patient who complains of a persistent and unproductive cough. The patient is told she has Irritable Cough Syndrome? Why? Because Irritable Cough Syndrome has as its core problem a persistent and unproductive cough. Somehow one feels that little is gained.

The 'broad' nature of the behaviours which characterise AD/HD remind me of a situation I encountered when studying for a Psychology oral exam. I asked a successfully licensed psychologist to engage me in a 'mock' oral. The exam consisted of a case vignette which briefly described the client and the problem. The examinee then formulated a 'tentative diagnosis', identified key issues, and designed an intervention. As we sat around the table, the psychologist started the mock exam ... 'Your client is feeling angry ... what are your impressions?' There was a long pause, as I waited for more information. The vignettes in the study manuals were typically a half-page in length and provided further detail. Surely I could not respond to such a brief vignette! Seeing that no further information was forthcoming, I fumbled my way through a response, all the while knowing that I did not have enough information to respond.

In retrospect, I should have been equally brief with the examiner and made up a diagnosis by turning the complaint into a disorder. I should have confidently replied 'Anger Disorder'. Nothing more to say. Receive a cryptic case, give a cryptic response.

Here is the parallel with AD/HD. It starts with a basic problem, 'short attention span'. This raises a red flag – Attention Deficit (AD)? After all, 'short attention span' is the foremost 'symptom' of Attention Deficit and we are talking about a deficit in attention. Add several associated behaviours (e.g., 'poor concentration', 'avoids mental work', 'easily distracted', etc.), and it may be AD/HD. So begins the investigation.

A formal assessment is the only way to precisely define and subsequently determine whether one meets guidelines for AD/HD. At this time, methods are used to determine if a child's impulse control, attention span, etc., is similar to his/her age peers. One way this is done is having adults rate AD/HD-type problems on a numerical index and then comparing their ratings to a group of similar children. In addition,there are tests designed specifically for measuring a child's attention span and impulse control.

6. SOME AD/HD BEHAVIOURS ARE PIVOTAL

Parents and teachers often speak of 'short attention span'. Attention span appears to be the centre of other problems, such as distractibility, lack of focus, poor concentration, homework battles, even forgetfulness (which could be considered as an intentional ploy to avoid homework). On the other hand, 'forgetfulness' by itself with no attention difficulties would likely come as a great relief to most parents and teachers. Essentially, attention span is a pivotal concept and it is no wonder why.

Consider the positive features associated with a healthy attention span. Children without attentional difficulties can amuse themselves for relatively long periods. In this respect, these children make less demands on adults, who in turn appreciate the lack of added tension. This leads to a 'win-win' situation for adult and child. When school work is required, children with-out attentional problems will undertake the work to the best of their capabilities. There will be minimal fuss so that adults can be confident that the minute they turn their back, children will not leave their seat, throw something at another child, or just look out the window, as if they never heard the directions.

Unfortunately, some children do not come pre-programmed with normal attention spans. The effects of inattentive children's behaviour on their families can be devastating. The incessant demands on parents coping skills creates an incredible amount of turmoil. A similar degree of tension is likely the case in the inat-tentive child's classroom.

As for Hyperactivity Disorder there is a dual emphasis on excessive activity and the need to constantly seek out new stimu-lation. The 'excess activity' is just that – perpetual movement and constant interruptions ('demanding'). Equally frustrating is the ease with which the child tires of one activity and thus requires new stimulation to keep amused. Thus, one activity is started, but stopped after a brief period; another activity started but stopped after another brief period, and so on.

One potentially dangerous feature of the need for novel stim-ulation is the disregard for danger and the bounds of acceptable conduct. A child might climb to the top of a dangerously high tree, paint the kitchen wall, overfill a sink, or drop toys out of the bedroom window to observe the effect. Parents are understand-ably miffed.

7. AD/HD – DICHOTOMY OR CONTINUUM?

This point relates to severity, which is generally considered on a continuum from 'mild' to 'severe'. In reviewing the characteristic behaviour of children with AD/HD, a child may demonstrate some but not all of the behaviours listed. Some children have par-ticular 'subsets' of problems but not all of them.

In general, the fewer the problems the more likely that AD/HD is of 'mild' severity or not a significant problem.

Sometimes a diagnosis is considered only if parents respond unequivocally (without qualifying statements like, 'it depends' or 'not so much anymore') to six or more problems in each category – Inattentive (AD) and/or Impulsive/Hyperactive (HD).

Here is the crux. There is an awkward mix of continuity and dichotomy with AD/HD. Some prefer to say 'yes, it is AD/HD, and it is of mild severity'. Note that the condition is present (yes), and the continuity follows (mild). But is it possible to not answer the 'yes' or 'no' question and still consider degree (mild to severe)? For example, AD/HD can be conceptualised along a continuum where 1 = Very Mild and 10 = Extremely Severe. No mention is made of the 'yes' or 'no'. Obviously, if one answers '10' than it logically follows that the condition is present ('yes'), but it is less clear if one answers '2'. In this case, is the condition present?

You might think this matter is one for professionals to ponder and not for public consumption. However, AD/HD does not appear on an X-Ray and there is no one test to diagnose it. Therefore, it remains a 'subjective' diagnosis, although subjectivity is reduced through comprehensive assessment. The point is that the informed consumer should be aware that the professional community has to cope with conceptual problems like dichotomy and continuity.

8. AD/HD – A DISORDER OR SYMPTOMS OF ANOTHER PROBLEM?

There was a recent dialogue in which a prominent psychologist took the view that AD/HD-type behaviour surfaces because the child does not receive unconditional parental love and affection. This led to a strong response from AD/HD support groups to the contrary – AD/HD was a medical problem and had nothing to do with parental love. Their message was that even the most loving and caring parents find themselves unable to manage the difficult behaviour associated with AD/HD. This type of debate is embedded in the larger difficulty of knowing when AD/HD is legitimate (all other causes can be ruled out except the inference of medical ones) and when AD/HD-type behaviour represents a response on the child to some other stressful situation (e.g., learning problems, social/relationship issues, family problems, etc.). A comprehensive and thorough assessment is the only mechanism by which an objective answer can be provided to this question.

With regard to any debate about AD/HD, it is important to know that mental health professionals are trained in particular theories of human behaviour. In some of these theories, the medical model (symptoms, diagnosis, treatment) is not viewed as a useful way to understand human behaviour. Therefore, the position advocated by any particular professional about AD/HD can be understood if one knows the type of theory of human behaviour the professional adheres to. As a case in point, a professional who adheres to the Humanistic theories, which stress unconditional love as the key to maximising human potential, is more likely to stress lack of unconditional love as an element in children's behavioural problems.

It is also important to realise that the polarised nature of the debate – AD/HD is purely medical versus AD/HD is a response to some environmental problem – is insufficient to explain the problem. There is certainly an interaction between a child's temperament and an adult's response to it. Children who are temperamentally wired for activity need constant stimulation, change activities often, can't wait, etc. are at high-risk for creating a generally negative response from adult caregivers (e.g., frequent use of punitive measures). Thus, an ingrained behaviour tempo can itself cause negative reactions from adults who manage the difficult child's behaviour. However, it is inaccurate to conclude that the adult's response to the behaviour caused the problem; rather, it is a reaction to the problem.

9. WHAT WOULD THE WORLD BE LIKE IF WE NEVER KNEW ABOUT AD/HD?

As you will see, if we did not detect and treat AD/HD there

would be more crime, early school leaving and family turmoil. Previous to our knowledge of AD/HD, there was inevitably more unnecessary suffering and pain. It is probably true that previously, more children were unable to complete school without ever knowing why (it certainly was not for lack of ability).

Take the issue of crime. The core characteristics of AD/HD – impulsive, restless, not afraid to take risks, high need for novelty – put some youth at risk for criminal behaviour. The link between AD/HD, especially the hyperactive type, and delinquent behaviour is well established (cf. Claude and Firestone, 1995). The link is especially increased if the child presents with AD/HD and another behaviour problem known as Conduct Disorder.

One can imagine that with increased awareness of AD/HD, early intervention, and ongoing support, it would be expected that some future anti-social behaviour would be prevented. In addition, parents and children would know the nature of the difficulties they experience and this would certainly assist the coping process. Since Attention Deficit Disorder is a recognised Special Educational Need, its early identification has obvious implications for schooling.

Yet, one of the biggest impediments to recognising AD/HD is that the disorder is not a physical one – there is no obvious physical sign that one has the problem. On the other hand, a child with a physical disability, like cerebral palsy, can be distinguished visually (e.g., spasticity, paraplegia, etc.). Because AD/HD has no obvious physical abnormality, the difficulties are recognised only through excessive behaviours (activity) or not enough behaviour (e.g., attention span). As such, the observed behaviour difficulties are easily interpreted as just that – a 'behaviour problem' or a 'bold child'. It is easy to ignore the possibility that difficult behaviour may have a genetic and biological basis. Consequently, early assessment and identification may be delayed, if done at all.

10. THE LONG-TERM OUTLOOK?

What do we know about the development of children with

AD/HD? Do these children become drug addicts, early school leavers, hardened criminals? Or is AD/HD better represented as a particular learning difficulty which makes school difficult but has little to do with later adjustment in life?

Like most issues related to AD/HD, it depends. What is clear is that AD/HD is not outgrown by adolescence (Fischer and Beckley, 1998). Indeed, the symptoms persist into adulthood, taking slightly different guises, but continuing to result in significant impairment.

In general, long-term outcome depends on the type and severity of AD/HD. It also depends on how problems related to AD/HD are managed when they do emerge. For example, some children with AD/HD also show signs of conduct disturbance (e.g., aggression, stealing, lying, lack of empathy about the feelings of others, etc.). This particular combination of AD/HD and aggression is typically related to a poorer outcome.

If the problems are confined to AD/HD, particularly the AD side, the picture is less pessimistic. Further optimism is warranted if the child's AD/HD is mild. Further still, there are several environmental variables which mediate long-term outcome.

At present, the accumulated research can be broadly grouped into two age spans – adolescence and adult. Adolescent aged children with AD/HD are at greater risk for the following (compared to children without AD/HD):

- academic difficulties (e.g., poor attendance, truancy, lack of response to school disciplinary procedures, suspension/ expulsion, learning problems, etc.).
- substance abuse (particularly cigarette smoking and alcohol) is noted but only when children present with both AD/HD and conduct disturbance (AD/HD without conduct disturbance does not appear to be related to increased substance abuse).
- relationship problems.

- low self-esteem and related problems with depression and anxiety.
- family conflict over and above what would be considered normal for adolescents.

The following factors appear relevant in predicting adolescent outcome.

- level of intelligence – the higher the score on an intelligence test, the better the outcome.
- socio-economic status – the higher the status the more favourable the outcome.
- peer relationship status – the more favourable, the better the outcome.
- parents with psychiatric problems, especially anti-social disorder, is associated with negative outcome.
- degree of conduct disorder in child (e.g., aggression, hostility, defiance) is related to negative outcomes.
- degree of conflict between parent and child – the more conflict, the greater the risk for negative outcomes.

The story does not end in adolescence. It seems that AD/HD persists into adulthood with some of the following consequences:

- greater likelihood for contact with police for offences such as assault, theft, and traffic offences.
- employment problems (lower ratings from supervisors, frequent job changes, etc.).
- relationship problems – quick tempered, verbally and physically abusive, etc.
- poor domestic management – difficulty doing basic household activities such as cleaning, food shopping, and laundry.
- poor financial planning – cannot manage accounts, spends money impulsively, etc.
- poor organisation skills – chronically late, unprepared, forgets appointments, etc.
- greater risk of depression and anxiety.

11. The good news ...
The picture so far is relatively negative. However, as with consistent negative themes, there are some positive features.

Positive Qualities from parents and teachers attributed to children with AD/HD
- Funny, good sense of humour.
- Imaginative/creative.
- Caring/nurturing.
- Happy and content with certain activities such as outdoor pursuits, construction, etc.
- Inquisitive – perceptive questions, want to talk about things.
- Can be motivated by video technologies (e.g., computer, Nintendo, TV, etc.).

In my clinical experience, adults often tell me that they can relate to many of the problems their children are experiencing. Yet,some of these same adults have achieved in a monetary/employment fashion beyond what would have been expected given their difficult time at school, with parents and with peers. This level of achievement, despite undiagnosed AD/HD, may be due to some of the positive features of the disorder. For example, perpetual energy and drive may be related to over-achievement. In addition, this drive, combined with imagination and creativity, gives the person with AD/HD a certain degree of entrepreneurial advantage relative to the 'normal population'. Unfortunately, this energy and zest is not without a type of maddening restlessness which continues to create relationship problems as well as personal discontent.

At the End of the Day
The observations of Dr. George Still at the turn of the previous century are as prophetic today as they were 100 years ago. How is it that some children, despite reasonable environments and

well-intentioned parents, cannot control their behaviour? Why do these children persist in being distracted and demanding when other children, given the same set of parents and environments, would not be so inclined? Further, are children who are inattentive, disorganised and lack impulse control necessarily AD/HD?

I recently watched a television programme which featured a well-respected children's guidance clinic. The programme dealt with the difficult behaviour of a four-year-old boy, his parents' view of their son,s conduct, and the interventions of the treating psychiatrists. Like any other viewer, I was struck by how the boy never settled with any activity for more than a fleeting second. He flitted from one object to another, and in most cases, played with objects that were not toys (e.g., door handles). When he did play with a toy, he typically threw it at an adult. Perhaps it was because of the cameras but neither parent took much notice of his behaviour. It was only when the boy did something that could result in property destruction (e.g., grabbing an electric mixer) that the parents repeatedly gave verbal reprimands (e.g., 'don't do that', 'put that back', 'that is not a toy', etc.). When the boy paid no attention to parental requests, the object was confiscated, the boy became upset and started to hit his parents. One got the feeling that this pattern was endlessly repeated.

After a few minutes of observing the youngster, I immediately concluded that he was very hyperactive, easily bored, and lacked impulse control. I waited for the psychiatrist to tell the parents that their son presented with all the core features of AD/HD. But this opinion was never rendered. Instead, the father's own childhood was explored with the connection between how his upbringing influenced his perceptions of his son, which in turn influenced his son's behaviour. The idea was that the father, by understanding his own childhood, would come to alter negative perceptions of his son and this would change the boy's behaviour. And amazingly, by both parents' accounts, this is exactly what happened (could it be that the parents told the psychiatrists what they wanted to hear, especially given that the entire procedure was filmed?).

Had I been wrong about the boy's behaviour? Perhaps the child did not have AD/HD, but was simply seeking his parents' attention, albeit inappropriately (even though the video footage suggested that his parents provided adequate attention and not just the negative kind)? What if the treating doctors did not believe in AD/HD? The psychiatrists in the clinic seemed to downplay formal psychiatric labels such as AD/HD. Instead, their approach centred on deeper analysis of parent issues which may contribute to their son's behaviour.

This boy was raised by competent parents in a reasonably stimulating environment. Yet his behaviour was far more problematic than other children his age reared in similar conditions. Why the difference? To me, AD/HD appeared a strong possibility.

Chapter 2

Problems Associated with AD/HD

AD/HD is considered a 'behaviour problem' mainly because of the excess behaviours associated with HD. HD-type behaviours (e.g., can't wait, over-active, tire of task quickly, etc.) are viewed as disruptive and interfere with the child's learning and social development. However, it is less clear how to classify AD (without HD). Since AD occurs mainly in regard to school work and mental activities, it could be seen as a 'learning problem'.

The point is that AD and HD may be linked with other behavioural and learning problems. Additional problems are known here as 'associated problems'. Another more medical term is 'co-morbid conditions' or 'competing diagnoses'. Data from my practice show that AD/HD rarely occurs in isolation. For example, I have considered AD/HD the sole problem in 25 per cent of cases, and mixed with some other behaviour or learning problem in the other 75 per cent of cases. In other words, three in every four children with AD/HD have an associated problem. Some of these problems may be more important than AD/HD or vice versa.

I have developed a particular grouping of associated problems. The names and labels of these problems will not be clear at this point but each will be explained:

General Problem	Sub-Groups
Externalising Behaviour Problems	Oppositional Defiant Disorder (ODD)
	Conduct Disorder (CD)

GENERAL PROBLEM	SUB-GROUPS
Internalising Problems	Depression Anxiety
Pervasive Developmental Disorder	Autistic-Type Asperger's Syndrome
Learning/Cognitive Problems	Specific Learning Difficulty (Dyslexia) Mechanics > Comprehension/ Reasoning General Learning Difficulty Language Related
Physical-Co-ordination Problems	Dyspraxia
Specific Problems (non-diagnostic)	_Psychological:_ •Erratic/Variable Performance •Increased Role of Interest Level •Frustration about Inability to Change _Health Habits:_ •Dietary issues •Sleep problems _Medical Factors:_ •Thyroid •Sensory Impairment (vision/ hearing) •Allergies/Asthma •Accidents/Injuries •Neurological Impairments (e.g., Tourette's Syndrome, seizure disorder) •General Health

All items previous to Specific Problems are viewed as 'competing diagnoses'. On the other hand, specific problems are those issues which may co-exist with AD/HD but are more descriptive (e.g., eating habits, general health) rather than formal and alternative diagnostic categories.

EXTERNALISING BEHAVIOUR PROBLEMS

The term externalising behaviour problems refers to excessive and inappropriate behaviours. The behaviours deviate with age-expected conduct in both quality and quantity. These behaviours are often viewed as disruptive and can be difficult to manage. Other terms related to this group are 'disruptive behaviour disorder' and 'challenging behaviour'. Specific examples are aggression, disobedience, teasing, argumentative, stealing, excessive activity, problems with impulse control, etc. The word 'externalising' implies an ongoing tension between the child and the outer environment – with parents, teachers, other children, relatives, animals, and objects. AD/HD is an example of an 'externalising disorder' particularly in its more severe forms and especially the HD component.

Oppositional Defiant Disorder (ODD) and Conduct Disorder (CD) are two of the most common Externalising behaviour problems. Of all the problems to be discussed, research suggests that ODD and CD are the most commonly co-existing problems. The estimates vary but the average for ODD is given as 35 per cent (Barkley, 1997). CD rates are about the same. My results are more conservative in that in the combined category of ODD and CD, the co-occurrence of AD/HD and either ODD and CD is thirteen per cent (the disparity is due to the rules applied to making the classification). Both problems are described next:

Oppositional Defiant Disorder (ODD)

The main quality of ODD is the hostility shown to authority figures. The hostility is expressed as frequent arguing and inflexible persistence with respect to getting what is desired. The child is reluctant to compromise and there is a sense of whining and persistent disagreement until the battle is 'won'. Other qualities are failure to take personal responsibility for misdeeds (usually blames others), disobedience, resentment, and sensitivity to corrective feedback (e.g., easily upset by requests to do or not do something).

Problems Associated with Oppositional Defiant Disorder

- Problems controlling temper.
- Argumentative.
- Stubborn.
- Blames others for mistakes.
- Purposely annoys others.
- Appears hostile, angry, sullen.
- Defies or refuses to comply with rules or requests.
- Touchy, irritable.
- Denies misdeeds.
- Often pushes adults to limits, tests patience.

Note that many of the behaviours relevant to ODD may also be relevant to AD/HD. For example, both problems will likely test an adult's patience and there is a degree of negativity in both areas. However, AD/HD and ODD are not the same. ODD children are not necessarily inattentive, impulsive or over-active. Also, if a child with AD/HD does not follow through on a request, it is not because of intentional defiance, as is true with ODD. Rather, failure to comply is due to inattention to the request, starting the request and not completing it, or doing only one or two parts of the command. These outcomes are due to the distractibility and difficulty listening which are so characteristic of AD/HD. Children with ODD fully understand and process the request but voluntarily decide to ignore or refuse to do it.

Although ODD is most commonly noted in the family context (e.g., parent-child), its significance is increased if oppositional features are observed in school. If ODD is observed in the home but less so in other situations, then there is a greater likelihood that family factors may be the root of the problem (e.g., harsh parenting, inconsistent limits, marital discord, parent mental health problems, etc.). On the other hand, if oppositional behaviour is observed in different situations (home and school) it is more likely a 'temperamental' feature of the child and in this case, a formal diagnosis of ODD may be relevant.

CONDUCT DISORDER (CD)

CD is perhaps the most troubling of the externalising behaviour disorders. It is most troubling because the behaviours associated with it are at greatest odds with societal mores. This is due to the core feature of CD which is the violation of accepted cultural standards. These violations are wilful and afterwards, the children with CD do not take responsibility for their actions (e.g., justify behaviour, blame another). In addition, there is a lack of compassion as to how their behaviour affects the 'victim(s)' of their conduct. A number of terms are used to describe the behaviours associated with CD, such as 'juvenile delinquent' and 'incorrigible' among others. I recall a newspaper article which covered CD titled, 'The Child from Hell'.

With CD, there is a central aspect of aggression directed to people or things. When directed to people, aggression takes the form of bullying, verbal abuse, physical fighting and sexual violations. Aggression can also be directed to things, such as damaging property, breaking and entering into a building, house, or car, fire-setting and vandalism.

Another element of CD is dishonesty in that children with CD can manipulate situations so as to avoid punishment, do tasks, or gain reward (e.g., ulterior motive). Stealing is another aspect of the deceit often noted in CD.

There are other behavioural patterns. Children with CD often disregard basic rules as set forth in school and home. At school, truancy and serious infractions of school rules are the most common problems. At home, there may be failure to obey household rules (e.g., curfew).

While some indications of CD can occur in children younger than ten, the full spectrum of difficulties do not typically manifest until adolescence. It does not auger well for the family if CD-type behaviours manifest early, as early indications indicate a poor outcome (treatment less likely to be effective).

Like AD/HD and ODD, true CD is not a reaction to environmental conditions but an inherent proclivity towards aggression and general misconduct. There are particular environmental conditions which may foster CD but a formal diagnosis is not warranted. For example, in some circumstances, children may engage in CD-type behaviours for survival purposes (e.g., extreme poverty, high crime areas, war-torn areas). There is also the need to disentangle CD from the 'resistant culture' dynamic by which inappropriate behaviours are viewed by a group as a form of acceptance (even initiation) into the group. In these instances, a child may be part of a larger group which takes part in an illicit activity. However, if 'caught', a child without CD will feel remorse and will feel relieved to make some form of restitution. Such is not the case with the a CD child, who will repeat violations without feelings of repentance.

PROBLEMS ASSOCIATED WITH CONDUCT DISORDER
- Bullies others.
- Physical fighting.
- Mean-spirited.
- Damages the possessions of others.
- Fire-setting.
- Stealing, forgery.
- Truancy.
- Deceit.
- Running away from home.
- Lack of empathy or remorse.

What sets CD apart from AD/HD and ODD is the serious nature of the conduct described. Children with AD/HD and ODD do not typically engage in the grievous offences associated with CD, although this is not always the case. Like ODD, research suggests that if AD/HD is present in adolescence there is a 50 per cent chance of co-existing CD. This high co-occurrence has led some to consider a subset of AD/HD as AD/HD–Aggressive Type. This particular combination is one of the most unfortunate because children with such a profile are very difficult to treat (poorest prognosis).

INTERNALISING BEHAVIOUR PROBLEMS

While Externalising behaviour problems are directed outward, Internalising behaviour problems are directed inward. Internalisers usually harbour excessively negative emotions, such as anger, frustration, fear, etc. The person appears inhibited, anxious, fearful, down on self, worried, retiring, removed, lethargic, bland, etc. Since the behaviours are not directed outward, the individual is not 'acting out' as is true of the Externalising child. This may lead many to overlook the Internalising problems because there is no behaviour disruption. However, other problems may arise, such as specific phobias, obsessive-compulsive behaviours (e.g., obsession with cleanliness and subsequent compulsion – excessive hand-washing), eating and sleep disruptions, maladaptive habits (e.g., nail-biting, picking at skin, etc.), school refusal, and psychosomatic illnesses (e.g., stomach aches, headaches, nausea, dizziness, aches/pains, etc.).

There are two common childhood Internalising Behaviour Problems – depression and anxiety.

DEPRESSION

I recently read where depression is considered the 'common cold' of the mental health profession. This is not surprising since we often use the term 'depressed' in regular parlance. In common use, being 'depressed' is more a transitive and non-clinical state which one could refer to in everyday conversation (e.g., 'You seem really depressed'). In psychiatric terms, Clinical Depression implies a significant degree of impairment. For example, clinical depression interferes with everyday functions, such as looking after self (e.g.,

hygiene), family tasks (e.g., managing the children), relationships (intimacy), job performance, to name just a few.

Clinical depression is one of several disorders related in the general group of 'Mood Disturbances'. Since this is not an exposé on 'depressive disorders' the focus is on the generic term of 'clinical depression'. The two important features of clinical depression are the significant impairment it causes and that it is the primary (or co-primary) focus of treatment. That is, if it is clinically significant depression, it requires professional treatment.

COMMON PROBLEMS ASSOCIATED WITH CLINICAL DEPRESSION

- Down in the dumps.
- Always sad.
- Negative beliefs about the world (e.g., pessimistic, fatalistic).
- Low self-worth (lack of self-esteem).
- Insecure (hypersensitive).
- May discuss self-injury (suicidal themes).
- Excessive self-blame.
- Irritability / anger (especially in children).
- Inability to concentrate.
- Fatigue, physical lethargy – move or talk slowly.
- Reduced interest in activities (one senses a shrinking interest in hobbies, activities).
- Increased involvement in non-productive activities (e.g., television).
- Possible sleep disturbance.
- Possible weight gain or weight loss.
- Loneliness.

After looking at the above, one could conclude that clinical depression is more applicable to adults than children (do children engage in excessive self-blame). While the age of onset tends to be the mid-twenties, clinical depression can begin at any age. As such, it is very relevant to children.

The discerning reader will note that some of the problems associated with clinical depression also overlap with AD/HD. For example, inability to concentrate is related to Inattention. Also, hypersensitivity and sleep problems are sometimes linked with AD/HD. And, it is possible for a child to be both Clinically Depressed and have AD/HD.

However, AD/HD and Clinical Depression are distinctly different. The core problems of each are antithetical in some cases – impulsivity versus inhibition, lethargy versus over-activity, etc. A thorough assessment will help clarify the picture.

ANXIETY

Do you recall the last time you had to perform a forbidding task, such as giving a speech, completing a job interview, or taking a test? If so, try to recall your state of mind. Common and 'normal' anxiety reactions are shortness of breath, heart palpitations, dry mouth, and shaking/trembling. Psychological responses are worry, problems concentrating, preoccupation about performance, difficulty sleeping, and so on. Interestingly, mild anxiety (or arousal) can be beneficial to performance. For example, before giving a speech or taking a test, a small amount of anxiety creates greater alertness which can lead to more successful outcomes.

These responses could be considered 'normal anxiety reactions'. Like inattention or low mood, anxiety is a mental state which is common to all individuals. However, a normal anxiety reaction is different from an anxiety disorder (to keep the terms consistent with the previous section, an anxiety disorder is referred to as 'clinically significant anxiety'). When we speak of clinically significant anxiety, the feelings are more intense, last longer and lead to impairment (e.g., disrupt life), whereas a similar level of discomfort is not observed in a normal anxiety reaction.

Like other mental health problems, anxiety can be considered both a disposition and a situational quality. When viewed as a disposition, the implication is that the individual is generally 'anxious' – worries often, concerned about the future, preoccupied, always asking questions, clingy/dependent, self-conscious, tense, frequently complains about feeling sick or having pains, perfectionist, appears shy and timid, and may have nervous habits such as nail-biting, scratching, etc.

On the other hand, anxiety may be situational. That is, the person may function in a non-anxious way in most situations but will become extremely distressed about a feared future event (e.g., performance in a school play). The individual may also react with great panic and shock when encountering the feared item. Abnormal anxiety responses to specific environmental cues are known as 'phobias', and can be triggered by animals, heights, water, flying or social events (e.g., fear of performing before an audience).

Finally, stress is an important mediating variable in anxiety. For example, the greater the pressure and stress the person feels, the more likely they will experience anxiety. But the equation is not this simple, because differences in coping skill determine how stress is managed. People with good coping skills may still feel anxious, but not to the debilitating degree those with poor coping skills will experience.

COMMON PROBLEMS ASSOCIATED WITH CLINICAL ANXIETY
- Nervous, tense, worried.
- Preoccupied.
- Recurring worries/thoughts (e.g., death, performing unacceptable act).
- Insecure.
- Timid/bashful.
- Fearful.
- Clingy/dependent (afraid to leave caregiver).
- Asks frequent questions about the future.
- Self-conscious.

- Frequently complain about feeling sick or having pains.
- Perfectionism.
- Nervous habits such as nail-biting, scratching, etc.
- High levels of conformity with the expectations of others.
- Difficulty concentrating.
- Sleep problems.
- Avoidance of particular situations (e.g., places, people).
- Intense fear which may consist of feelings of choking, sweating, dizziness, chills, shortness of breath, etc.
- Irritability.
- Restlessness.
- Fear of losing control.
- Repetitive behaviours (designed to reduce anxiety) such as hand-washing, gestures, etc.

EXTERNALISING OR INTERNALISING: THE CHICKEN OR THE EGG

A child may first show signs of an externalising disorder. As time passes, and anger and frustration build, the person's mental state may become more internalised. Children with AD/HD can show this course. For example, a youngster may be described as inattentive, easily distracted, impulsive, over-active, etc. If the problems are not dealt with early, children with AD/HD may wonder why their behaviour is out of control, why they are not reaching goals, and why getting along with others is difficult. They may become increasingly frustrated, angry and defeated. A sort of learned helplessness may set in and this may manifest as one of the internalising problems just discussed.

It is important to repeat a point made earlier regarding whether AD/HD is the central problem or the result of another more important issue. For example, if parents state that the primary problems they encounter are temper flare-ups, irritability, low self-confidence and lethargy these issues do not seem related to AD/HD. Temper and irritability fit better with ODD and low self-esteem and lethargy match with clinically significant depression.

These categories may be more appropriate than AD/HD. However, if one follows the logic of the previous paragraph, anger control, moodiness, etc., could be the result of chronic and heretofore unrecognised AD/HD. Again, a thorough assessment will help to disentangle these issues.

PERVASIVE DEVELOPMENTAL DISORDERS

The operative word in Pervasive Developmental Disorders (or PDD for short) is 'pervasive', because these disorders are the most impairing of all of the problems mentioned in this chapter. Children with PDD are very different from their same-age peers in that they do not relate to the world as other children do. For example, a PDD child will not be able to relate to others in age-expected fashion. Instead, they seem to be locked in their own world whereby they can stimulate themselves or are stimulated by one or two repetitive inputs (e.g., restricted interests). There is little interest in companionship and greater involvement with objects and solitary activities (e.g., playing imaginary games alone).

Speech and language development is generally restricted (e.g.. small speaking vocabulary – repeating certain words, phrases, etc.). The PDD child typically does not participate in conversation, as one would expect. One might ask the child what he/she is doing and the child may respond without understanding the input (e.g., 'hello'). Typically, great effort is made to teach the child to respond with grammatically correct phrases in response to particular questions.

One of the most atypical aspects of PDD is the eccentric behaviours these children can display. For example, the child may be playing with a toy, then make a peculiar gesture or vocal sound. The child may flap his hands, make an intense grunt, pace, or do any combination of odd movement and sound.

PDD children also demonstrate limited and unusual play behaviour. There is typically little imagination in play and there may be a fixation with a minor detail of a toy (e.g., repeatedly opening and closing a toy car door).

A final aspect of PDD is that a majority of cases also present with Moderate to Severe General Learning Difficulty. This means that there is significant impairment in intellectual functioning, as well as performance of activities of daily living (e.g., taking care of self).

There are different types of PDD but two of the most common are autism (also known as Autistic Disorder, and Autistic Spectrum) and Asperger's Syndrome.

AUTISM

Autism is the most commonly recognised PDD. The word 'autism' is derived from the Greek word for 'self'. This term conveys the extreme reliance on self-stimulation and the concomitant absence of attachment with people. In fact, the earliest sign of autistic tendencies may be the disinterest an infant shows in others, and a possible dislike of affection (e.g., when cuddled, they may arch away from caregiver). Autistic infants are typically described as 'good babies' because they can entertain themselves for long periods and do not cry or place demands on parents.

Autistic toddlers remain indifferent to others and there is a notable lack of attachment with people. Instead, there is a fascination with inanimate objects, such as light switches, toy parts, door handles and washing machines (to name a few).

Language development is atypical. The autistic toddler may repeat words, but there is usually no spontaneous speech. Rather, the child may repeat a certain word, phrase, or sound. As it turns out, the amount of speech and language the autistic child develops by the age of five is a good predictor of later adjustment (Schwartz and Johnson, 1985). It is estimated that about 50 per cent of autistic children do not learn to speak.

The activities and interests of autistic children are described as peculiar, repetitive, even obsessional. Play is one area where these autistic characteristics are evident. For example, the autistic child may continually repeat a certain play activity (e.g., align a large row of cars, break the line, realign the cars, etc.). Also, a pre-occupation with parts of toys is evident (e.g., pushing the play button on a tape recorder). There is little in the way of imaginary play (e.g., giving a doll a cup of tea). As the autistic child develops, narrowed interests may be seen in the continued pursuit of one activity (e.g., do same activity in the playground) and the dislike for any other endeavour.

Another behaviour which marginalises the autistic child is self-stimulating body movements, such as rocking, hand flapping and other unusual gestures. These movements are not constant but occur periodically throughout the day. Self-stimulation may occur in response to external demands (e.g., when the child is learning a new skill).

It is often noted that autistic children have a strong need to preserve 'sameness'; this means that the child adheres to specific routines and is greatly upset if the routine varies. For example, the child may show extreme upset if a door in the house is locked whereas previously it was accessible. The introduction of novel objects or a change in the environment (e.g., rearranging household furniture) can also have catastrophic consequences.

One of the most interesting aspects of autism is that many autistic children show a particular talent. One is reminded of the film 'Rain Man', where the particular talent demonstrated was extraordinary computational skill. Likewise, autistic children may be exceptionally detailed when drawing, or they may have great factual knowledge about a specific subject. Some of their exceptional talent may be due to the aforementioned narrowed interests.

However, surrounding this talent is significant delay in reasoning and comprehension. Roughly 75 per cent of autistic children function in the General Learning Difficulty range of overall mental ability. The term 'overall' is important because autistic children may perform somewhat better on non-verbal tests (e.g., matching shapes) than verbal tests. This makes sense given that speech and language problems are one of the core features of autistic children.

AUTISTIC-TYPE SYMPTOMS

- Significant problems in relating to others (e.g,. impaired ability in various social skills, such as showing interest in another, recognising another person's feelings, etc).
- Lack of interest in companionship and attachment to people.
- 'Aloneness' – only interested in inner world, self-absorbed.
- Focus on inanimate objects.
- Delay in speech, and often no functional speech.
- Speech/language may be characterised by repetition of words, sounds, jingles.
- Unusual voice quality (high pitch, squeaky, dysfluent, etc).
- May entertain self for long periods engaged in ritualistic play (e.g., pushing play button on recorder).
- Preoccupied with parts of objects (e.g., small part of large toy).
- Upset by changes in environment.
- Obsessional and narrowed interests (one type of play, one subject, etc).
- Fascination with facts (schedules, statistics, etc).
- Self-stimulating behaviours (e.g., body swaying).
- May be skilled in one area (e.g., good word reading, but lack of comprehension).
- General learning difficulty (e.g., problems with reasoning and comprehension).
- Maybe relatively better at visual activities (e.g., jigsaw puzzles) compared with language ability.
- May engage in self-injurious behaviours (e.g., picking skin).
- May show excessive and inappropriate emotional reactions to events (e.g., become 'hysterical' if corrected, or given a request).
- Does not recognise the feelings or emotional states of others

(e.g,. does not understand non-verbal cues like frowns, tears, anger, etc).

ASPERGER'S SYNDROME

Asperger's Syndrome consists of two core symptoms also noted in autism – significant impairment in social relationships and narrowed/restricted interests. However, unlike autism, Asperger's syndrome does not include delays in Speech and Language. That is, the child with Asperger's syndrome will usually have single words by twelve months, and meaningful phrases by two years. Likewise, there is not the pervasive delay in mental ability as is typically the case with autistic children. There may be some delay in attainment of motor milestones. 'Clumsiness' is also associated with Asperger's Syndrome. Some consider Asperger's Syndrome to be a 'mild' form of autism.

One of the main features of Asperger's Syndrome is general difficulty relating to people. Children with Asperger's syndrome are seen as socially detached. These children typically do not form age-expected friendships, and may socialise only in a stereotyped fashion (e.g., asking the same questions). There is a notable lack of social skills, such as the ability to discuss a topic of interest to the other person, a general indifference to other children's interests and accomplishments, difficulty initiating or maintaining conversation, inability to pick up cues as to the other person's emotions, lack of eye contact, and a general neglect of behaviours which typically regulate conversation (e.g., gestures, facial expressions, etc.).

Impaired social interaction, by itself, is difficult to distinguish from clinically significant shyness. Children who are extremely shy have difficulty approaching peers, do not know how to start conversations, find it hard to express their needs, and are socially inhibited. If shy children are not anxious and their social interaction problems are the result of social skill deficits, then clinical shyness is very much the same as the qualities that represent Asperger's Syndrome.

However, shy children typically do not have the restricted interests noted in Asperger's Syndrome. Usually, a child with Asperger's Syndrome will be over focused on a specific topic (e.g., historical facts), and disregard all other activities or interests. There is an adherence to routine (e.g., wake at same time, same breakfast, etc.) which is more rigid than normal. Again, the positive side of preoccupation with a single interest is that this interest can become an area of talent (e.g., computers, chess, model making, etc.).

In later school years, the child with Asperger's Syndrome will typically remain isolated from his peers. The child may be quiet in classroom, and perceived as shy. There is concern that these children may be targeted for bullying, especially exclusionary tactics. Academic outcomes may be reasonably good.

PROBLEMS ASSOCIATED WITH ASPERGER'S SYNDROME
- Socially detached.
- Passive, socially inhibited, and vulnerable to being the 'scape-goat'.
- Problems in social-relational skills, such as:
    - initiating a conversation.
    - showing an interest in the activities or achievements of others.
    - difficulty maintaining social interaction by lack of spontaneous comments, lack of animation, poor eye contact, etc.
    - lack of empathy and ability to understand another person's perspective.
    - difficulty expressing needs.
- Limited interests (pursue one activity to the extreme).
- Preoccupied with facts, records, statistics.
- Strong preference for routine and may be anxious by changes in same.
- Odd, or stereotyped movements (e.g., unusual posture, head position, etc).

- May demonstrate good mechanics (word reading, computation, etc) but have difficulty solving more complex, abstract problems.
- May achieve fair to good academic outcomes.
- May appear clumsy.

LEARNING AND COGNITIVE PROBLEMS

So far, the difficulties have been predominately behavioural (e.g., oppositional, conduct) emotional (e.g., anxious depressed), or reflect significant developmental delays (autism and Asperger's Syndrome). The next set of issues pertain to children who relate in socially appropriate ways and do not suffer from behaviour problems, but who demonstrate significant learning problems. These problems may be specific to a certain skill (e.g., reading, spelling, maths, language, etc.) or more general learning problems (e.g., behind in most subjects).

SPECIFIC LEARNING DIFFICULTY (DYSLEXIA OR DYSCALCULIA)

Specific Learning Difficulty (aka Dyslexia) has various definitions but the one I find most descriptive is an unexpected delay in reading and/or writing. The delay is unexpected because the child is able in many areas, such as communicating ideas orally, visual reasoning (e.g., seeing how parts fit, construction/assembly, etc.), and usually maths.

Dyslexia is fundamentally a problem of processing the printed word – a phonological, or sound-symbol fault. Teachers, parents and other professionals may suspect a reading/writing problem around the age of six to eight when children are first expected to read and develop a reading vocabulary. At this time some children (estimated to be one in ten), may memorise words (e.g., 'cat'), but when faced with similar looking words (e.g., 'hat') will not have the phonic awareness to pronounce them. Writing and spelling may also be delayed. Another common problem is letter reversals (e.g., 'p' for 'q'), mispronunciations of similar looking words (e.g., 'that', 'then', 'this', 'them', etc.), slow reading rate, organising thoughts in written form, omissions/additions of words during reading, dysfluency, etc.

Another enigma of dyslexia is that dyslexic children may be well able to use spoken/oral language (e.g., the ability to converse and 'talk') and yet not be able to read this language once codified in print. For example, a child may not be able to read 'volcano' yet, when asked what a volcano is, reply with a comment like, 'a volcano is a mountain with a hole at the top which can explode with lava, hot rocks and fire.'

The contrast between spoken language and the ability to decode this same language in written form is not surprising. After all, if we did not transcribe our spoken language into written form there would be no dyslexia. However, in the process of translating ideas into printed symbols, a new set of complex skills is required. One must recognise individual letters of the language, know the sound these letters make, and then know how letters sound in various combinations (e.g., 'baby' ▶ 'buh-aah-bee'). Further, a beginning reader has to know where to break the word into it's constituent parts and then be able to blend these sounds ('unique' ▶ u/nique' not 'un/e/que'). If that is not enough, the same letter has different sounds, depending on the letters around it (e.g., the letter 'a' sounds different in 'at', 'are', 'Jane', 'was', 'saw', 'ball' and 'father').

While word decoding and the development of the sound-symbol system is vital for one to read, it is not the only system required in reading. Some children can get pronunciation clues from their knowledge of syntax and semantics. Syntax refers to the 'grammar' of the language, or how words are arranged to make sense. For example, the sentence, 'we got a new dog', is hardly interpretable as 'a we new got dog'. Semantics is the understanding one brings to the printed material; does the reader have a background which will enable him to make sense of the information. Finally, and perhaps the most basic reading system is motivation – without desire, interest, or purpose, there is no reason to read, even if the child is capable of making sense of the material (the other three systems are available). And, one of the most devastating cycles with delayed readers is that their difficulties with reading result in avoidance of reading, which consolidates the delay.

Dyscalculia is another specific learning problem, whereby mathematical computation and or reasoning skills are unexpectedly delayed (but not reading or spelling). Essentially, dyscalculia is 'maths dyslexia'.

Dyslexia is one of the more difficult problems to coherently assemble a list of 'symptoms' because there is such variety in the 'breadth' of problems listed in the 'dyslexia' rubric. The list of 'peripheral' problems (peripheral to the core problem of phonology) is immense and can include activities of daily living (dressing), motor skills (e.g., clumsiness, dexterity, confused laterally, etc.), language (e.g., delay in spoken language, articulation difficulties, problems recalling verse, confused syntax, etc.) to a variety of specific cognitive skills (e.g., sequencing, visual memory, etc.). As most of these problems are more appropriately covered in separate categories (e.g., delay in activities of daily living is a core feature of General Learning Difficulty; Language problems are discussed later on, etc.), only the myriad forms of sound-symbol weakness will be highlighted below.

PROBLEMS ASSOCIATED WITH SPECIFIC LEARNING DIFFICULTY
- Unexpected delay in reading, spelling, written composition (delay is unexpected because child is able in many way other areas – oral language, maths, etc).
- Uneven attainments – some areas at age standard (e.g., math), while others are below standard (reading).
- Specific reading problems include:
  - difficulty pronouncing words which child of similar age would recognise.

- may memorise word pronunciations but not be able to decode unfamiliar words.
- erratic retention of words; easily forgotten.
- substitute words based on visual similarity (e.g., 'when' for 'what', 'this' for 'then'.
- invert words (e.g., 'saw' for 'was').
- insert words which are not in text.
- omit words in text.
- dysfluent reading – word-by-word, not pausing, re-reading words or lines.
- specific phonetic weaknesses (e.g., not pronouncing short vowels, unable to blend sounds, etc.).
- mis-reads words with meaning units (e.g., 'rivers' as 'river', 'completely' as 'complete').
- doesn't understand what was read.
- misunderstands written questions or instructions

- Specific spelling/writing problems which include:
  - over-reliance on sound (e.g., 'wisel' for 'whistle').
  - does not recognise vowel sounds (e.g., 'pag' for 'pig', 'jomp' for 'jump', 'crls' for 'careless'.
  - sequencing errors (e.g., 'pitcrue' for 'picture').
  - inverts letters or numbers ('q' and 'p').
  - in written compositions, substitutes small words for larger, more enriching words, which may be in the child's oral vocabulary (e.g., instead of using 'gigantic' the child will use 'big').
  - slow writing speed (misses information on chalk board).
  - unaware of capitalisation/punctuation.
  - difficulty with grammar and sentence construction.
  - generally immature writing compared with oral language.
- Specific cognitive weaknesses, such as forgetting instructions, difficulty recalling sequences, problems listening and

concentrating, etc.

It is important to note that dyslexia is not due to social disadvantage, hearing/vision problems, faulty education, or lack of general intelligence. Instead, there appears to be a faulty process in the brain pertaining to phonological processing. Dyslexia is life-long, although when assessed and treated early the prognosis is more favourable.

GOOD MECHANICS BUT POOR COMPREHENSION/REASONING

This is a very subtle and largely overlooked learning difficulty, mainly because children seem to be academically able. For example, the child may read accurately and no problems in maths computation are evident.

To a degree, word analysis and computational skills are mechanical; they can be learned through drill and practice and there is a certain method and routine to pronouncing words and calculating sums. However, the child may encounter difficulty when deeper analysis is required, such as understanding what was read, or reasoning with numbers (e.g., solving mental mathematical problems). In these situations, flexibility and critical thinking skills take precedence over mechanics. And, for some children academic difficulties may lie solely in the area of abstract reasoning, deduction and problem-solving.

To clarify the distinction between mechanical, rote learning and abstract conceptual learning, the table overleaf provides examples of tasks considered mechanical and those considered more abstract (e.g., reasoning).

Another good contrast between mechanics and reasoning is found in the activity of 'sorting'. When one is confronted with a large variety of objects (e.g., toys, tools, etc.) and one wishes to organise the objects, it is inevitable that the objects be categorised for purposes of sorting into boxes, trays, etc. So for example, a child's room might be strewn with different toys and this might be

Mechanics		Reasoning	
Activity	Task	Activity	Task
Word Reading	Word pronunciation; reading accuracy.	Verbal Reasoning	How are two concepts alike (e.g. train and a boat, ice and steam, etc.), responding to practical questions (e.g. why should children be vaccinated...)
Spelling	Accuracy of oral or written spelling	Visual Reasoning	Fitting jigsaws without a model; arranging picture cards to make a sensible story, etc.
Number Calculation	Maths computations (e.g. 756 x 21 =)	Logic/Inference	n is fatter than l; l is fatter than s; is s fatter than n?
Simple Memory	Repeating numbers, facts, etc.	Reading Comprehension, Written Expression, and Maths Reasoning	These activities are the more conceptual/abstract counterparts to word reading, spelling, and number calculation.

the impetus for helping the child to be more organised. To do this, a parent could purchase three containers with each containing a various category of toy (e.g., all the cars, trains, figures on one box, lego and building material in another, etc.). A mechanical form of this task is to tell the child which box is for what type of toy, and have the child sort the toys as specified. On the other hand, if the child were asked to develop the categories and justify each one, then the task is more conceptual, abstract, and requires critical thinking skill.

PROBLEMS ASSOCIATED WITH COMPREHENSION AND REASONING DIFFICULTIES

- May lack flexibility in thinking (e.g., keep applying an

ineffective problem-solving strategy).

- Require more practice to learn material.
- May lack practical problem-solving skills (e.g., may perform household tasks in a way that complicates what should be a simple routine).
- May confuse concepts (e.g., name the season of the year with a month; may define the alphabet as a set of numbers, etc).
- May show limited concept development (e.g., define 'brave' as 'when you are brave').
- May not see errors in problem solutions, even when given an opportunity to correct a mistake.
- May have difficulty seeing how concepts or objects relate to one another.
- May do well on memory tasks.
- Can demonstrate good word mechanics (basic reading and Spelling), as well as number mechanics (calculations) but may show more difficulty with reading comprehension and numerical reasoning (maths word problems)
- May learn quicker when concepts are made more 'tangible and concrete'.
- May find mental work tedious and tiring.
- Performs best on reasoning-reduced tests (e.g., repeating back numbers, copying letters, factual information, etc).
- May not learn from experience (e.g., repeat the same mistake).
- Performs best when allowed ample time to rehearse and study information.
- May have difficulty generating solutions to novel problems.

GENERAL LEARNING DIFFICULTY

As the name implies, General Learning Difficulty (GLD) refers to widespread delay in cognitive development. Many areas of development may be delayed, such as physical functioning, communication, social/emotional, thinking and problem-solving, and performing activities of daily living (e.g., dressing, hygiene, eating, etc.).

What separates GLD from all other learning difficulties is that the nature of the learning problems are more general and more serious. In terms of more general, most cognitive skills are below average, whereas with SLD, many areas are at, or above, average. Likewise, children with good mechanics tend to score close to average on word reading, spelling, computation tests, and measures of rote memory (e.g., immediate recall of numbers).

The term GLD has several different namesakes, such as Mild Mental Handicap, Mental Retardation, and Intellectual Deficiency. There are also four different levels of severity of GLD, based on the degree of cognitive delay (as determined by intelligence tests). The most debilitating level of GLD is known as 'Profound' and constitutes the smallest per cent (roughly 1 or 2 per cent) of all individuals with GLD. If you recall, reference was made earlier to the hospital unit this author visited during his undergraduate psychology studies. The children in this unit were considered 'Profoundly Retarded'. The next level is called 'Severe', and also defines a small per cent of the total GLD group. Children with Severe GLD have minimal communication skills, and require caregivers to manage most activities of daily living (e.g., dressing, grooming, etc.). Another level is referred to as 'Moderate' a designation which accounts for about 10-15 per cent of the GLD population. Children with Moderate GLD have basic communication skills (can converse) and are able to manage activities of daily living. Special schooling is typically indicated.

By far the largest group of individuals, roughly 85 per cent of the entire GLD group, are referred to as 'Mild' GLD. Children in this group develop communication and self-help skills as young children, although the attainment of major milestones may be delayed (e.g., late to speak). The child will normally progress through regular schooling, although academic work will be difficult and the child may fall behind in all academic areas. The child usually finds homework very difficult and the completion of academic work may take an inordinate amount of time. Secondary schooling is even more challenging, and, at this time, behaviour and emotional difficulties may arise from the mismatch between the child's limited cognitive resources and the demands of regular secondary school. Academic attainments usually reach the end of the primary school learning objectives. Adults with mild GLD usually manage independent living, although self-autonomy may be stressful (e.g., managing domestic matters, work, social life, etc.).

The cause of GLD is unknown in about 35 per cent of cases. In those cases where a cause is identified one of the most common are chromosomal abnormalities (e.g., such as trisomy 21 which leads to Downs Syndrome). Other causes are pregnancy and perinatal complications (e.g., infections, trauma), infant or early childhood medical events (e.g., infections, poisoning), gross understimulation/neglect, and the fact that GLD may be due to another condition (e.g., autism – as 75 per cent of autistic children function in the GLD range).

The problems associated with Mild General Learning Difficulty are provided below.

PROBLEMS ASSOCIATED WITH MILD GENERAL LEARNING DIFFICULTY
- Significant homework difficulties.
- Lags behind classmates in most or all academic areas.
- Needs more time to process information and formulate an answer.
- Slower to grasp concepts.
- Have difficulty with reasoning and comprehension.
- Require over-learning to ensure material is retained.
- Make progress, but gains tend to be slower than peers.
- Have standardised cognitive test results in the lowest percentile band (e.g., tenth percentile and below).

- Easily confused.
- Find academic work strenuous and tire easily during mental work.
- May have delays in attaining basic developmental milestones.
- May exhibit emotional displays which are out of context for the particular situation (e.g., laugh at something sad, over-react, etc.).
- Find it difficult to achieve some basic self-help tasks (e.g., tying shoelaces, eating cleanly, etc.).
- May have difficulty with social and interpersonal skills.
- May be emotionally immature.

Language Related

The term 'language-related' refers to many different types of communication problems. Speech delay or language-related problems are one of the most frequent reasons parents first seek professional assessment. There are clear markers for the development of speech, beginning with pre-word communication such as babbling, cooing and crying. Well before one year, infants are typically making partial speech sounds (e.g., 'bah', 'dah' etc.). Around twelve months speech sounds become clearly articulated words, which are followed by more and more words. In a matter of six more months, two word utterances are made in a variety of forms (e.g., the declarative – 'mean dog', a question – 'where doll', etc.). In another six months, longer and more sophisticated sentences begin (e.g., 'I want more drink'). Expressive language continues to mature and by four years of age most adult-like grammatical structures are fully formed.

Parents may be aware that something is amiss in the child's speech and language development. In some cases, the concern may be related to lack of speech (e.g., no clearly articulated words by eighteen months). In others, the speech/language concern may be related to specific problems such as minimal vocabulary, difficulty finding the right word, jumbled syntax (e.g., confused order of words), articulation/pronunciation problems, etc.

There are different types of speech and language problems. One of the most common is articulation difficulties, which is the failure to correctly produce speech sounds. In some cases, when articulation problems are severe, it is very difficult to understand the child's speech. In other cases, the articulation difficulty may represent certain consonants (e.g., l, f) or consonant blends (e.g., th, str, etc.), and it is well known that certain speech sounds are acquired later than others (thus, some articulation problems may be developmentally appropriate). There may be problems in the speech mechanism (oral-motor responses which control voicing, accent, etc.) which result in mis-articulations.

In addition to articulation problems, some children may find it difficult to orally express themselves. These difficulties may be broadly considered as 'expressive language'. Some of the common elements of expressive language problems are limited vocabulary, unusually short and/or simple sentence structures, repetitive use of words or phrases and confused word order ('ball I want').

There are many issues which arise in relation to speech/language. Some of the most common comments relate to cause and prognosis. In regards to cause, a number of hypotheses are ventured for delayed speech such as other family members talking for the child, personality factors (e.g., shy, timid), ear infections, hearing problems, and other medical factors (e.g., tonsils, adenoids, dental problems, etc.).

SPEECH AND LANGUAGE PROBLEMS
- Delay in attainment of speech/language milestones.
- Articulation/pronunciation problems (e.g., certain per cent of words are distorted – 'airspoon' for 'airplane', 'fye' for 'fly', etc).
- Lisp.
- Low volume (e.g., whispering).

- Great effort required to communicate ideas.
- Simplified grammar and sentence type for age (e.g., four-year-old with two-year-old grammatical structure).
- Confused morphology (e.g., 'I runned' for 'I ran').
- Disorganised syntax ('seatbelts safe you keep').
- Simplified vocabulary.
- Difficulty finding correct word (e.g., effort to retrieve correct word). This can result in the constant repetition of a phrase (e.g., 'the yoke that goes here', 'the thinga-ma-jiggy that should be here', etc).
- Misunderstanding verbal instructions (frequently receives a different message from the one intended and one which would be correctly identified by most children).
- Frequent use of gestures instead of words.

PHYSICAL CO-ORDINATION PROBLEMS

The two initial topics covered in this chapter can be generally grouped as 'behaviour disorders'. The next two can be broadly categorised as 'emotional problems'. We then reviewed two 'Pervasive Developmental Disorders': Autism and Asperger's Syndrome. Subsequently, we turned our attention to four groups of 'Cognitive/Learning' related disorders. Each of the aforementioned ten topics emphasises one or the other basic area of human functioning – behavioural, emotional, social and cognitive. One general area of development which has yet to be discussed is that of physical development.

DYSPRAXIA

Most readers will not recognise the formal title of 'dyspraxia', as the term is a clinical, professional one. However, in plain language, dyspraxia is known as the 'clumsy child syndrome' or 'co-ordination disorder'.

Like most of the other difficulties discussed, dyspraxia is complicated by factors such as whether the child has other problems (e.g., significant learning difficulties, speech problems, etc.) which may overshadow dyspraxic tendencies. And, like the other concerns mentioned, dyspraxia occurs with varying levels of severity. Dyspraxia is typically noted when the child is unable to perform expected physical tasks, such as using a knife, running, throwing a ball, buttoning shirts, pouring a drink, etc. The prevalence of dyspraxia is estimated to be about 6 per cent in a five to eleven age group (Diagnostic and Statistical Manual of Mental Disorders, Fourth Edition). In general, dyspraxia is considered a motor disorder. However, it is not due to some of the more serious motor disorders such as Cerebral Palsy or Multiple Sclerosis. In other words, the child with dyspraxia does not have an obvious physical (e.g., paralysis) reason for why they have difficulty performing physical activities.

The cause of dyspraxia is usually attributed to damage or immaturity to any one of a number of brain systems that control motor function. The system is highly complex and includes the spinal cord, brainstem and motor cortex. Lesions in any area can effect motor development, as can a general immaturity in motor neurons.

One way to explain dyspraxia is to consider the various tasks that most of us have mastered. For example, consider the case of tying a shoelace. We can do this quickly and efficiently. However, if you have ever tried to show a child how to tie his/her shoe, you must take an 'automatic' skill and re-package it for the novice. When you do this, you might realise the complexity of tying a shoe. For example, one must have an idea of how to approach the task, what to do and what the completed product should look like. This is the mental component of physical tasks (referred to as 'ideation'). Once the idea (or mental framework) is in place, there is the next step of planning – what movements does one make and in what order – to complete the task. Finally, one executes the plan. An analogy would be building a new home – what does the person want the home to look like (idea), what are the steps involved to create the home (planning), and then the execution of the plan. All three components must be closely linked and occur rapidly and smoothly.

Unfortunately, something goes awry with dyspraxic children. The error may occur in any one area (e.g., faulty idea, problems sequencing the movements, etc.) or in the connection between the components. Thus, the teaching of a skill like tying a shoelace, using a knife, etc., may occur slowly and with more difficulty.

If you are familiar with comic strips, some of you may recognise that Charlie Brown, of 'Peanuts' fame, was probably dyspraxic. The episode depicted is an example of Charlie Brown's difficulties.

DIFFICULTIES ASSOCIATED WITH DYSPRAXIA
- May be late in attaining motor milestones (e.g., sitting up, walking, catching a ball, etc.).
- Bumping into things.
- Falling and dropping items.
- Difficulties with activities of daily living (e.g., pouring a

drink, using a knife, tying a shoe, buttoning a shirt, etc.).

- Not keeping pace with the physical development of same-aged peers (e.g., when other children are playing catch, child may not be able to throw or catch a ball like peers, etc).
- By virtue of co-ordination delay, may not be selected for games, or will be teased about lack of athletic skill.
- Problems with writing, drawing (e.g., messy, disorganised, lines slanted, letters uneven, etc).
- Does not run, climb, hop, throw like same-age peers.
- Lacks muscle tone; muscles may appear underdeveloped.
- Messy, disorganised, forgetful.
- May experience problems with visual, perceptual, spatial tasks (e.g., sentences off-centre, runs out of room on the page, etc).
- Hesitation before executing a motor movement (e.g., child may consciously stop, pause and concentrate for a second before executing a physical activity).
- Poor posture.
- May be defensive to touch.
- May be distractable, poor attention.
- Activity level may be excessively low (withdrawn, listless) or high (hyperactive).
- Lack of self-esteem (aware of co-ordination shortcomings and others perception of same).
- May be socially excluded (due to difficulty with physical games).

SPECIFIC PROBLEMS (NON-DIAGNOSTIC)

There are a number of specific physical and mental health problems that are commonly associated with AD/HD. Since many of the previous eleven associated problems contains a number of specific problems, some of which overlap with the core symptoms of AD/HD, no attempt is made to repeat them. For example, children with AD/HD may be prone to temper outbursts. As problems with anger control are a core feature of ODD, and since ODD often overlaps with AD/HD, temper problems will not be repeated here. Instead, the discussion that follows concerns topics which are neither the core symptoms of AD/HD as discussed earlier, nor common to any of the previous topics in this chapter. These 'other' problems are divided into psychological, health habits and medical factors.

PSYCHOLOGICAL FACTORS

There are at least three observations that are often made about children with AD/HD.

Erratic and variable performance. Children with AD/HD are inconsistent in their performance of a variety of tasks. Parents and teachers are often perplexed at why a child's application is on one day, off the next, etc. Many skills are exhibited, and just as easily gone the next day, or even on the next problem. This type of variability is not observed in children without AD/HD, at least not to the same degree.

In addition, erratic and variable performance extends to longer periods of time. For example, parents often report that the child with AD/HD may experience learning and behaviour fluctuations many times within a day, or experience several good days, then as many bad days, with this inconsistent cycle repeating itself.

Increased importance of interest level: Most children show some difference in attention and concentration, depending on whether they are interested in the task. For example, most children will be able to concentrate for considerable periods when engaged in self-selected activities, such as watching television, playing computer games, playing with lego, etc. However, while these children may not fancy writing an essay, they will do so without a significant degree of distress and trauma.

Such is not the case with AD/HD children. The role of interest is so strong that tasks of low interest are avoided or performed only under strict supervision. Performance of low interest tasks (e.g., homework) is usually done quickly, with children taking the path of 'least mental effort'. The completed task may be done carelessly and without sufficient deliberation or planning.

Frustration at inability of others or self to change problem behaviour. Imagine doing many things wrong, know your doing them wrong, yet not be able to change the situation. This inevitably leads to frustration which may express itself through anger and decreased self-esteem ('I'm no good at anything'). The child may also be doubly frustrated that adults are unable to change his or her problems.

Adults may be equally frustrated because even the best intentions to assist the child may be ineffective. Take the two basic consequences which alter behaviour – reward and punishment. For some reason, children with AD/HD are less inclined to respond to reward and punishment. This is not to say the child with AD/HD is impervious to reward and punishment, only that these consequences must be delivered in a more immediate, consistent, and intensive manner if any change is to be observed.

HEALTH HABITS

Health habits are defined here as basic human activities such as sleeping and eating.

Sleep disturbance. In my clinical experience, somewhere between 25 and 50 per cent of parents refer to problems related to bedtime routine. Delaying bedtime and difficulty falling asleep appear to be the most common complaints. Sleep problems may be noted during infancy where sleep/wake cycles are arhythmical (without pattern). Reference is rarely made to sleep difficulties after the child is asleep but problems arising in the morning are common complaints. So too are the 'early risers'. In general, it appears that children with AD/HD do not require as much sleep as their non-AD/HD counterparts.

Dietary Issues. In America during the mid 1970s, a causal view of AD/HD was advanced that suggested nearly half of childhood

AD/HD could be attributed to allergic-type reactions to various food additives (e.g., dyes, preservatives, etc.). A dietary intervention known as the 'Feingold diet' was promoted and became extremely popular. Unfortunately, when the diet was put under the scientific microscope, little evidence of its benefit was found.

Another popular idea relates excessive sugar intake to AD/HD, such that AD/HD-type behaviours are noted when the child consumes chocolate, drinks soft drinks, etc. (all food stuffs with any of a number of potentially offending substances). At first glance, this seems a straightforward connection but upon deeper reflection, the connection is not at all clear. For example, all children who have excessive sugar intakes will have lower attention spans and be excessively active, regardless of whether the child has AD/HD or not. Also, the degree to which sugar produces AD/HD type of behaviour depends on other dietary factors (e.g , protein intake), the actual excess of sugar, and whether the child may have an intolerance to sugar.

In my experience, sugar intake is only a small part of the dietary issues relevant to AD/HD. For example, parents often report that the child with suspected AD/HD may have a more restricted diet and tend to be finicky about what they eat. It is common sense that a balanced and healthy diet will have a positive effect on the behaviour of all children. Most parents know this and aspire to achieve healthy eating habits. If such is not the case, the reasons for non-optimal diets need to be determined.

MEDICAL FACTORS
A number of medical factors have been associated with AD/HD. *Thyroid functioning.* The thyroid gland is close to the base of your neck lying just below the larynx (voice box). It produces a major hormone known as thyroxin. When thyroxin is over-produced the person may appear fidgety, hyperactive, restless, irritable, unable to concentrate, have problems with sleep and have a large appetite (yet not gain weight due to a faster metabolic rate). When

thyroxin is under-produced, the individual may be lethargic, slow to react, tire easily, have problems concentrating, seem depressed and may be overweight.

In sum, problems with thyroid functioning may mimic AD/HD symptoms, although such difficulties are not very common. Nonetheless, there are blood tests which indicate whether the thyroid is operating within normal limits.

Sensory impairment (vision, hearing): in some cases, AD/HD-type behaviours are the result of deficits in basic sensory processes. For example, a child in classroom might be considered a day-dreamer and frequently off-task, especially when asked to read or copy information from the chalkboard. This child may hold their head close to the page when reading or show an awkward posture when writing. These may indicate problems with visual acuity.

It is even more common to hear that children with problems similar to AD/HD suffered frequent ear infections. Variable hearing can result in many of the indicators of AD/HD, especially not seeming to listen when spoken to. The more subtle effects of hearing are possible loss of certain tones or sounds. Thus, the child may hear part of an instruction and perhaps try to fill in the gaps, by guessing at the direction. This may lead to not completing the request, or only completing part of it, which is a common complaint about children with AD/HD. Researchers have noted that children with AD/HD may be hypersensitive to sound; that is, they may be more distracted and distressed by loud sounds and more easily distracted by background noise.

Allergies/Asthma. There are a number of substances in which an individual may react adversely. These substances may be related to diet (food allergies) or environmental particles which can aggravate breathing (e.g., dust, pollen, pets, lead, smoke, etc.). Anyone who suffers from allergies and related illnesses knows that these health problems adversely affect concentration and persistence. Try reading a book or writing a letter when your breathing is laboured, or you are wheezing and sneezing.

The research to date regarding allergies and asthma is equivocal. Some researchers find that children with AD/HD are more likely to have recurring allergic-type reactions. The presence of asthma is similarly unclear. However, one must be very vigilant about possible toxins and seasonal discomforts, and make sure that these concerns are assessed by a medical specialist.

Accidents/injuries. It may come as no surprise that children with AD/HD are far more likely to be considered accident prone and are at far greater risk for serious injury due to accidents relative to non-AD/HD children. By virtue of being more active and less inclined to be aware of danger, the child with AD/HD is an accident waiting to happen. No tree is too tall to climb, running is appropriate no matter where or when, and there is a type of thrill seeking which inevitably leads to accidents and injuries. As adults, there is a clear relationship between AD/HD and driving offences, like traffic accidents and speeding.

Neurological Impairments. Neurological factors are central to the cause of AD/HD. Some 70 per cent of children with 'tic disorders' have AD/HD. This is an extremely high rate of co-occurrence and suggests that for this group of children their brain difference creates two separate entities – tics and AD/HD. A tic is a sudden, rapid, spasmodic and involuntary movement. Tics are classified as motor (e.g., eye blinking, facial grimaces, squatting, tongue protrusions, etc.), or a vocal (e.g., yelp, grunt, throat clearing, cursing, etc.). The most serious tic disorder is known as Tourette's Syndrome. Children with tic disorders without AD/HD will normally not have the learning and behaviour problems associated with AD/HD.

Tics and AD/HD are also entwined by the fact that a small per cent of children with AD/HD who do not have tics may develop them with the use of psycho-stimulant medication (estimate of 1 per cent). Psycho-stimulant medication is the most common medication for AD/HD. Medical practitioners typically will inquire about family history of tic disorder before prescribing medications for AD/HD. Also, if tics do develop during the course of medication, the type and dosage of the medication can be altered to reduce this problem.

Most people associate epilepsy with grand mal seizures where the individual falls down, loses consciousness, turns blue, the eyes roll back, etc. However, there is a more subtle type of seizure known as the petit mal, in which there is no loss of consciousness. In fact, the small seizure may be missed. It may seem as if the individual stares blankly into space, or daydreams. Around 20 to 30 per cent of children with epilepsy have co-existing AD/HD. Anti-seizure medication can create AD/HD symptoms and a change to different medication can make a big difference.

General health. One might ask whether children with AD/HD are less healthy relative to their peers who do not have AD/HD. Starting from the beginning, it might seem reasonable to suspect that pregnancy and labour/delivery complications are more likely in children with AD/HD compared with children without AD/HD. Such is not the case. For example, toxaemia and foetal distress are not substantially different among AD/HD and non AD/HD samples. However, one consistent finding is that children with low birth-weight are more at risk for AD/HD compared with normal birth-weight babies.

Infant health is consistently found to be less optimal in AD/HD children compared with non-AD/HD groups. AD/HD children do not differ significantly from other children regarding weight. Height appears to be lower in AD/HD children but this difference is not noted during adolescence. There is no significant difference between AD/HD children and their non-AD/HD peers regarding bowel or bladder difficulties.

SUMMARY

The message is this – AD/HD is difficult to diagnose! Imagine all of the preceding issues and how they intertwine with each other and you can get a sense of the complexity of the problem. In my mind, 'pure AD/HD' is the case where parents and teachers do not report any other externalising or internalising problems, no pervasive developmental disorders, no learning problems, no delays with speech and language, no problems with physical co-ordination, and no health concerns. Of 100 cases in my files, 27 per cent would fit this description. The other 73 per cent include one or more of the associated problems discussed in this chapter.

As a general guide, it is wise to start with medical examination in order to rule out the physical problems discussed. Medical evaluation and subsequent intervention may solve the problem or at least greatly reduce its impact. If the child has a clean bill of health and the problems persist, then it is wise to obtain psychological and psychiatric assessment.

Chapter 3

FACTORS RELATED TO CAUSE AND RISK

AD/HD would be a very simple topic if one could assume that whenever anyone reported that a child demonstrated AD/HD type behaviour the child was in fact AD/HD. Unfortunately, it is not this straightforward.

First, behaviours characteristic of AD/HD may occur erratically, only under certain conditions, or only with certain individuals. Perceptions about the occurrence of a behaviour may be based on mistaken notions about the behaviour itself (e.g., a six-year-old child should sustain attention for 30 minutes without any disruptions during a sustained mental task). What if inattention only occurs at home but not school? What if a child can control his behaviour with one parent but not another? A comprehensive discussion of AD/HD must address these issues.

To initiate this deeper investigation, I have come to view AD/HD as somewhat akin to an iceberg. As you know the vast majority of an iceberg lies underneath the waterline. A relatively tame looking chunk of ice can actually be enormous if its totality is viewed. Similarly, a relatively cryptic and seemingly tangible problem like AD/HD is only this way when we view the part that is showing; the small surface symptoms which lie above the watermark. As you will see, the issues which relate to AD/HD are vast and represent the material submerged and not so readily apparent. For example, there are five areas of contributing factors – medical, family, culture, education and child. The five areas can be viewed as the roots of the problems noted.

When viewed only at the surface level, AD/HD is easy to assess, diagnose and treat. There are some professionals who do just that – view only the surface of the iceberg (there are probably just as many who do not see the iceberg at all!).

However, AD/HD is difficult to assess and diagnosis. Likewise, simple, one-channel treatment approaches are unlikely to succeed. This sentiment is widely gaining momentum, as noted by writer Paul Cooper in his aptly titled paper 'Biology, Behaviour and Education; AD/HD and the Bio-Psycho-Social perspective'. Basically, AD/HD is a multi-factored problem, not just for the child but for society in general. Attempts to confine it as only a 'within-child' disorder are naïve. On the contrary, AD/HD has a ripple effect. It usually begins with adult concern about a child's learning and/or behaviour. Unfortunately, the behaviours associated with AD/HD place great demands on parents and teachers. As a result, significant energy is re-directed from other children, other adults, from work, and so on. As this happens, tension emerges which then spreads through homes and classrooms and into the larger societal fabric. We can greatly reduce this tension if we are properly informed about the problem, its causes, and what can be done to help.

THE NAME AND BLAME GAME

The search for the basis of AD/HD is not one of seeing who is at fault for the problem. In this regard, it is important to avoid the tendency to look at a particular context (e.g., home) as the 'cause' of AD/HD. In fact, a more constructive way to answer the question, 'what causes AD/HD?' is to re-phrase the question as, 'what contributes to AD/HD?' The connotation of cause is that someone is doing something to make a child have AD/HD. Inevitably, children and/or parents may feel they 'caused' the problem and they are to blame. However, when searching for causes of child behavioural problems, the goal is not to name or blame but to analyse ways one can contribute to a problem and, through this knowledge, make required changes. That is why I prefer 'contributions' to 'cause' as the former implies that people can withdraw or change their contributions. What follows is a brief sample of each of the five contributing factors which may be at the root of AD/HD (the topics below the watermark).

As an example of a parent contribution, a youngster was referred to me for an assessment because she was creating havoc in school. Her behaviour was totally inappropriate (spilling paints, leaving the school grounds, etc.) and the cause of great distress to the school and other students. During the evaluation, I discussed the child with her parents. The parents did not report similar problems at home. They noted that the child played for long periods in an adjacent field. I started to suspect that the child was generally unsupervised and allowed to wander and roam (hence no problems at home). During the parent meeting, the child was left unattended in the waiting room (even though I request that young children wait with another adult). The child subsequently left the waiting area and 'explored'. She went to an upstairs kitchen, soaked the floor and got water inside a seemingly airtight light bulb casing. The lack of supervision during the appointment supported my suspicion about the same lack around the house. This meant that the child had no limits about behaviour and probably perceived that her school should likewise have no rules or boundaries.

In this situation, I would not say the parents 'caused' the child's AD/HD. Certainly, the parents 'contributed' to the problem by not providing closer supervision of behaviour at home. Without proper parental guidance, the child's behaviour was largely unstructured and rule-free, with little parent attention given to differentiating right from wrong. Interventions to improve this situation could help the parents change their influence in a more positive manner.

Along these lines, a similar analysis could be directed to teachers in order to help them identify effective methods for managing the child's behaviour. In this child's case, the school was challenged to place boundaries on a child who did not have similar limits at home. Likewise, the child's 'self-influences' cannot be ignored. Perhaps this child lacked internal regulation and required instruction in methods of self-control. Similarly, instruction might require special emphasis on the difference between appropriate and inappropriate conduct.

Also, I would regard the attitude among some educators that they are not responsible for individualising instruction, discipline, or assessment to suit the needs of a child with AD/HD as an 'educational contribution' to the problem. I repeatedly hear stories that children need to 'conform' to the educational system rather than the other way around. There are many books and research articles which provide information about how teachers can assist AD/HD children to learn and behave to their utmost capacity. However, this information will not be taken on board if there is a prevailing ethos against individualising learning.

Let us not forget the primary players, children. Can one say that children contribute to their difficulties? Not intentionally, at least not to begin with. For example, it is increasingly believed that children with AD/HD have a neurological impairment involving the area of the brain which regulates attention. It is also noted AD/HD (and thus the neurological deficit) are inherited. Thus, if children are pre-programmed to be inattentive, easily bored, constantly active, demanding, etc., this is a medical condition out of their control.

Later, children may develop negative 'behaviour habits' such as learning that it is fairly easy to control teachers and parents through the types of negative behaviours associated with AD/HD. There is a concept known as 'negative reinforcement' which occurs when adults inadvertently reward AD/HD-behaviours while overlooking more positive, non-AD/HD conduct (simply because appropriate behaviour is expected). This is another adult contribution. However, one can find that even when parents display good 'reinforcement' skills, some children with AD/HD continue to seek negative attention. I recall one family who informed me that they considered their child a 'control freak' because of the ingenious ways he was able to manipulate others. In situations like these, one could argue that this particular child learned a negative behaviour pattern which could be legitimately classified as a 'Child Contribution'.

Other child contributions are not learned but reflect a lack of awareness. For example, it is often the case that children who lose attention quickly and for lengthy periods do not know they have not listened or worked for ten minutes during a fifteen-minute lesson. I notice this problem often when children perform a computer attention task. When told they were inattentive, some find this conclusion very different from their subjective self-assessment, which usually takes the form of, 'I thought I concentrated the whole time'. Thus, lack of self-awareness of inattention could be considered another child contributing factor.

Medical contributions are perhaps the most solidly established. The history of the AD/HD title clearly prioritises the brain-behaviour relationship. In many fact sheets about AD/HD it is referred to as 'neurobiological disorder', a problem related to 'brain chemicals', or 'neurochemistry', etc.

Even though the brain basis for AD/HD is the most likely explanation, no one has yet to lay out the exact biological mechanism of AD/HD. This is not surprising because attention is one of the most complex of all cognitive functions and is likely to be regulated by many interwoven neurological structures and processes. Until the day that the biological basis of AD/HD is known, AD/HD is considered an 'aetiological' deficit – that is, there is no single known cause at present.

Also, AD/HD can be an indirect result of many medical issues. Stephen Garber outlines the following medical problems in need of examination:

- Vision difficulties
- Hearing difficulties
- Thyroid dysfunction
- Diabetes/Hypoglycemia
- Asthma and allergies

The contributions of culture are heretofore the most overlooked aspect of AD/HD. Only recently has the popular press introduced the idea that AD/HD is a by-product of western culture with its emphasis on speed and stimulation. But the contributions of culture extend in far more ways than increased cultural tempo. Particular groups of people (e.g., cultures) have unique views about acceptable behaviour, expectations, child-rearing habits and methods of discipline. In addition, people in certain societies may exhibit a strong desire to be approved by others and would therefore avoid drawing attention to difficulties experienced by family members. All of these factors are essential to a discussion of AD/HD. For example, consider the last point – desire for approval and acceptance. In this situation, managing the 'family appearance' is very important, and hostile interchanges would need suppression until the 'appropriate time'. However, we know that children with AD/HD require immediate feedback about their behaviour. If we do not respond to negative behaviour with immediate and effective behaviour management strategies, we miss the opportunity to alter the behaviour.

Consider this scenario. A family has a meal in a local and popular restaurant. The parents know many of the diners. Shortly after sitting down, one of the two boys begins his usual giddiness display. Parents do or say nothing because they do not wish to draw attention to the boy's behaviour (even though the behaviour is already getting public notice). The meal arrives and the child continues to make noise and has difficulty sitting still. The family 'survive' the experience, with the parents expressing their anger towards the child in a more 'private' context. Perhaps, under the same circumstances, this child's behaviour would be dealt with differently depending on the cultural context in which it occurs.

Now, more than ever, we need to include cultural factors in the discussion of AD/HD. There is more interconnectedness among people from various parts of the world. As we become more 'multi-cultural' it is imperative to understand the unique contribution of culture.

What follows is an elaboration of the five areas of contributing factors noted earlier. Let's begin with the most widely researched and accepted contributing factor.

MEDICAL CONTRIBUTIONS

Since neurological and genetic factors are the most compelling explanations for AD/HD, each is discussed as a medical contribution. The two areas provide a strong biological basis for AD/HD, with neurological factors indicating how the brains of AD/HD individuals are atypical and why their brains may be this way (inherited).

AD/HD: IT'S A 'NEUROBIOLOGICAL THING'

The history of AD/HD is laced with references to the brain and its regulation of attention, self-control and activity level. As you might recall, AD/HD was once classified as 'Minimal Brain Dysfunction'. Now, the question is not so much about the role of the brain in AD/HD, but about where, how and why. It is useful for the reader to understand the basic neurology of AD/HD, especially since some of the most common and validated treatments are aimed at 'hot-wiring' the neurochemistry of children with AD/HD. Let's look at the human brain.

The brain is divided into four basic lobes, each covering a different region and with unique functions. Relative to AD/HD, the Frontal Lobe is the one most implicated (recall Phineas Gage). Patients who have suffered frontal lobe injuries tend to exhibit many of the core symptoms of AD/HD. For example, individuals with frontal lobe damage tend to respond carelessly, have trouble inhibiting behaviour, show disorganised thinking, are reckless, etc.

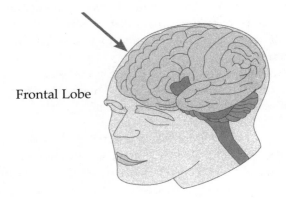

Frontal Lobe

Another consistent finding is that children with AD/HD tend to have smaller frontal lobes compared with a normal comparison group. These conclusions are based on studies using brain scanning techniques (e.g., MRI, CT, etc.).

Equally important is that brain activity is regulated by different chemicals referred to a neurotransmitters. As the name implies, these chemicals transmit information from one brain cell (specifically known as a nerve cell) to another.

Consider the diagram on the following page. When nerve one 'fires', it sends chemicals to nerve two at their 'synapse' which is the small gap between the dendrites of each cell. The dendrites are the branch-like projections from each axon. The information travels through the axon of nerve two to its dendrites and on to the left side synapses (not shown in the diagram) where it connects with another nerve and so on.

Although there are several types of brain chemicals which nerve cells transmit, Dopamine and Norepinephrine are the two most consistently implicated in individuals with AD/HD.

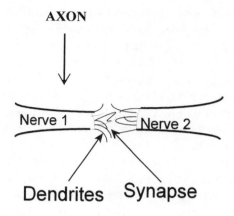

Two Nerve Cells

Specifically, there is some evidence to suggest that children with AD/HD have lowered dopamine and norepinephrine levels relative to those without AD/HD. It is not clear why this difference exists, but two hypotheses are (a) lower production of these chemicals in the nerve cell, or (b) inefficient passage of the chemicals between the synapses (imagine two relay racers dropping the baton during their interchange).

Dopamine and norepinephrine happen to be critical to attention. Specifically, these chemicals regulate what input is important and what is not. Obviously, individuals with lower levels of these neurotransmitters will be at risk for attention problems. Knowledge of neurotransmitters provide the necessary background to understand how and why stimulant medications are effective in helping children with AD/HD.

THE ROLE OF GENETICS IN AD/HD

Genetics play an increasingly important role in society. We often hear about genetically modified food, genetic engineering, etc. Similarly, researchers are looking at the genetic basis of mental health problems, and AD/HD is no exception. It is important to link our previous discussion of neurotransmitters with genetics because there are specific genes involved in neurotransmitter functioning. For example, researchers refer to the Dopamine D2 Receptor Gene as one particular gene which impacts the function of this neurochemical (Horacek, 1998).

In general, AD/HD is very much inherited; that is, there is a genetic component which runs in families. This conclusion comes from several corroborating lines of research. For example, in family studies, researchers note that if either parent has AD/HD, there is a 50 per cent chance that the child will also have AD/HD. In addition, if a child has AD/HD there can be a 30 per cent chance that a sibling will also have the condition.

Researchers have also studied adopted children. These studies clarify the role of nature and nurture because obviously adopted children are genetically similar to their biological parents yet reared by adoptive parents (who bear no genetic resemblance to their adopted children). The nature aspect of AD/HD is strengthened if adopted AD/HD children show similar behaviour patterns to their biological parents instead of their adoptive parents. And this is indeed the case – researchers find that the child's attention and activity levels are similar to their birth parents compared with their adopted parents.

Finally, twin study research is also relevant to AD/HD. Note that identical twins have the same genetic code so the co-occurrence of a disorder provides information about its genetic basis. With AD/HD, if one identical twin has AD/HD there is, on average, an 80 per cent chance that the other twin will also have AD/HD. This is an extremely high risk and much higher than the general prevalence in the population (about 3 to 5 per cent). There is also an increased risk among fraternal twins such that if one twin has AD/HD the risk for the other twin is about 30 per cent.

In sum, there is a clear genetic component to AD/HD. This fact, combined with the brain abnormalities highly associated with AD/HD, suggest a strong biological basis. When a disorder has a strong biological basis, a number of implications can be derived. First, if a child exhibits the core features of AD/HD – inattention, impulsivity, and over-activity – then these behaviours cannot be seen as wilful or voluntary behaviours. That is, the child is NOT misbehaving to purposely annoy adults or other children. Rather the child's difficult behaviour is the result of a biochemical disturbance that results in less self-control. When viewed as such, adults and children may experience a great reduction in frustration and annoyance if the true purpose of the behaviour is understood and recognised.

Another implication of the biological basis of AD/HD is that biological causes require biological treatment. So, for example, if ever the day does come when a particular gene for AD/HD is identified, there may, some day, be a method for genetically correcting the fault, thereby reducing or eliminating AD/HD. As for neurotransmitters, there are medications which make dopamine and norepinephrine more accessible for uptake by the adjoining nerve cell. For example, Ritalin is the most common medication used to treat AD/HD and this is precisely its purpose.

Finally, while biology is important, this does not mean that environmental factors are irrelevant. The way we respond to challenging behaviour can either aggravate it or reduce its impact. For example, effective behaviour management can greatly assist in everyday coping. Likewise, environmental programming (reducing distractions during homework time) can also assist the child to be more academically productive. There are many effective and non-medical approaches to AD/HD. To understand these approaches it is necessary to elaborate other sources of contributing factors.

FAMILY CONTRIBUTIONS

What seems clear is that poor parenting does not create AD/HD. However, it is commonly reported that a child with AD/HD can create poor parents. That is, parents typically adopt non-optimal strategies for dealing with the difficult behaviour confronting them. However, they do not create or cause the difficult behaviour. Instead, the way parents react to the difficult behaviour can intensify it. Let me give you a case example.

From the details, one could infer possible pitfalls in the parents' management of Steve's behaviour. However, a child with AD/HD is usually difficult to manage at home because the consequences which are normally effective with other children (e.g., ,rewards, punishment) are less effective when applied to children with AD/HD. This is one of the greatest sources of frustration for adults who manage children presenting with AD/HD.

A discussion of family and parent factors in regards to AD/HD is essential for several reasons. First, although stimulant

---

THE PERPETUAL NAG

Steve is persistent. Unlike his older sister or two younger brothers, he does not give in until his demands are met. For example, if he does not want to do something asked of him, his parents typically do not make him. Their feeling is that it is not appropriate to force him into compliance and it is easier to reduce domestic stress if they do what he does not do (e.g., put away his toys, pick up his school work, remove the dishes from the table, etc). If he wants something from his parents (e.g., money to go tothe shop and get a snack) he will repeat the request until he gets his way. Steve's parents feel that it is easier to cope if they give in because Steve will only nag and persist and drive everybody crazy. At times, they have ignored his requests but he only intensifies them (e.g., repeats them more frequently, louder). At other times, they have lost their cool and smacked or yelled at him. But he does not respond to these types of punishment. In fact, his behaviour only gets worse.

There are isolated moments when Steve does play appropriately. There are even times when he complies with a request. He might go a day and not demand anything from his parents. There is never a time when he will complete his homework

---

without complete supervision. Otherwise, the homework will not be completed or it could take two or three hours (when it should be 30 minutes). Steve's parents are fed up and desire professional consultation to deal with the situation.

medication may be the single most effective treatment approach, many parents are justifiably concerned about the use of medication to control behaviour difficulties. Some of these concerns relate to the side-effects of medication, the long-term use of such medication, and the fact that 'pills do not teach skills'. Thus, parents may desire non-medical interventions to address the behaviour difficulties associated with AD/HD. Further, it is important to outline what family factors may exacerbate behaviour difficulties so that these factors can be addressed in a comprehensive treatment plan.

A second reason why family process is critical to AD/HD is the general consensus that prognosis is partially dependent on specific parent and child issues. For example, parental mental health problems typically lead to a poorer prognosis for children with AD/HD. Likewise, harsh and conflict oriented parent-child relationships are associated with less favourable outcomes in adolescence.

AD/HD IN THE FAMILY CONTEXT
In recalling the early development of children with AD/HD, it is often the case that parents remember a stressful infancy. For example, they may note that the child did not have a regular sleep/wake cycle, or required less sleep than the siblings. Feeding habits may also be difficult. Reference is usually made to behavioural descriptions such as 'active', 'alert', 'curious', 'fussy', 'into everything', 'less need for affection', etc. Parental response to these behaviours becomes an important factor, as this is the time when parents and child develop habitual patterns of interaction. It is understandable that more negative impressions of the child emerge because of demanding behaviour, its persistence and the

lack of successful interventions (nothing works, or works only minimally). For example, if the child has less need for affection and requires constant supervision, the obvious consequence is a reduction in parent affection and an increase in reprimands (and general stress).

As toddlers and pre-school children, the most notable difficulties are an excessive activity level and a difficulty maintaining a focus on toys for any significant duration. Intensity of emotion may emerge in the form of low frustration tolerance, irritability and emotional upset (tantrums). Parents are required to be extremely vigilant because the toddler will go from one activity to another, and may escape the play area altogether (e.g., roam out of the house to an adjoining road, as I have heard on several occasions). In addition, the toddler is at risk for accidents (e.g., falling down stairs) and damaging property (e.g., pulling down lamps).

At this time, difficulties interacting with other children may also emerge. The child may have problems with social interaction skills, such as sharing, and aggressive behaviour may occur. On the other extreme, the child may be withdrawn and anxious. Typically, there is something problematic about social interactions and these concerns are not restricted to other children. Parents and other family members may also experience negative social behaviour.

During early and middle childhood, the major parent complaints are not complying with requests, negative emotional states, lack of persistence, difficulty entertaining self, intrusiveness (e.g., not respecting privacy), and the need for constant adult supervision during academic work. Parents report that discipline techniques are usually ineffective and the child seems more in control of parent behaviour rather than the other way around.

As I have stated before, the observation of difficult behaviours in infancy, toddler, pre-school or school aged children do not necessarily mean the child will develop clinically significant AD/HD. What is important is the number of problems, the severity of the problems, and their persistence across time, setting and people. The more problems noted and the longer they persist, regardless of setting, the more likely the child will meet formal criteria for AD/HD.

It is also important to note that early problem behaviour is not the only factor in predicting childhood AD/HD. Difficulties with behaviour management, parenting style, family relationships, and parental mental health difficulties are also important.

BEHAVIOUR MANAGEMENT

After stimulant medication, the next most frequently referenced treatment is parent training. Parent training refers to teaching parents methods to cope with AD/HD-type problems.

The most difficult and frustrating issue for parents is that no matter how they try to alter problem behaviours, every method adopted is typically unsuccessful. Many times, parents report that the use of particular strategies intensifies the problem. Some of the ill-fated techniques referred to are loss of privileges, loud reprimands, reasoning and isolation (going to room). Parents may mention 'praise' and 'rewards' for positive behaviour, but these consequences do not result in any significant success. However, there a number of factors which will increase the success of behaviour management techniques, discussed in Chapters 5 and 6.

Again, even the best intentioned parents may end up contributing to behavioural difficulties, usually without knowing this is the case. Consider the use of 'reinforcement'. Reinforcement refers to consequences (how we respond to behaviour) that increase (e.g., strengthen) the behaviour they follow. Thus, any adult action which increases a child's behaviour is generally known as 'reinforcement' (the opposite of reinforcement is punishment). There are two types of reinforcement. Positive reinforcement involves favourable consequences, such as praise and rewards. Saying 'well done' or giving the child a sticker after good behaviour are examples of positive reinforcement because these consequences strengthen behaviour (make a particular behaviour more likely to occur again).

Negative reinforcement, like positive reinforcement, also strengthens the behaviour it follows. However, the behaviour is strengthened because a negative event is avoided or terminated. The best way to understand the concept is through example, three of which are provided below:

- remove the car keys from the ignition to turn off the warning sound.
- a teacher gives in to a student moaning to have a test postponed.
- a staff meeting is missed because of a conflicting responsibility (which conflicts intentionally to allow the individual avoid negative interactions).

Notice that all of the behaviours involved will increase (fortify). For example, we will be more likely to automatically remove car keys, students will be more likely to moan about tests in the future, and the employee will find ways to miss potentially unpleasant meetings.

Of these examples, the second one is the closest to describing the interaction between parent and the child with AD/HD. For example, take the core symptom of impulsivity. By definition an impulsive individual has difficulty waiting and delaying his or her needs. Thus, when the child with AD/HD wants something, they may pester, whine and nag until it is received. After a period of child discontent, parents may give in. This action inadvertently strengthens a child's whining and nagging. Of course, parents do this to terminate an unpleasant situation. Yet this action intensifies the behaviour one wants to reduce.

Likewise, short-attention span typically makes homework periods very difficult. Parents may request the child to begin their homework. However, the child may leave their seat often and repeatedly ask if they can go outside and play. The parent may refuse this request and re-direct the child to the homework. A similar re-directive prompt may be issued several more times. The parent usually has some other activity to manage and the incessant demands may ultimately be allowed simply to maintain calm. Again, this is an example of negative reinforcement.

Another pitfall in parenting children with AD/HD is the general drift to negative relative to positive attention. In time, it emerges that almost all parent energy is directed at negative behaviour (e.g., accidents, aggression, school problems, homework difficulties, etc.). Negative child events understandably meet with negative parent attention. The most common form of negative parent attention is the repeated use of reprimands (e.g., 'don't do that ...'). Eventually, verbal reprimands lose impact because there is no tangible consequence associated with the reprimand.

Parenting Style. Parenting style is very much at the core of how we relate to our children, how we manage their behaviour, and the general element of discipline and child-rearing. The way in which parents respond to challenging child behaviour is largely a function of two factors–control and acceptance. Control refers to strict rule enforcement whereas acceptance pertains to empathy and reasoning. Both control and acceptance can be categorised as 'low' or 'high' which results in the following outcomes:

PARENTAL ACCEPTANCE

		High	Low
PARENTAL CONTROL	Low	Permissive parents	Neglectful parents
	High	Authoritative parents	Authoritarian parents

101

The four parenting styles referred to are briefly described as:

- *Permissive parents*: Positive feature is high acceptance –
  caring, warm, etc. The problem with this style is that
  children may be 'spoilt'; no demands are made of the child
  and most of the child's requests are met, even though these
  requests are unduly frequent and excessive. Permissive
  parents tend to over-emphasise autonomy and let the child
  make decisions, with comments such as, 'whatever you
  want ... you decide'. Ironically, children reared in this type
  of climate can lack autonomy and may have problems with
  self-control. Problems with self-control touch on the
  AD/HD factor, as lack of self-control is synonymous with
  impulsivity, over-activity, and demanding-ness.
- *Neglectful parents*: An extremely unfortunate situation arises
  when control and acceptance are both lacking. Parents in this
  group tend to be distant from the child, showing little interest
  in child-rearing and avoiding parenting responsibilities. In
  these situations, the child appears to be an 'inconvenience'.
  Children treated in this manner usually demonstrate quite
  serious behavioural difficulties early in life.
- *Authoritarian parents*: The positive element of this approach
  is that parents set rules and expect co-operation with same.
  However, the difficulty here is that rules are excessively
  enforced, with potentially harsh punishment for relatively
  minor rule infractions. In addition, no attempt is made to
  reason with the child. Instead, children are expected to obey
  authority figures, with no questions asked. A sample parent
  response might be, 'you are going to do what I say.
  Understood!' These parents may be perceived as strict,
  harsh, and overly critical. Children's typical response to the
  authoritarian parent is the opposite of what this parent
  expects – more challenging of authority and rebellion.
- *Authoritative parents*: This is the ideal parenting style,

because it combines the best of both worlds – high acceptance and high control. This approach could variously be considered as 'tough-love'; or 'child-centred'. The positive features of this style are the setting of limits, but an attempt to enlist the child's support in both determining the limits, explaining consequences, and generally discussing the implications of various behaviours. Parents are warm and encouraging, but when problems occur, the response is firm yet reasonable. A typical response might be, 'I know you like sweets, but I won't let you have any right now. You can have a bar for dessert if you wish. That way we can keep strong and healthy.' This style is associated with the most favourable child behaviour outcomes (e.g., reliant, self-controlled, content, curious, etc.).

In most books about AD/HD, the above-named parenting styles are not construed as 'causes' of AD/HD. As was noted earlier, these styles may be maladaptive attempts of parents to cope with the challenging behaviour of a child with AD/HD. It is also relevant to include parenting style because parent-related interventions are the second most common form of intervention. Thus, recognising the above parenting styles may help individuals recognise less ideal strategies and seek to try the most advantageous child-rearing approach.

Family Relationships. The negative effect of AD/HD on family functioning must be emphasised, as the daily demands on coping skills are immense. In response to AD/HD, a number of relationship patterns can develop. Elaine McKewan (1995) outlines potential parent coping styles, some of which are provided below (notice the connections with the aforementioned parenting styles):

- *denial* – either one or both parents deny the existence of behavioural problems. If one parent denies the problem, then the other is typically left alone to fight the battle (e.g., seek help).

- *abuse* – one or both parents may respond to stress via aggression towards the child, such as physical, emotional, or verbal abuse.
- *over-involvement* – one or both parents become excessively entwined with the child (e.g., nagging, spoiling, cajoling, charity, etc.).
- *emotional bankruptcy* – one or both parents 'check-out' of the problem (leave responsibilities to partner or third party).
- *one-upmanship* – one parent feels he/she has adopted the better coping method. The partner is then critiqued.

These relationship patterns creep in slowly, but gradually. Parents then have the added burden of dealing with problems with their partner while simultaneously managing the child with AD/HD.

What about other children in the family? Because of the negative attention devoted to the child with AD/HD, parents may neglect the positive accomplishments of other children. That is, parents are so often putting out the proverbial fires the child with AD/HD creates, they may not have the energy to devote to their remaining offspring.

One can see how the difficult behaviour associated with AD/HD creates a tremendous amount of stress for all family members. The added burden of coping with AD/HD is often more than families can tolerate. Mary Squire (1994) reports research indicating that the separation and divorce rate of families rearing a child with AD/HD is three times that of families without a child with AD/HD. Strained relationships with extended family members are also reported to be more common in families where AD/HD is present relative to its absence.

One often cited relationship factor is the early attachment between infant and parent. For example, in situations where a newborn is placed in a long-term residential facility, and where there may be frequent changes in the primary caregiver. Similarly, if a child is placed in different foster care environments, this may prevent the formation of a typical carer-child attachment. In addition, if a parent suffers from a mental illness during their child's infancy, the quality of the attachment may be compromised.

One of the consequences of these types of disruptions in normal attachment is a disorder known as Reactive Attachment Disorder (RAD). Essentially, children who experience unusual neglect (e.g., basic physical and emotional needs not met) may reveal inappropriate behaviour in childhood. As might be expected, the inappropriate behaviour is related to social interactions, such that the child may be very inhibited during social interaction or conversely, very uninhibited (e.g., excessive familiarity with a new acquaintance). It is the lack of inhibition that sometimes gets confused with AD/HD, because lack of social restraint looks like impulsivity (e.g., frequent interruptions, cannot leave adults alone, etc.). However, the cause of the problem and the resulting behaviours are quite different.

Parent Mental Illness. If one recalls that AD/HD has a family pattern, then a childhood diagnosis of AD/HD translates to an increased risk that either parent will have the condition. Such is the case. Research indicates that 15-20 per cent of mothers and 20-30 per cent of fathers of children with AD/HD may also be effected. This statistic is relatively benign until one considers the various problems that co-occur with AD/HD. Some of the most common problems which persist into adulthood are depression, alcoholism, anti-social behaviour and learning difficulties. We thus have the unfortunate scenario where adults with significant difficulties rear children at risk for similar difficulties.

It is also known that one predictor of the course of AD/HD is the degree and type of parental mental health problem. For example, the prognosis tends to be poorer for a child with AD/HD if a parent presents with anti-social behaviour (e.g., unlawful behaviour, deceit, lack of remorse, aggression, etc.). This makes logical sense in that (a) the parenting style of a parent with an anti-social personality is likely to be maladaptive, and (b) there is an increased risk that the child will show conduct disturbances if a parent has anti-social tendencies.

EDUCATIONAL CONTRIBUTIONS

If there was one context in which one should observe AD/HD-type behaviour it would be school. Children with AD/HD often say they dislike school; parents say that if there was no requirement for formal schooling, than life would be much more satisfying. No wonder that the age of onset for AD/HD is roughly four to seven years, the age at which children begin formal schooling. Certainly, it is the classroom teacher who bears the brunt of AD/HD, because in the classroom, children are expected to wait their turn, remain seated, listen, be academically productive, etc. These are precisely the situations where children with AD/HD are at risk for problems. The entire compilation of AD/HD behaviours is at odds with the typical expectations of classroom conduct.

THE EFFECTS OF EDUCATIONAL ENVIRONMENTS ON THE CHILD WITH AD/HD

What follows are some of the school factors which influence the behaviour of the child with AD/HD. It is important to recognise that none of the variables to follow operate in isolation, much like the ingredients in a recipe merge to form the final product. For example, take the first topic – class size. It is intuitively attractive to believe that the larger the class size the more adverse effect on the child with AD/HD. True, but only if it is assumed that most, or all, of the other factors are also not favourable. Teachers with positive teaching, relational and discipline styles can compensate for a large class size, relative to a smaller class with a less effective teacher.

Realise that while the variables to follow effect all children, these variables are especially relevant to the child with AD/HD. Thus, in a large class, the child without AD/HD may be less attentive, but not to the degree of his/her AD/HD classmate.

Class size. Assuming all else is equal, the larger the number of students under the direction of a teacher, the more difficult it is to manage the child with AD/HD. The size of the class is the single most important class arrangement. It is easy to see why. Imagine a classroom of 25 students. Assume that the class teacher identifies one student with behaviours similar to AD/HD. This student is frequently off-task and may disturb other students, and is greatly demanding of teacher attention (which the teacher provides in order to reduce the disruptive effects of this child on other children). In this scenario, this child can greatly disturb normal classroom process, mainly because the teacher must direct extra time and energy to this particular child at the expense of other children.

However, the same degree of disruption is less damaging in a small group because the teacher can provide more attention to any particular student without losing track of the larger group. The child also benefits from closer contact with the teacher because more academic work is completed, the child is less likely to be off-task, and there is a greater chance that the teacher can get to know the child on a personal/individual level. The opportunity for personal contact is especially important because the teacher may increasingly realise that the child's inattention, impulsivity and excessive activity are not borne out of malice or boldness. Rather, these behaviours reflect medical factors as noted earlier.

The issue of class size is central to the larger issue of appropriate education for children with AD/HD. The question is often raised whether children with AD/HD can be educated in a regular, mainstream class. Or is a special education, special class, or special school the most appropriate form of education? As you might predict, the best response to this question is – it depends. It depends on some of the issues previously raised, such as the severity of the condition, and the degree to which other learning and behavioural problems may supercede AD/HD. It also depends on the educational services/placements available under relevant legislation.

Ideally, educational placements vary on a continuum, from least restrictive (regular, mainstream class) to most restrictive (special school). There are alternative forms of educational services which may combine elements of each, such as bringing special services to the regular class, or having a special class within a mainstream school. There is typically an attempt to match the type and severity of the child's problem to the relevant placement. For example, children with significant autism are usually educated in a special school. In this context, other children may have similar degrees of the same problem (this is referred to as a categorical classroom, as all children share the same condition). This placement is the most appropriate for a number of reasons, not the least of which is more individual attention, specialised equipment (e.g., learning materials, playground material, etc.), individual education plan, and specialised teacher training.

A child who presents with significant AD/HD may also be best served in a similar arrangement and with similarly disposed children. Such is the case in some countries where specialised and categorical AD/HD classrooms (or schools) exist. The least viable option for this child is to continue regular schooling without some form of educational modification. The severity of the problem(s) is usually specified after professional assessment, as are the type of educational modifications.

Conspicuously absent in the discussion is what exactly defines an optimal versus non-optimal class size. Hopefully, you will understand that an exact number is difficult to justify, mainly because of all other factors which need consideration. It should be noted that special classrooms for children with specific learning and behavioural needs usually vary in size from six to twelve pupils.

When it comes to traditional academic homework requiring written output, most parents and teachers will note that even with one-to-one supervision, the child with AD/HD will lose focus and persistence, and will tire more easily relative to other children without AD/HD. That is, if you can get the child to initiate academic work!

Specialised Learning Materials. Children with AD/HD require educational materials (books, workbooks, etc.) which differ from regular education materials. Because these children tire quickly and lose focus, the classroom should have different learning materials. Ideally, teachers have the resources to purchase different types of colourful, novel and interesting materials in order to increase attention and productivity.

In the absence of specialised materials, much can be done to individualise available materials. For example, children with AD/HD are likely to lose attention and become distracted when presented with a workbook which contains numerous items crammed onto a page (e.g., different sets of maths problems co-existing on a single page). Instead, one may improve on-task behaviour and productivity by creating an index card booklet with a single problem on each card. When the problem is completed, the child can turn to the next problem. In this way, the child with AD/HD will not be overwhelmed by the amount of work required when presented with a conventional worksheet.

One can almost sense the 'shut-down' of the concentration system upon realising there is more work to do. For example, say you provide the child with ten computation problems, well within the skill level of the child. When the child reaches the final problem, there is a feeling of relief and accomplishment. But what if the homework actually required ten more computations, all of which are on the reverse side of the worksheet. When the page is turned over and the request is made to complete ten more similar problems, the child with AD/HD will usually resist the work, or rush through the problems in a careless fashion.

Assignments and Homework. In addition to the quality of the materials used, quantity is also a factor (as the last point clearly indicates). In the best case scenario, the teacher will individualise the workload to match the child's mental stamina, balancing the amount of work without compromising the syllabus. A close scrutiny of the child's educational programme will likely indicate where material can be pared down. For example, if a particular learning objective is accomplished using three different worksheets (over-learned) perhaps only one worksheet is necessary for the child with AD/HD. Similarly, instead of asking the child to complete 30 problems of three-digit addition, have the child do every other problem. The idea is to reduce repetitive work, as the child with AD/HD finds repetition very difficult. There is a related principle regarding class tests. Instead of having the child spell all twenty words on a weekly spelling test, require ten. In the absence of these alterations, the child with AD/HD may come to dislike school and find homework particularly stressful.

Teaching Approach. Ideally, teachers will use different media and adopt an active approach to learning. Different modalities are tapped, such as the visual, auditory and tactile senses. There is also a distinction between active and passive learning, such that passive learning requires the child to sit still and listen, whereas active learning allows the child to move around and be a more active participant in the learning process. You can guess which approach is more effective with the child with AD/HD.

The worst case scenario is the reliance on one mode, usually auditory, and the tendency to require a passive learning approach. This approach will not typically trouble non-AD/HD students, but it will trouble those with AD/HD. The classic 'lecture' format is one most likely to be difficult for children with AD/HD. Likewise, in class assignments, where a certain amount of work is expected, are also risky for children with attention deficits and hyperactivity. If the child with AD/HD is not closely supervised, it is likely that in-class work will not be completed.

Oral versus written work. Children with AD/HD are especially prone to inattention and restlessness during written work. Since most school output is in the written form, this is particularly disadvantageous to the AD/HD population. Parents and teachers report that during written work, the child may only complete one or two lines of work before losing focus. On the other hand, a greater barometer of skill is typically obtained in the oral – question and answer – format (discussion). At this time, the child with AD/HD may be particularly motivated to share information and do so quite capably. When you think of it, part of the oral skill attributed to children with AD/HD is one of the very symptoms of it – excessive or incessant talking. One advantage of this 'symptom' is that children frequently use the oral media and become quite sophisticated with it.

Looking for positives. Children with AD/HD are exposed to daily negativity in school situations. Their school work may be incomplete or inaccurate, behaviour is a cause for reprimand, and the child may find it difficult to relate to classmates. However, no matter how difficult, a teacher should strive to find one positive aspect of learning, behaviour or social relation on a daily basis. This may not be easy when so many issues are present. It requires a concerted re-direction of energy, but the long-term benefits are great.

Specialised equipment. An array of attention training, impulse control and activity devices are available. These devices can be used to help children learn more about 'attention' and 'concentration' as these terms are relatively abstract. Children's behaviours are recorded by the particular piece of equipment and many experts say that timers are of great advantage.

Of course, computer-assisted instruction is one type of instructional mode which may also be relevant. The advantages of computers are their visual nature, the ability to present learning in a game-type format, and the programmed learning materials which adjust difficulty level and can be easily modified to suit a particular child's skill, etc.

Classroom environment. There are many ways to arrange the classroom for the child with AD/HD. Particular seating arrangements can be used, with certain types of tables/desks. Partitions and study carols may also be useful. Reminder cards, lesson cues, and other organisational aides can all be part of the modified classroom environment.

One classroom environment issue which sometimes comes to the fore is the combination of classes. For example, in smaller schools, it is often the case where children are combined in the one room, even though the pupils are in two, three, or more class levels (e.g., first, second and third). The query is whether the child with AD/HD is better suited to a single-class cohort (all children of the same class level) relative to mixed classes. The concern is that the child will be distracted when the teacher assigns seatwork to the child's classmates, then proceeds to teach another class their content. Does this distract the child with AD/HD and result in lower academic productivity?

Again, this depends on other factors, such as the size of the classes, teacher style, the severity of AD/HD, the classroom environment, etc. Each situation will have pros and cons, and parents and teachers should collaborate to find the best educational arrangement for a particular child.

Parental involvement. This last point ties in with this point, because one of the most effective approaches to the education of children with AD/HD is close collaboration between teachers and parents. Daily home notes can be part of this plan. Organisational aides and behavioural modification strategies can be discussed and plans made to solve particular problems.

In sum, nine aspects of an educational programme are outlined. In the best case scenario, all of these options are implemented as necessary. In the worst case scenario, none of these points are implemented at great cost to the child, parent or teacher.

Child Contributions

This is a tricky idea because it is unfair to say that someone with a genuine genetic-biological brain disorder intentionally acts the way they do. Imagine the silliness in thinking that a person with epilepsy consciously behaved in a way to induce a seizure. Children are not purposely inattentive, impulsive and over-active because these behaviours are somehow appropriate or valued by society. Just the opposite – the behaviours of a child with AD/HD create ongoing friction with other children and adults. It is essential that the behaviours associated with AD/HD are recognised as the result of the medical factors outlined earlier.

What makes AD/HD even more demanding is that children, families and teachers adapt to the condition in non-optimal ways. A child with AD/HD presents significant challenges for all involved and in the process of coping, a number of secondary problems emerge. These problems are not the primary characteristics of AD/HD but they develop as natural side-effects from the condition.

Children's Maladaptive Coping Mechanisms

The following topics are best considered as ways a child with AD/HD learns to adapt to their difficulties. Many refer to the topics that follow as a secondary list of the psychological problems associated with AD/HD. It must be stressed that most children know very little about AD/HD. Children are not aware that their problems (e.g., inattentiveness, difficulty finishing work, disorganisation, restlessness, etc.) have a name and a cause. Thus they either do not take notice of their difficulties, or, if they do, have no understanding of why they occur. Yet, there is no mistaking the difficulty these children encounter on a daily basis.

Looking for negative attention. A child with AD/HD soon learns that conflict earns attention, even though the interaction may be hostile and negative. This happens because the child has relatively few behaviours which earn praise or positive attention. Thus, there is a natural dynamic where the child behaves negatively and receives attention for this behaviour (e.g., reprimand, negative comments, etc.). In the unusual case where an instance of positive conduct occurs, the child rarely earns positive attention, because those who interact with the child do not expect non-negative behaviour, and therefore, overlook it when it does occur.

Take for example a family relaxing after a meal. The restless and inattentive child sits down momentarily to look at a book. This behaviour is ignored. Next, the child wrestles with his younger brother, which eventually leads to tears. This draws parent attention in the form of a loud verbal reprimand. What bothers parents is that this behaviour (e.g., rough and tumble play, running, always demanding something, etc.) occurs over and over again, despite their attempts to curb it.

What the child learns is that positive conduct is ignored and negative conduct leads to attention, albeit negative. In the ideal situation, parents might 'catch' the child engaging in appropriate behaviour by telling the child how much they like it when the child sits down to look at a book. Nonetheless, even if parents do make a concerted effort to praise the child with behaviours as challenging as those associated with AD/HD, it is often difficult because of a general negative perception of the child. This perception develops over time and is derived from repeated and failed attempts to reduce problem behaviour.

There are several terms that parents sometimes use to refer to the pattern of looking for negative attention, such as 'controlling' and 'manipulative'. In the case of true AD/HD, 'control' and 'manipulation' are not due to intentional malice; rather, the core behaviours of AD/HD prevent the child from achieving success in ways other children gain positive notice, such as completing work, succeeding in school, relating well to others, etc. It is sometimes the case where deceit and manipulation are the rule but these qualities may be more associated with Oppositional Defiant

Disorder or Conduct Disorder.

Common Psychological Defence Mechanisms. If someone points out a weakness in your character, how do you respond? Most of the time, one argues that this is not the case, or says 'maybe' but then justifies why the problem is not really a problem. Basically, we defend ourselves, which is as natural as a cat hissing and raising its fur when approached by a dog.

Therefore, it is only natural that children with AD/HD will resort to psychological defences in order to protect their 'self', their 'ego'. One of the most common is denial, which is observed when a child simply says there is not a problem. With AD/HD, denial is not as much a conscious attempt to remove painful self-examination as it is a lack of self-awareness. That is, children with AD/HD are often unaware that their behaviour is a problem!

A similar mechanism is defensiveness, which refers to the child's irritability and touchiness surrounding the notion that a problem exists. This sense of irritation is often the case, even when the hint of a problem is made indirectly and subtly. A parent might say, 'I'm concerned about how you are doing at school', to which the defensive child may reply, 'I'm doing fine ... you always think there is a problem ... why don't you say that to,' etc.

A final defence is rationalisation. This is more often the case in children who are older and of average to above average verbal ability. These children may acknowledge a problem, but then give ten reasons why one should not be worried (e.g., 'I get notes from another student ... there is a free period when I can do work ...' etc).

Low frustration tolerance. Attention and concentration are fundamental to learning, because they lead to persistence and productivity. Work completed leads to notice and accomplishment. If you have problems concentrating and sustaining attention to mental work, you may rush through the task, give up before it is finished, make impulsive and careless errors, have an overly quick response tempo, etc. If solutions are not immediate, the mental effort required to achieve them is overwhelming. These are examples of low frustration tolerance. The final result is that performance suffers and negative feedback ensues.

It is during performance tasks, that one realises how behaviour interferes with learning. Children with AD/HD are impatient and tire quickly during mental work. Thus they are easily frustrated, even though they may have the ability to solve the problem at hand. These children literally 'shoot-themselves-in-the-foot'.

Take for example, a word reading test, where children read a list of words which increase in difficulty. The goal is to determine the child's basic reading skill – how many words they have in their reading vocabulary, how they approach words not immediately recognisable, etc. Children without AD/HD approach the task with care and deliberation. Each word is read clearly, then the next. When a word is unfamiliar, there is a pause, the word is inspected, and the child may resort to sounding it out. On the other hand, the child with AD/HD may rapidly respond to each word, with their mind ahead to the next word, before the last one is sufficiently inspected. The result is careless errors, such as leaving off the 'ly' in 'completely' or reading 'shut' as 'shout'. When you ask the child to go back and carefully review the misread word, the mistake is typically noticed.

There are many examples of performance tasks where it is clear how low frustration tolerance effects problem-solving – solving problems on computers, putting puzzles together, and in interpersonal situations (e.g., how to respond to conflict, etc.).

Low self-esteem. Imagine the frustration in knowing you have the ability to achieve, but for some inexplicable reason, are failing to do so. Further, imagine that others are disappointed or frustrated by your lack of success to date, and you are keenly aware of this. You do not have an obvious physical problem by which one can explain underachievement (e.g., cerebral palsy). Nobody seems to know what the problem is.

This is the scenario for children with AD/HD and it is a

recipe for self-loathing. In younger children, this sense of dislike may manifest in a number of ways–anger, refusal to go to school, problems relating with peers, and physical symptoms (e.g., stomach aches, toileting problems, etc.). As lack of success continues with a lack of explanation for same, self-esteem continues to suffer. In adolescence, low feelings of self-worth can result in significant depression and its corollary problems.

Illogical thinking. Illogical thinking refers to the type of 'thinking' errors we make when analysing our behaviour. One specific thinking error is called 'over-generalisation'. For example, while it may be intuitively reasonable to think that because one has a reading problem one is 'not smart'. One mistakenly over-generalises reading as the definition of 'smart' when in fact 'smart' could be defined in any of a number of ways, some of which the person may be quite skilled in. In fact, a measurement definition of 'dyslexia' is a gap between intelligence and reading with the latter far lower than the former. This implies that a child with a reading problem is delayed in reading not through lack of mental ability. In fact, the measurement definition of dyslexia suggests that a 'dyslexic' individual is one who is mentally able but for some unexpected reason finds it difficult to analyse words or express themselves in the written medium. Thus, the 'dyslexic' child is by definition of average to above average ability. It is important for dyslexic children to understand this so they do not over-generalise their specific academic difficulty.

In a similar manner, children with AD/HD can over-generalise their difficulties and not be able to find any bright spot in their character. It is very important for adults to correct this error whenever it occurs.

Lack of social skills. It is often noted that children with AD/HD have problems relating to their age peers. For some reason, these children relate better to either a much younger or older age group. I find that children with AD/HD and a clear pattern of CD tend to relate better to older children. On the other hand, other children with AD/HD relate better with younger children. Interpersonal problems are usually related to social skill deficits, such as not sharing, domineering, being bossy, grabbing objects from other children, teasing, making hurtful remarks, argumentativeness, boasting, and not showing interest in the accomplishment or joy of others.

It is sometimes the case that children with AD/HD are socially isolated. One notes this through lack of close friends or the development of age-expected relationships. On a more conspicuous level, children with AD/HD may be excluded from social events such as birthday parties.

CULTURAL CONTRIBUTIONS

Anyone who has lived for a significant period away from their country of origin will know how cultural differences dictate perceptions, attitudes and behaviour. Certainly, differences in language present obstacles, but even among people who supposedly speak the same 'language', there are subtle differences which effect how we interpret each other's thoughts and actions. Now, more than ever, we need to include cultural factors in the discussion of AD/HD, especially since there is more inter-connectedness among people from various parts of the world.

As just one example of cultural differences in 'road behaviour', I recently indicated to turn into a parking spot, when a child was standing in the spot. I realised that he was standing there to reserve the space for his parents. I had never encountered this behaviour and noticed that the car registration was different from the country in which this event occurred. Perhaps, this is a common and accepted manoeuvre in this child's country. The point is that I may interpret this behaviour as 'abnormal' or even 'defiant' but such might not be the case if I were accustomed to the ways of this child's country.

There are two specific ways to connect culture to AD/HD. One is the notion of 'cultural tempo'. The other is knowing whether AD/HD is even in the vernacular of people from different countries (e.g., do Fijians refer to children as AD/HD?). That is, how different are perceptions of AD/HD in the global stage?

CULTURAL TEMPO

Cultural tempo is a general term referring to the change in lifestyle and pace of daily life in the present generation compared with that of previous ones. Cultural tempo is not culture specific because one could guess that people from all parts of the globe are influenced by fundamental changes in lifestyle which arise from the current age as opposed to previous ones.

For example, information technology is profoundly changing our lives – mobile phones, internet, television, etc. Also significant are changes in child-rearing patterns, with an increase in the number of families where two parents are working. The issue of childcare is central to many countries. Intuitively, it would seem that there is far greater stress today than previously. That is the message one gets when communicating with more senior members of society, where one hears, 'things are so much more complicated today than in my time ...'

Generational changes in stress and the possible adverse effects on children have not gone unnoticed. David Elkind (1982) observed that children were exposed to a significant amount of stress related to the current generation. He mentioned the different ways in which children were 'overloaded'. For example, some children may be expected to carry out tasks that parents cannot, due to work demands, such as minding younger children, cleaning the house, or preparing meals. Parents may express their frustration with their overload by quarrelling or arguing in the presence of their children. This is another source of potential stress for the child. The title of Elkind's book, *The Hurried Child*, reflected the prevailing message to children – 'hurry and grow up'.

An objective, scientific determination of the influence of cultural tempo on children, and specifically, AD/HD, is difficult to determine. As far as this psychologist can tell, the idea of cultural tempo, while appealing, is at present, too diffuse and vague a concept to be amenable to research. Even if it were, it is hard to imagine how one could actually pinpoint cultural tempo as the cause of AD/HD. Barkely reasons that if cultural tempo is valid, we should see a rise in the prevalence of AD/HD. However, the actual prevalence of AD/HD varies depending on the methods and criteria used in diagnosis. In sum, the present status of cultural tempo is comparable to shooting at a moving target with an unpredictable gun. One could say that cultural tempo is an interesting speculation, but the verdict is far from clear on its relation to AD/HD.

CULTURAL DIFFERENCES

Where cultural tempo is a global phenomenon, cultural differences pertain to societal differences in the perception of AD/HD. In this regard, one can ask how AD/HD relates to different cultural groups. Is there more or less AD/HD across cultures? How do various societal groups deal with the problem of AD/HD? Only through close inspection of these questions can we see how cultural variables influence AD/HD. Some of the most relevant cultural variables are education, health, diet, child-rearing practices, and more complex psychological variables, such as group differences in beliefs about children's behaviour, perceptions of what defines a behavioural problem, the cause of the problem and what can be done to correct it.

Cultural factors relevant to AD/HD were largely ignored until recently, despite the general acceptance of cultural differences in attitude and behaviour. There are stereotypical notions of groups of people which to some degree are based on true differences in attitudes and behaviour. Some of these differences are captured quite humorously and some pertain directly to children's behaviour. For example, Hans Kaldenbach's *Act Normal! 99 Tips for Dealing with the Dutch*, notes that children who may otherwise be considered, 'bold' or 'cheeky', are seen by the Dutch as 'amusing little rogues who demonstrate a healthy precocity'.

There are clear and culture specific interaction patterns between children and parents. These interactions start at birth and significantly influence what behaviour is valued and whether or not any particular behaviour is viewed as a 'disorder'. As an example, consider a study by Arbiter, Sato-Tanaka, Kolvin, and Leitch (1999) which explored differences in the behaviour and temperament of Japanese and British toddlers who were living in London. One of the more interesting items concerned 'bedtime routine' where Japanese children were rated by their mothers as 'sleeping with parent'. This same item did not occur in the British sample. Further, 'sleeping with parent' was viewed as a sign of disturbance and this contributed to what appeared to be a greater sign of parent-child dysfunction among the Japanese relative to the British toddlers. However, the authors rightly point out that Japanese families value family cohesion and interdependence among family members. One way this value is demonstrated is co-sleeping arrangements where it is common for part, if not the entire family, to sleep in one bed. This bedtime routine would be viewed as more disturbing by traditional 'Western' culture, only because the Western view is to emphasise separateness and individuality (manifest as different beds for each person from birth). The Japanese could easily perceive this view as 'disturbing'.

In terms of cultural specific factors related to AD/HD, Lawrence Diller is concerned about the fact that 90 per cent of the worldwide use of Ritalin (the most common prescription drug for AD/HD) is in the United States. He questions whether the imbalanced use of Ritalin is a sign of progress or does it represent shortcomings in American society, like readiness to accept a biological basis of behaviour, and the corollary belief in medical interventions for behaviour difficulties.

As AD/HD has grown in prominence, it seems that an increasing number of professionals are questioning either the existence of AD/HD, or its treatment with medication. For example,

William Pollack (1998) believes that much of what we call ADD (Attention Deficit Disorder) is really Male Deficit Disorder and stems from societal issues related to truly understanding boys – their feelings, needs and conflicts.

If the basic meaning of AD/HD is called into question, then a number of other authors are appalled at the rise in use of medication to treat AD/HD. A good example, is David Stein's *Ritalin is not the Answer* (1999). Dr Stein is concerned about the 'disease' model behind AD/HD, and argues that AD/HD (or general misbehaviour, as he would call it) can be treated through non-medical techniques (e.g., different parenting techniques).

Do some cultures value, even encourage behaviours associated with AD/HD? One way to answer this question is to examine the prevalence of AD/HD in different countries. If AD/HD is culture bound, its prevalence would vary greatly depending on the country of focus. Ultimately, higher rates of AD/HD in a particular country might provide insight as to what contributes to the problem in these countries relative to countries reporting a lower incidence.

Russell Barkley (1997) summarises prevalence data worldwide. Prevalence data is available for European countries (Netherlands, Germany), China, India, New Zealand, Puerto Rico and the United States. He concludes that AD/HD is a 'worldwide phenomenon, found in every country in which it has been studied'. However, Barkley also mentions the wide variation in research methods used to determine prevalence as well as the different composition of the samples (different age groups, gender, etc.). This makes it very difficult to compare prevalence across countries, let alone with a country (e.g., the prevalence rate for AD/HD in the United States varied from 1.8 per cent to 13 per cent, depending on the location of the sample, type of sample, and method used). Further, there are many countries in which no prevalence data exists.

Thus, even where prevalence rates vary, it is difficult to conclude that there are culture specific factors which account for the difference. One cannot conclude with any confidence that the India data, where a startling 29 per cent AD/HD prevalence rate is reported, shows that there are factors unique to Indian culture which exacerbate the development of AD/HD. Neither can low prevalence rates imply culture factors which inhibit AD/HD. Interestingly, one of the lowest reported prevalence rates for AD/HD was the Netherlands (1.8 per cent). Perhaps children with AD/HD are viewed as showing a healthy precocity, as Kaldenbach revealed.

My personal view, and it is entirely speculation, is that as the topic of culture specific factors and AD/HD are more thoroughly explored, the impact of culture will relate to differences in early parent-child interactions (as the Japanese study mentioned earlier showed) and that some of these differences might aggravate AD/HD. Certainly, if one believes that AD/HD is a medically-based, biochemical disorder, cultures, per se, do not create AD/HD, but they certainly may play a key role in how society responds to it.

In the two countries of which I have personal and professional experience, I would see errors on a single attitude continuum – 'willingness to accept AD/HD'. On the one hand, I found that one culture was too accepting of AD/HD while the other was too dismissive. Both errors have equally grave societal consequences. In 'quick-to-detect AD/HD' societies, as Lawrence Diller makes clear, there is risk of over-identifying with the problem, where one is the 'victim' of the disorder, one uses passive, disease-language ('I have AD/HD'), and where medication and support groups are the inevitable outcome. In this situation the real problem and its treatment may never be exposed. And, where AD/HD is perceived as non-existent or extremely rare in occurrence, there is a danger that children with a bonafide special need will not be recognised and will go through life wondering why they misbehaved and never achieved their goals, despite having the ability to succeed. As the frustration mounts for these children, adolescence can be particularly hazardous, such as drug taking, early sexual activity, criminal behaviour and early school drop-out.

There is much to learn about culture and AD/HD. What seems obvious is that the role of culture-specific factors in the promotion or suppression of AD/HD remains largely unexplored. As a result, it is difficult to formulate how culture-specific factors relate to AD/HD. The toddler study mentioned earlier provides the type of research design which may clarify the association in the future. I would certainly concur with Lawrence Diller's notion as it relates to the American situation. He proposes that cultural factors specific to the United States require further exploration to determine whether the American approach to children's behaviour problems signifies development or misguided expectations about children, families, and school.

SUMMARY

This chapter began with the lofty aim of setting out explanations for AD/HD-type behaviour. These explanations were grouped into five categories – medical, family, education, child and culture. Of these five, the most consistently proven is medical factors. It is relatively clear that AD/HD is a biologically based disorder. The other four categories can be seen as parts of the 'nurture spectrum'. That is, the response to AD/HD is generally influenced by family, educational, child and cultural variables. To conclude this chapter, consider a best and worst case scenario.

In the best case scenario, Mr and Mrs Smith have a new son, John. He is the youngest of their four children. Early in John's life, the Smith's note that John's temperament is very different from his older siblings. By contrast, John is always on the go, flits from one activity to another, leaving all activities unfinished, dislikes mental-type activities, such as listening to stories, following instructions, and is disorganised in action and thought.

When John begins pre-school, his teacher, Mrs Jones, notes these same qualities and meets with the Smiths to share her perceptions. She is aware that these behaviours form the larger constellation of AD/HD. She notes this possibility to the Smiths who have also heard of AD/HD and wondered if John might have these characteristics. They seek a comprehensive assessment of AD/HD and, after thorough investigation, it is concluded that John meets the guidelines for AD/HD. A treatment team, consisting of psychologist, social worker, psychiatrist, paediatrician, and other therapists, as needed, form the least invasive treatment programme. The programme consists of parent training in behaviour management. Also the pre-school John attends is provided with an additional, part-time assistant to work with John on attention and behavioural programmes in school. John is four at this time.

The interventions lead to significant improvement. However, as John starts primary school, difficulties continue, especially as the academic work becomes more tedious. His medical doctor is aware of a number of medications for AD/HD and begins with the least toxic at the minimal dosage suggested. A vast improvement is noted. Parent and school needs are periodically checked by the treatment team. John does reasonably well in school and finds a career he enjoys and lives happily ever after ...

In the worst case scenario, the Smiths recognise John's behaviour as difficult. They do not understand why he does what he does and why his behaviour does not change despite their efforts to direct him otherwise. They are mystified as to why John does not respond to the same discipline methods which were needed in far less frequency with his siblings. In turn, they lose their patience. They may start to argue with each other about what to do. They make take their anger out on John, which only aggravates the situation. Then John begins school. His teacher sees John as disruptive, disturbing other children, always seeking attention through negative, inappropriate behaviour, and rarely engaged in academic work. As with John's parents, discipline techniques prove ineffective. The teacher meets with John's parents and suggests a professional assessment. However, the parents do not wish to attend a psychiatrist or psychologist as this is perceived as embarrassing and potentially 'shameful'. Instead, they get assistance from a dietician who provides an alternative diet. This has no effect on John. Meanwhile, they believe that John's problems will improve with time. They don't. In the meantime, John is suffering at school. He is now starting to feel great anger about his inability to get from A to B, even though he is as bright as any of his classmates. He loses confidence in himself, which is little wonder, given that his parents and teachers are always reprimanding him. His behaviour does not improve. His school work declines.

John is fifteen. He has done poorly in his exams, which is expected as he never studied. He is starting to affiliate with a 'resistant peer culture' – adolescents who share in risky behaviour – drugs, vandalism, etc. John is expelled from secondary school at sixteen. He tries several vocational training programmes but to little avail. He is alienated from his parents and has little contact with his older siblings. When these siblings try to 'talk' to John he does not listen. He seems full of rage and hopelessness. He does not live happily ever after ...

Chapter 4

ASSESSMENT AND DIAGNOSIS

It should be obvious that AD/HD is not a clear-cut and tangible disorder like other medical problems. For example, there are no medical tests – X-Rays, blood tests – which indicate the presence of AD/HD. Realise that while there is substantial evidence to support the brain basis of AD/HD, there are as yet no neurological tests (e.g., MRI) which definitely indicate its existence.

What this means is that AD/HD is a 'hypothesis' about why specific learning and behaviour problems are occurring. However, there are many reasons why such problems occur. Hopefully, it will be obvious from reading the preceding material that problems can be classified in more than one way, and each classification carries with it a different behaviour pattern and a unique reason for its manifestation. And it is inaccurate, as well as naïve, to think that a particular problem resides entirely 'within' the 'difficult' child. There are external factors (e.g., parenting style) which can intensify the situation.

In this context, the main purpose of an assessment is to clarify the problem and its seriousness, and, in doing so, to formulate reasons why the problem exists. When these matters are clarified, it is possible to make recommendations to improve the situation. This is why a formal, comprehensive assessment is the precursor to effective planning.

Another way to stress the importance of an assessment is to consider what happens when such an assessment is not undertaken. For example, parents may not fully understand the purpose and scope of an assessment. There may be fears that child evaluation is shameful to the 'family', even damaging to the child. Or they be under advice from relatives, friends or other professionals that an assessment is not necessary. These inhibiting factors may persist for years, resulting in untold and unnecessary suffering for all involved. In the absence of a thorough analysis, the long-term consequences are weighty, not only to children and their families but to society in general (e.g., school, community).

Another mistake is prematurely seeking help before the problem has been properly investigated. For example, parents may report a number of alternative 'treatments' for academic and behaviour problems, ranging from reflexology to herbal tea. These 'remedies' may have temporary, or no effect, which is understandable because the exact and true nature of the problem (or problems) has never been properly outlined.

The major goal of this chapter is to identify what is meant by an 'assessment'. To do this, the most frequently used measurement devices for assessing AD/HD are outlined. The pros and cons associated with each measure are discussed. Later, practical information is covered, such as what to tell a child prior to an assessment. First, we need to define 'assessment' and relate this term specifically to AD/HD.

ASSESSMENT OF AD/HD – DEFINITION AND OVERVIEW

The concept of 'assessment' is a generic one referring to the process of collecting information. The actual process may involve a number of techniques, such as talking with parents and child, observing the child, having the child complete various types of tests, as well as reading and analysing information already gathered by other professionals.

All assessments are undertaken to answer questions. The questions range from the specific – does my child have ...? – to more general ones – 'what does my child have?' If questions are medically based, one seeks a consultation from a medical doctor. If one is concerned about behaviour, one might obtain a psychiatric or psychological assessment. If the problem is learning related, an educational assessment will be most useful.

Obviously, different professionals have unique knowledge bases which determine how they view problems and the types of methods and tools they use to collect information. The assessment of AD/HD is a good example. A medical assessment involves a medical specialist, such as a neurologist or paediatrician, who has a particular frame or scope by which to assess the problem. Certainly, it would be expected that a medical assessment would involve a medical work-up (e.g., physical exam) and specific tests as necessary (e.g., blood, X-Ray, etc.). With regards to AD/HD, medical consultation is critical, namely because AD/HD is primarily a physical disorder (keeping in mind that the exact medical basis for the disorder is unknown at present). In addition, there are a number of medical problems which may result in AD/HD-type behaviour but in fact are due to medical complications (e.g., thyroid problems, hearing deficits, etc.).

A psychologist would adopt a slightly different perspective, perhaps focusing more on behavioural themes, family issues, or the psychological needs of the child and family. The assessment procedure might require an extensive interview with parents, child-based tests and any other information as needed. The psychologist is looking for behaviour/psychological themes which may confirm an AD/HD pattern, may be consistent with another pattern, or both.

An educational analysis is also critical to a complete AD/HD assessment, because educators have daily contact with the child. In addition, the classroom involves social and academic factors which may be related to behavioural problems. Further, teachers can comment on the types of learning problems which are often tangled with AD/HD, especially the AD part.

What follows is a discussion of the psychological assessment of AD/HD. Initially, the reasons for an assessment of AD/HD are outlined, followed by a discussion of the methods and tests a psychologist might use in a specific AD/HD evaluation.

THE PSYCHOLOGICAL ASSESSMENT OF AD/HD

In the majority of cases, the general aim of an assessment is identifying the child's learning and behavioural needs. Learning needs cover many of the specific categories discussed earlier, and behaviour needs would cover those which do not pertain to learning and cognitive problems. In other words, the psychologist is trying to determine which problems pertain to the child (if any), and to what degree. Given the categories noted in Chapter 2, one can imagine how challenging it is to make the right decision.

One potential folly in the assessment process is focusing only on AD/HD and not examining other types of problems which often co-occur with it, or may supercede attention deficits and hyperactivity. It is suggested that any attempt to assess AD/HD be multi-faceted, comprehensive and thorough. Multi-faceted refers to more than one profession. In the case of AD/HD medical and psychological consultations are vital. In addition, the assessment should be intensive, with no stone left unturned.

In addition to identifying what the problem is, a psychological assessment has two additional rationales. One is to speculate as to why the problem is a problem. So for example, in situations where AD/HD is the most obvious problem and there are no other difficulties co-existing with it, then the psychologist should be prepared to cover possible reasons for the existence of AD/HD. The typical explanation is the biochemical one as outlined in the previous chapter. However, other contributing factors should be outlined, as necessary.

Finally, the nuts and bolts of an assessment is to assist in formulating a treatment plan. This is where the assessing psychologist can outline individual programmes to address the needs identified.

The methods and tests which are relevant to the psychological assessment of AD/HD are outlined next. The methods are grouped into two general categories–formal, standardised tests and informal measures.

FORMAL TESTS

The definition of a formal test is one which measures particular abilities or perceptions through numerical scales. The child's performance evaluated relative to a similar age group, the end result being a score which provides information on the child's skill level. In this category fall all norm- referenced (child compared to similar age children) and standardised tests (each task given the same way with the same materials). These tests cover a variety of general abilities, such as intelligence, achievement and aptitude, as well as numerous and specific skills (e.g., attention span, memory, co-ordination, listening, visual reasoning, etc.).

However, not all formal tests pertain to a child's cognitive performance. Some formal tests measure perceptions of adults about a child's functioning in specific areas, as well as the child's self-perceptions. These measuring tools also yield numerical information, are norm-referenced and standardised. In this category fall rating scales and self-report questionnaires.

One of the most essential components of a psychological assessment is the measurement of intelligence.

INTELLIGENCE TESTS

Intelligence tests are often part of an AD/HD assessment. These tests measure mental ability and are useful in determining what, if any, cognitive difficulties are relevant. These tests tend to be time-consuming, because intelligence is such a broad concept that for it to be measured adequately, a number of different tasks are usually administered. Of course, one not only gets information about the child across specific cognitive tests, one also gets to observe how the child responds to various tasks – frustration level, organisation, learning strategies, risk-taking, etc. The types of observations made during an assessment will be covered under 'informal' measures.

Although there are different types of intelligence tests, the most commonly used is known as the Wechsler Intelligence Scale for Children-III (third edition). This test is commonly known by its acronym – WISC-III. The WISC-III is perhaps the most well developed and extensive test available to psychologists.

The WISC-III consists of thirteen different tests (known as subtests) six of which define the Verbal scale and seven the Performance (or Non-Verbal) scale. Users of this test typically administer anywhere between eight to twelve of the subtests. Children receive scores for each of the subtests, and these scores are then combined to yield a general Verbal score, a general Non-Verbal score, and a total, Full Scale score. To illustrate the types of verbal items on tests like the WISC-III, consider the following.

TYPES OF VERBAL ITEMS ON INTELLIGENCE TESTS
1. What is the capital of Australia?
2. In what way are celery and spinach alike?
3. Steve has twelve marbles. He loses eight. How many does he have left?
4. What does arrogant mean?
5. Why do we have police?
6. Repeat these numbers: 6   3   5   9

The general theme in verbal measures is to assess how fluently people can reason and express themselves in the oral medium. The questions typically come in sets and measure different types of verbal skills (e.g., memory, word concepts, fund of knowledge, classification, practical knowledge, etc.).

In contrast with verbal items are non-verbal tasks. These tasks are visual and the individual does not have to make an oral reply (answer a question). Several examples of non-verbal items are provided in the following Figure:

1. Making designs with multicolored cubes.

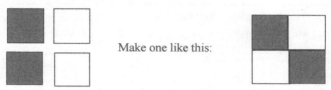

Make one like this:

2. Find the missing piece in the picture:

There are many other types of non-verbal items, not illustrated above. However, one gets the general idea that non-verbal tests measure visual reasoning; the ability to fluently and quickly manipulate visual images. Most non-verbal tests have a time limit and there is an element of eye-hand coordination. Some of the eye-hand tasks require paper and pencil and involve copying symbols or scanning symbols to determine a match. Children with attention and learning problems typically score lower on these tasks relative to other types of non-paper-pencil visual items.

When the entire battery of WISC-III tests are completed, one has a large amount of cognitive performance data such as the information that follows.

WISC-III OUTCOMES

Overall Full Scale Intelligence Score = 116 (average is 100)

Verbal Score = 117 (thinking, reasoning, expressing self with words)
Verbal subtest scores (subtest average is 10):

Subtest name	Description	Score
Information	General fund of factual information	13
Similarities	Logical, abstractive, categorical thinking	16
Arithmetic	Computations skill (mental math); **concentration**	11
Vocabulary	Word knowledge; word concepts	13
Comprehension	Understanding of social norms, practical knowledge	11
Digit span	**Attention; short-term memory (auditory)**	8

Performance Score = 113 (thinking with visual images)
Performance subtest scores (subtest average is 10):

Subtest name	Description	Score
Picture Comp.	Visual inspection skill	12
Coding	Copying speed; **short-term memory; concentration**	7
Picture Arrange	Synthesising visual parts; temporal sequencing	18
Block Design	Analysis of whole-parts; abstract visual reasoning	11
Object Assem.	Relationships among visual pieces; flexible thinking	12
Symbol Search	Visual search and scan; **memory; concentration**	8

This shows that this individual scored above average on the general scales – Full Scale, Verbal and Performance. This means that the child's general, verbal, and non-verbal ability is above what is typically the case for similar aged children.

A closer inspection of the subtest scores is revealing. Note that the child scored above average on the vast majority of subtests (scored above ten on all but three tests). The tests that the child scored lowest on all relate to memory and concentration. Thus, this child may have specific difficulties when asked to perform tasks that require sustained and focused attention. This information may support AD/HD.

When the WISC-III was revised in America, it was administered to children with specific learning and attention problems.

The WISC-III manual (American version) shows the performance of 68 children diagnosed with AD/HD. A Table in this document shows the average Verbal, Performance and Full Scale score. The averages are 98, 101 and 99. In other words, this tells us that for this sample, children with AD/HD, on average, tend to score near exact age norm. However, this sample tended to score lower on specific tests of attention and concentration (as in our example).

Attainment Tests. Attainment tests are used to measure school learning. Unlike intelligence tests, attainment tests cover basic academic skills typically learned in school. For example, the three 'Rs'– reading, writing, and arithmetic – are classic attainment areas.

Although there are different ways to measure reading skill, one of the most common is having the child pronounce individual words. Typically, the list starts with simple, frequently encountered words and then more difficult ones. Individuals who construct these tests take great pains to select words with different phonetic patterns (e.g., blends, digraphs, short and long vowels, etc.). The number of correctly pronounced words provides an indication of the child's word reading skill.

HYPOTHETICAL WORD READING LIST

In
For
Park
Helping
Adjust
Loan
Inept
Frequently
Generation
Hypothetical
Epistemology

Realise that the list is far shorter and 'non-scientific' in comparison with an actual word sample on a true reading test. However, the list is purely for illustration. For young children who are pre-readers, reading tests may include letter recognition activities, such as letter decoding (see Figure below).

how   car   man   elephant

The child is asked to point to the word with the same beginning sound as in the picture – 'cow'. Children with letter-decoding skills will recognise 'car' as the right answer, whereas children who do not have this skill will make an incorrect choice.

Spelling speaks for itself. Typically, the individual hears a word, is given the word in a sentence (in order to select the right word in case of homophones – 'pray' and 'prey'), and may hear the word a third time. The person then spells the given word. Spelling lists are constructed with the same attention to detail as are reading lists.

Like reading tests, number tests come in different forms. The most basic type of number test is asking the child to answer written computations – 5 + 3, 18 - 9, 354 x 30, .453-.034, 4y + 15 = 55, y = , etc. And, like reading tests, number concepts can be geared toward the four and five age ranges—counting, identifying numbers, more/less, etc.

As attainment tests indicate the degree to which children have mastered educational skills, one would expect AD/HD children to perform lower on these tests relative to the typical performance of their classmates. This prediction is based on the premise that the very nature of attention deficits is contrary to learning. After all, how can a child who has difficulty listening, has problems concentrating, and is frequently off-task, be learning at the same rate as his/her peers. This prediction is borne out by many studies as cited in Barkley's text. He refers to studies which show that the academic attainment scores of AD/HD children typically fall ten to 30 points below the norm. For example, if the average score is 100, the performance of children with AD/HD can vary between 70 and 90.

This psychologist has collected similar academic attainment data. The average performance (100 is exact average) of a sample of children referred for assessments of AD/HD is noted to be (N = number in sample): Reading = 93 (N = 98), Spelling = 93 (N = 98), and Maths = 92 (N = 40). These results are closer to the norm and less negative than those Barkley cites.

Attention specific tests. The interest in AD/HD has led some researchers to develop standardised tests of attention span, vigilance, reaction time, etc. These tests are usually computer based. One of the most common tests of attention span is the Continuous Performance Test (or CPT for short). The CPT is a fourteen minute task where the person views letters at differing intervals. The person must concentrate with the goal of pressing the space bar after each letter, except a particular letter (X). The task is monotonous and places a premium on concentration, reaction time, and ability to withhold impulses (e.g., not press the space bar when the letter X appears).

One advantage of the CPT is that it contains norms (or standard performance) for different age groups. For example, a six-year-old is not expected to have the same attention span as a ten-year-old. Thus, a person's performance is compared to a similar age group (as is the case with all the other measures previously discussed).

Another advantage of the CPT is novelty. Children usually think of the CPT as a computer game. Thus, motivation is enhanced. However, it does not take long before the routine and tedium are apparent.

Related to the last point, it is when the person realises that the CPT (or other similar test) is not a 'Play Station' type game, that certain behaviours indicative of loss of attention may emerge. For example, the first sign is when the person looks away from the screen. Another indication of attention loss is random pressing of the space bar. Still another indication is when the individual asks questions about the game, especially how much time is left. The time between the start of the test and behaviour indices of loss of concentration give a rough approximation of the person's attention span. For example, if a ten-year-old queries how much time is remaining at the four-minute mark, then four minutes is a rough estimate of attention span. One would predict that this individual will persist for four minutes before losing mental focus in the context of academic work.

Rating scales. These types of scales require an adult familiar with the child to assess the target child on various dimensions of learning and behaviour. Usually, these scales contain a statement and a number scale next to it. The rater is instructed to circle the number which describes the child's current behaviour with respect to the item.

EXAMPLE OF AD/HD RATING ITEMS
1. Is easily distracted.
2. Often leaves tasks (chores, school work) unfinished.
3. Does not seem to be listening in class.
4. Finds it difficult to sustain concentration.
5. Does not remain in seat when it is expected.
6. Has difficulty waiting turn.

One frequently used rating scale is the Conners' Rating scale. This measure includes a parent and teacher form. Basically, the rater reads a statement like the example and then circles a number (0 = Not at all to 3 = Very Much True) which describes the child's behaviour regards the target behaviour. These items are then grouped into different areas of learning and behaviour. For example, the Conners' Rating Scales measure four basic areas:

- Oppositional Behaviour – likely to break rules, have trouble with authority, easily annoyed and angered, etc. (five items).
- Cognitive Problems/Inattention (CP/I) – difficulty completing homework, trouble concentrating, learn more slowly (five items).
- Hyperactivity (HYP) – Always on the go, difficulty sitting still, more impulsive and restless than most individuals their age (seven items).
- AD/HD Index (AD/HD) – identifies those at risk for AD/HD (twelve items).

The raters numerical scores are summed to obtain normative information. That is, the ratings of the particular child are compared with a large sample of similarly rated children and divided into various age groups. The scale used to make these comparisons has an average score of 50. If the rater's scale score is 50, then no problems in that scale are perceived/observed. However, if the rater's score for a scale rises above the 60 point mark, then difficulties are noted. It is a subjective decision at which point the score indicates a clear problem. However, there is a statistical rationale for using the 65 score level as indicative of a problem. Realise that scores of 63 or 64 also indicate notable difficulties, although technically, this score is below the 65 mark.

To further clarify the scale, consider the following Figure:

AVERAGE PARENT AND TEACHER SCALE SCORES FOR A SAMPLE OF 94
CHILDREN

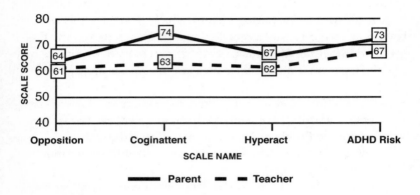

The data in the chart is based on a sample of 97-parent completed
forms and 94-teacher completed forms. The children were
referred for AD/HD assessments, which explains the high averages for both parent and teacher raters. Parent ratings tend to be
slightly higher for all scales, especially the Cognitive
Problems/Inattention scale. This score difference is due to the fact
that the parent form emphasises inattention, whereas the teacher
form stresses cognitive problems (e.g., reading, spelling, math
delay). The score differences for the other scales is minimal (three
to six points).

In general, rating scales are an important part of the assessment of AD/HD because they provide a numerical, standardised
and norm-referenced tool for measuring the perceptions of adults
who interact with the child on a regular basis. These scales are
economical because they are not time-consuming and do not have
to be completed with the assessing clinician present.

Perhaps the most basic reason for the use of rating scales is
the assumption that for a child to be truly AD/HD, problem
behaviours should be viewed in a variety of contexts – across

people, places, and time. Thus, many rating scales include a teacher edition (like the Conners' Scale) for completion by the child's classroom teacher (or other educational specialists who have regular contact with the child). Ideally, one should obtain ratings from parents and teacher (or teachers). This will help clarify the learning and behaviour pattern at home and school.

Self-report questionnaires. The term self-report means 'child' ratings. That is, there are different types of questionnaires for children to complete. The purpose of these measures varies greatly; some measure personality types (e.g., outgoing, passive, etc.), while other items are designed to assess specific problems (e.g., anxiety, depression, etc.).

In relation to AD/HD, there are newly-developed self-report scales which assess a child's self-perception of specific AD/HD-type behaviours (e.g., short attention span, always on the go, problems completing school work). Usually, the items are read to the child and the assessing clinician records the child's response. An example item: 'Do you have a hard time sitting still and being quiet?' The child's response is scored as 'not at all', 'rarely', 'sometimes', or 'usually' (or similar wording).

I find it useful to get a measure of the 'emotional' life of the child. Towards this end, I usually include a self-report scale covering aspects of self-concept (e.g., how one feels about oneself). The particular measure is known as the Piers Harris Children's Self-Concept Scale (PHCSCS). It measures general self-concept as well as six specific self-concept areas as follows:

- Total Score = Overall Self-Concept (total evaluation of self).
- Behaviour = Self appraisal of behaviour at home and school.
- Intellectual/School Status = Self-view of cognitive skill.
- Physical Appearance = Belief about physical attractiveness.
- Anxiety = Degree of perceived worry, preoccupation.
- Popularity = Perceived status with peers.

•   Happiness / Contentment = Self-perception of overall mood
    and satisfaction.

As with the Conners' Scales, this psychologist has kept statistical
records of the average scores for children who were referred for
AD/HD assessment.

The information in the Chart below is based on a sample of 78
children referred for AD/HD assessments. Thus, it is not altogether surprising that the lowest areas of self-concept relate to
Behaviour/Conduct, and Intellectual and School Status. That is,
children with suspected learning and behaviour issues tend to
acknowledge same. On the other hand, children's self-perceptions
are adequate in all others not directly linked to learning and
behaviour (e.g., popularity, not anxious, not dissatisfied, etc.).
And, the overall Total Self-Concept score tends to be right at the
average line, which means that in general, children with suspected AD/HD have reasonably positive self-concepts.

AVERAGE PHCSCS SCORES FOR CHILDREN REFERRED FOR AD/HD
ASSESSMENTS

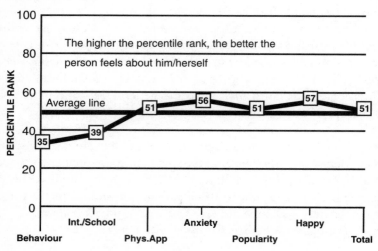

INFORMAL MEASURES

Whereas all the previous instruments have standardised instructions for administration, normative samples which allow for comparison, and scientific evidence that the test consistently and accurately measures what it purports to measure, informal measures could be considered 'non-scientific'. This does not lessen their importance. Rather, informal measures allow for subjective impressions on the part of the informant and the assessing clinician. For example, general discussion of a problem area with parents (or child) is informative and invaluable. One typically does not obtain a 'score' for these measures, and the information is not collected the exact same way from one person to the next. However, informal measures are not confined by a pre-selected set of questions or tasks, which means that the information is more individualised and sometimes more 'in-depth'.

A classic example of the difference between formal and informal measures commonly occurs with the Conners' Rating Scale. For example, a teacher completing the form is responding to say 28 statements related specifically to oppositional behaviour, inattention, hyperactivity and general AD/HDRISK (refer to the sample item set provided earlier in this chapter). However, it is not uncommon for teacher rater to note at the bottom of the scale (PTO) with a narrative report handwritten on the back of the scale. Teachers occasionally remark that they feel 'confined' by the rating items and that the particular set of descriptions does not fully and accurately depict the particular child's needs. The teacher may then provide a narrative report which includes the conditions in which misbehaviour or learning difficulty are likely, the form of the problem (what actually happens) and any previous attempts to correct the problem. As you can see, the narrative report, which is 'informal' in classification, allows the person to individualise perceptions and achieve a depth that is not always possible with formal, standardised tests.

With this overview in mind, let's look briefly at some of the informal methods of data collection used in the assessment of AD/HD.

Parent/Teacher (Other) interview. Perhaps no other data collection method has a brief as large as the interview. An interview is the formal name given to the discussion between clinician and parent (parent will be used throughout, although the reader should recognise that other family members can be interviewed, as can other people familiar with the child – teacher, other professional, etc.). The discussion can be structured or unstructured depending on the preference of the interviewer. The more organised inter-viewer usually follows a prescribed list of questions in a certain order. The unstructured interview allows the parent and inter-view to move in different directions, change pace, go into some detail more than another, etc. As the conversation is not struc-tured, it tends to be more spontaneous.

In the context that this psychologist operates, the goal of the interview is predominately diagnostic. That is, the interview, along with all other sources of information, is combined with an eye towards pinpointing the type of problem, its severity, and what can be done to address the issues emerging in the assess-ment. There is a necessity to obtain as much information as possi-ble in the shortest period of time. In the assessment of AD/HD, there are general areas which require discussion.

Developmental history begins with pregnancy, labour/deliv-ery and antenatal health. Infant temperament follows (e.g., easy/difficult baby, sleep/wake schedule, activity, feeding rou-tine, etc.) and then toddler milestones (e.g., walking, talking, toilet training, etc.). Pre-school behaviour/learning is the next topic and refers to first experiences in group learning situations (e.g., play school).

School history is a related line of inquiry. Parents usually describe adjustment to school, learning skills, behaviour concerns, social connection, outside learning support, etc. It is important to determine how the child responds to academic work – does the child initiate academic work? Can the child maintain focus without individual supervision? Are there different types of mental work that the child responds to differently?

A separate topic is health history. Has the child suffered any significant health problems, accidents or injuries, or hospitalisations of note? What is the status of the child's current general health? Any problems with hearing/vision? What are the child's health habits like – eating, sleeping, exercise, etc.?

The emotional-social life of the child can also be explored. Is the child content, anxious, frustrated, irritable? How does the child react to correction, praise? How does the child relate to same-age peers? What are friendship patterns like?

Parents may report specific behaviour issues and these issues require further exploration. For example, if the parent says the child is 'lively' or 'busy' it is necessary to define what these terms mean. If it comes to bear that the child is restless, cannot remain seated for long, and wants to be involved in everybody's affairs, then this pattern has obvious diagnostic implications (e.g., hyperactivity).

Family structure and process is an essential part of the interview. This includes size of the family, ages and names of siblings, etc. In single-parent families, it is useful to know if there is contact with the non-custodial parent, as well as the quality of the relationship with this parent. Family relationships can be enlightening. Who does the child relate best and worst with? What are the methods of discipline? How does the child respond?

In the case of AD/HD, issues related to attention and activity require further clarification. For example, regarding attention, it is useful to know if the child can play for extended periods with non-academic materials (e.g., dolls, lego, toy cars). How does the child play? Quietly or boisterously? Does the child play for extended periods with the same toy, or flit from one toy to the next? All of the questions provide useful diagnostic information.

Far from being just a fact-finding mission, the interview serves other important functions. One is diagnostic – does the child present with a problem which can be categorised according to diagnostic guidelines? A more specific question (which some parents wish to know) is whether the child meets specific guidelines for AD/HD?

During the interview, parents may gain insights as to the nature of the problem and what they can do to clarify or change a particular aspect of the situation. Comments like 'I hadn't thought of that', or 'I don't feel I spend enough time with ...' etc. can be important revelations which are more likely during a professional discussion.

Sometimes it is clear that other aspects of the situation are important. For example, frequent and contentious disagreements between parents may highlight marital discord as an exacerbating factor. Unrealistic expectations, unfavourable comparisons with siblings, and differing beliefs about the importance of the problem are just a few of the many points which may require comment.

In addition, the interview may include a 'de-briefing' element where results from instruments the child and parents have completed are shared with parents (and child in some situations). For example, this psychologist usually covers outcomes on formal tests (e.g., intelligence, attainment, attention, self-esteem, rating scales, etc.). Parents can then integrate assessment data with their own experiences and this can lead to further insights for parents and the assessing clinician.

Finally, it is during the interview that parental knowledge of various interventions can be explored. These interventions, which will be detailed in the next chapter, allow for further and important discussion. Parents may mention that a particular technique has proved ineffective (e.g., behaviour management). However, it may turn out that the procedure was not implemented correctly or for sufficient duration. Parents may gain useful tips at this time.

Review of Records. An often overlooked source of information is that gleaned from other professionals – teachers, doctors, social workers, speech and language therapists, etc. Other professional assessments may include reports which summarise test results and other sources of data as discussed. If these reports are available, it is useful to consult these documents.

Behavioural Observations. Much of the information discussed so far is that gained from standardised testing. How the child responds to the test situation – separating from parents, co-operation, persistence, ability to respond when uncertain, communication, interpersonal style, sense of humour, activity level, impulsiveness, mood – are equally important sources of information.

Research studies and the experience of most professionals show that children's behaviour is typically much less challenging for assessing clinicians than it is for parents. In other words, it is frequently the case that children behave within normal limits in the assessment context relative to home (and/or school). With regard to AD/HD, it is well established that behaviour in the assessment context will be improved relative to the child's daily environments. That is, children who are assessed with a specific query about AD/HD are less likely to engage in AD/HD-type behaviour during professional evaluation relative to the natural context of home, school and other frequently encountered environments.

This discrepancy is not surprising. After all, the assessment environment optimises novelty (novel adult, new tasks), pace (frequent change of tasks to prevent monotony) and demand characteristics (children are usually highly motivated to perform well because of salience of appointment – travel, length of meeting, uncertainty about 'real' purpose of the assessment, etc.). In most assessment situations, there are minimal distractions and one-to-one supervision. Thus, it is not surprising that children behave better in the assessment context relative to the home and/or school environment.

When problem behaviours emerge during an assessment then

important information can be found in the nature of the behaviour, the type of task which reliably predicts the behaviour, and what is done in response to the behaviour. For example, let's assume that an assessing psychologist senses lack of effort (e.g., loss of focus, less interest, less likely to persist, etc.) to a particular task. It is important to note whether the child's effort varies depending on the task (e.g., high on visual tasks, low on conversation activities). This is very revealing information.

Also, when effort declines, what does the psychologist do to increase motivation? Are incentives considered? Is guessing encouraged? Is praise provided for effort (even if unsuccessful)? What prompts, if any, are used to maximise persistence? Are these techniques effective?

Medical examination. In the case of suspected AD/HD, a medical evaluation is part of a complete assessment. In some respects, this type of examination is incorrectly placed as an 'informal measure' because of medical tests which are precise and well standardised (e.g., blood pressure, measurement of height and weight, eye and ear examination, reflexes, blood tests, etc.). Other types of medical information are more characteristic of informal measures (e.g., patient report). The importance of medical assessment must be re-iterated especially since there are some medical problems which mimic AD/HD.

ISSUES IN THE ASSESSMENT AND DIAGNOSIS OF AD/HD

The purpose of this section is to address typical concerns (e.g., 'will the assessment damage my child's self-esteem?') or practical questions (e.g., fee) about the assessment process. Some of the issues raised are borne from this writer's clinical experience (e.g., accuracy of the information received).

NO SINGLE TEST FOR AD/HD

Although AD/HD is believed to have a medical basis, there is no 'X-Ray' which shows the presence (or absence) of the condition.

Normally, a medical evaluation may include medical tests but these tests are to rule out other medical conditions which may mimic AD/HD. Even if children do undergo intensive medical investigation (e.g., MRI) there is no guarantee that the procedure will detect the exact neurological fault (it does not help that we do not know with complete certainty what the fault is).

The accuracy of an assessment depends on many factors, some of which are influenced by the assessing clinician. For example, a psychologist can require ratings from several people, the minimum of which are the child's parents and teacher. This will increase the comprehensiveness of the assessment. Likewise, at least two professional inputs are needed – psychological and medical (e.g., neurology and/or psychiatry). Finally, the clinician can select only the most reliable and valid instruments in the assessment and diagnosis of AD/HD.

SUBJECTIVE AND OBJECTIVE

Occasionally, people inquire about the types of tests used in the assessment of AD/HD. The previous content of this chapter elaborates the types of instruments, both standardised (relatively more objective) and less standardised (relatively more subjective) which are frequently used in an assessment of AD/HD. Both types of instruments have advantages and disadvantages. Ultimately, the accuracy of the assessment depends on comprehensiveness and the ability of the diagnostician to integrate different data sources to form reasonable conclusions.

The Assessment Process Depends on Where You Go and Who You See
The assessment procedure will naturally vary depending on the type of professional who provides it. Obviously, medical doctors have knowledge and assessment devices specific to their profession. Likewise, mental health professionals have a different array of tools.

The nature of an assessment will also vary depending on the place of service – hospital, private office, specialised clinic, etc.

For example, consider the following scenarios. In situation one, parents may be concerned about the difficulty they are having managing a particular child. They first seek medical assessment from their general practitioner, who refers the child to a child psychiatrist. It is recommended that the child be placed in a play group, special school or some other service. In this context, the child may be observed by more than one profession (e.g., psychology, speech and language, nursing, etc.) and the assessment may be on-going (one week, one month, etc.).

Contrast this with example two, where a parent makes direct contact with a service provider – neurologist, allergist, psychologist, etc. This professional conducts an assessment. At the end of the assessment, the parent may be advised to seek another consultation from another specialist. The parent does so. This may conclude the referral process, or ongoing services with a third professional may be suggested.

The Quality of an Assessment Depends on the Quality of the Information

I'm reminded of a statistics professor I knew who often used the adage – 'garbage in/garbage out'. In this context, he meant that no matter how good the statistical technique, one cannot use statistics to transform a poorly conceptualised research study into a proper investigation.

A similar point can be made regarding assessment of AD/HD. The quality of the self-report made by parents is vital in coming to accurate conclusions about the presenting problem. If information is withheld or greatly altered, then a golden opportunity to change the 'real' problem is lost.

Self-Assessment: An Important First Step

It is often the case that people first learn of AD/HD through the media – television programmes, internet, magazines, etc. In this context, a brief overview of AD/HD is provided, and this overview typically includes a list of behavioural difficulties associated with AD/HD. Relatedly, people may say that the list of behaviours matches well with the child's behaviour. Hence the desire for, and importance of, further investigation.

HOW DOES AN ASSESSMENT AFFECT THE CHILD?

Occasionally, the question is raised as to how children react to an assessment. For the vast majority of children, they soon realise that the assessment is somewhat like being at school, especially as far as attainment tests are concerned (e.g., reading, spelling, math). Further, because some of the tasks are novel (e.g., arranging picture cards to make sensible stories, working on a computer, etc.) interest and motivation is usually optimised.

A child's adjustment to an assessment also depends on the emotional status (e.g., predisposed towards anxiety, negative mood, etc.), the way in which parents explain the assessment in advance of the appointment, and the ability of the assessor to establish rapport and make the child 'comfortable'. Let's briefly look at each factor.

If the child has difficulty adapting to new situations, is easily upset by change in routine, is prone to worry excessively or has problems relating to unfamiliar adults, there is a greater risk that the child will react negatively to the assessment process. In this examiner's experience, negative reactions take the form of significant inhibition (e.g., little communication, or crying and upset). In the past five years, I can count the number of children who have reacted poorly to an assessment on one hand (say one child per 150 assessments). Of course, there are several strategies to encourage participation even when a negative reaction occurs (e.g., allow the parents to comfort and be present during the assessment; normally the child is assessed without parents present).

How and when parents introduce the appointment to the child is another important factor. In the ideal situation, parents are encouraged to explain why the assessment is necessary (e.g., to get the right kind of help for reading/spelling, to help teachers know how to teach better, to help parents help the child at home, etc.). Subsequently, parents are advised to tell the child exactly what they will do – little bit of reading, spelling, maths, blocks, puzzles, etc.). Answer the child's questions honestly and alleviate any erroneous beliefs (e.g., emphasise that the process is fun). If resistance is encountered, then parents have the challenge of reducing this resistance and encouraging co-operation. While there is no single way to achieve this, honesty is the best policy.

When parents tell the child about the assessment can also be important. I understand that in some cases, the child is not informed about the assessment until the morning of it. This psychologist would not advise this action, unless parents are completely confident that significant resistance will occur if the child is told about the appointment in advance. The reason that such an action is ill-advised is that the child may react negatively just before the assessment, and this reaction could carry-over during the assessment. If children are told in advance, then negative reactions can be dispelled and parents have time to enlist co-operation.

Finally, an assessor's ability to establish rapport upon initial meeting is another key variable. I find it valuable to discuss non-academic matters at the outset (e.g., favourite toys, pets, sports, hobbies, brothers/sisters). During this time a sense of 'lightness' and humour typically pervades. Personal disclosures and compliments are also useful. Once the child is involved in casual conversation, it is almost a given that the results of the assessment will reflect the child's true abilities.

Even if the child is quiet or anxious at the outset (e.g., little communication), once the child begins with a familiar task (e.g., reading words or passages), it is likely that any timidity will gradually fade. Also, during the administration of standardised tests, the assessor can praise effort and make other complimentary observations in order to enlist rapport.

WHO DIAGNOSES AD/HD?

AD/HD is considered a 'psychiatric' disorder. As such, medical doctors (e.g., neurologists, child psychiatrists) play a significant role in the diagnoses of AD/HD. However, AD/HD is most accurately diagnosed using a 'multi-disciplinary' approach. Multi-disciplinary means at least two different professionals assess the child. A diagnosis by one specialist would not be regarded as 'comprehensive' and obviously it would not be multi-disciplinary.

Perhaps the most common tandem is psychologists and psychiatrists. This is not to say there cannot be additional professionals (e.g., speech and language therapists, social workers, teachers). Rather, the basic minimum would be a comprehensive psychiatric and psychological assessment.

To underscore the importance of a comprehensive assessment one only has to return to Chapter 2, where some of the problems commonly entangled with AD/HD are noted. Realise that some of these problems require specialised assessment from particular specialists (e.g., dyspraxia).

ASSESSMENT IS NOT TREATMENT

One potential misconception about assessment is that it is not a treatment programme per se (e.g., individual therapy with child; family therapy). A 'therapeutic' effect can occur in some cases (e.g., improve self-esteem, parent insight, etc.).

AN ASSESSMENT REPRESENTS THE CHILD AT A SINGLE POINT IN TIME

The data collected during an AD/HD assessment is gathered during a fixed time frame, typically between one hour (e.g., a single medical consult) or one day (a complete psychological assessment). However, realise that during parent interview a great amount of historical information is related. Likewise, the Conners' Rating Scales are based on observations of parents and teachers in the past month. Finally, many of the procedures used have the scientific quality of 'reliability' which means that scores on the tests used do not vary greatly over time.

COST

The fee for assessments depends on the type of service. In the case of public health facilities, an assessment may be free. If independent practitioners are involved, the fee will vary greatly depending on how long the consultation and by what type of professional. The fee may be €80 to €150 if an independent child psychiatrist is consulted. Consultant paediatricians and neurologists may have a similar fee scale.

A full psychological assessment usually requires a complete day and this is more expensive, as the practitioner is involved for an entire day with the family. The fee scale may vary from €300 to €500. In some cases, psychologists and medical practitioners work together in a co-ordinated service. Fees can vary from €600 to €1,000.

It is also important to note that fees may be slightly greater in cases where the professional completes a full-report and forwards this to the parents. These reports can be time-consuming, especially if one considers how much data must be analysed and integrated. Reports can take between one and three hours to write, proofread and correct.

PUTTING IT ALTOGETHER–A CASE REPORT

To get an idea of an assessment and report, a complete Psychological Report follows. It is based on the report style this psychologist uses for an AD/HD assessment. However, the actual information in the report is completely fictitious.

PSYCHOLOGIST'S REPORT

(Personal and Confidential)
Name: John Doe
Address: 123 Main, Anytown, Anywhere

D.O.B.: 12 September, 1992   *Age at Testing*: 10 years, 3 months
Date of Evaluation: 1 January 2003   *Date of Report*: 3 January 2003
School: Any School   *Year*: fourth

REASONS FOR ASSESSMENT

1. To identify John's learning and behaviour needs.
2. To provide recommendations given the needs identified.

EVALUATION PROCEDURES

Parent Interview
Behavioural Observations
Wechsler Intelligence Scale for Children-III (WISC-III)
Wechsler Individual Achievement Test (WIAT)
Continuous Performance Test (CPT)
Conners Rating Scales (Parent and Teacher Forms)
Piers-Harris Children's Self-Concept Scale (PHCSCS)

OUTCOMES

Parent Interview (with Mr and Mrs Doe)
Health and developmental history are as follows. Mrs Doe reports a full-term pregnancy and uncomplicated labour/delivery. Infant/toddler health and behaviour were without issue. No delays regarding developmental milestones were noted.

John's current health is generally good. No long-term illness is noted, vision and hearing are without complication, and diet is generally good. Some difficulties were reported with sleep (e.g., difficulty settling before bed).

The present referral was school initiated and is based on

concern about possible learning and attention difficulties. Apparently, the report from school is that John is frequently off-task, cannot seem to concentrate for more than a few minutes, is resistant to school work, and tends to complete academic work quickly and without attention to detail. His school behaviour is not considered disruptive. Academic delays in all areas are reported and John receives learning support in school for his academic difficulties.

At home, parents note a similar pattern. John requires constant supervision to complete homework, and is it is difficult to get him to initiate academic work. However, his concentration is said to be far better for independent play and recreational activities (e.g., lego, arts/crafts, sports). He is described as affectionate, sensitive, and imaginative.

John is the middle of three children. He has one younger sister, Jean (six) and an older brother, Joseph (thirteen). No learning or behavioural difficulties are noted with the other children. John is said to relate well with Jean although a more contentious relationship is noted with Joseph (argue frequently, tease, etc.). Parents report no difficulties with discipline or John's response to same.

BEHAVIOURAL OBSERVATIONS
John separated from his parents without difficulty. Rapport was established easily, as John was chatty, friendly, cheerful and relaxed.

John co-operated with all standardised tests. Although he appeared motivated to perform his best, he did not persist on challenging problems. For example, he often gave up quickly even though with greater perseverance he may have achieved a correct solution. There was no observation of excessive activity or impulsivity. However, John's mental stamina appeared low as noted in the previous comment. John's complete WISC-III results are given overleaf:

OVERALL FULL SCALE INTELLIGENCE SCORE = 104 (AVERAGE IS 100)		
SCALE NAME	SCALE DEFINITION	VERBAL SCORE = 100
VERBAL	Thinking, reasoning, expressing self with words.	Percentile rank = 50
PERFORMANCE (NON-VERBAL)	Thinking in visual images and manipulating them with fluency, flexibility and speed.	PERFORMANCE SCORE = 108 Percentile rank = 70

VERBAL SUBTESTS (score average for subtests is 10)		
Name	Description	Score
Information	General fund of factual information; long-term recall	11
Similarities	Logical, abstractive, categorical thinking	10
Arithmetic	Computational skill (mental maths); concentration	8
Vocabulary	Word knowledge; word concepts	11
Comprehension	Common sense, practical knowledge	10
Digit Span	Attention; short-term memory (auditory)	7
PERFORMANCE SUBTESTS		
Picture Completion	Visual inspection skill	11
Coding	Copying speed; short-term memory (visual); concentration	8
Picture Arrangement	Synthesising visual parts; temporal sequencing	13
Block Design	Analysis of whole into parts; abstract visual reasoning	12
Object Assembly	Seeing the relationship among visual pieces; flexibility in thinking	12
Symbol Search	Speed of visual search and scan; short-term memory (visual)	8

John's WISC-III Full Scale, Verbal, and Non-Verbal are considered in the Average to High Average range. In other words, his general mental ability, as well as his verbal and non-verbal ability, are either at age standard or slightly advanced, compared to similar aged children.

Profile analysis shows a clear SCAD Index. SCAD consists of four WISC-III subtests – Symbol Search, Coding, Arithmetic and Digit Span. Children with specific learning and attention difficulties typically achieve lower scores on SCAD tests relative to their Perceptual Organisation (PO) scores (PO = all Performance subtests except Coding and Symbol Search). John's PO average was twelve while his average SCAD subtest score was eight.

WIAT

John's results on three WIAT subtests are Table below (standard score average = 100; AE = Age Equivalent):

Scale Name	Task	Standard Score	Percentile	AE
Basic Reading	Individual word pronunciation	98	70	7.9
Spelling	Writing spoken words	93	68	8.3
Numerical Operations	Performing written computations	95	94	9.9

John's WIAT scores are in the 'average' band. This means that his reading, spelling, and maths skill is about the same as the average performance of a similar-age reference group. His WISC-III/WIAT scores do not suggest specific or general learning difficulty.

Continuous Performance Test (CPT)

The CPT is a fourteen-minute computer administered test which requires the person to react quickly to letters and to withhold impulses by not reacting to a selected letter. The purpose of the test is to provide norm-referenced scores which measure attention span, reaction time, perceptual sensitivity, etc. The CPT automatically produces a report and the general summary statement taken from this report says, 'Numerous indices from the Conners' Continuous Performance Test suggest that John Doe has attention problems. There is strong evidence from the Conners' CPT to suggest attention difficulties'. Observations of John during this test show that he became increasingly restless (fidgety) and inattentive (looking away from the computer monitor) as the test progressed.

Conners Rating Scales-R (Parent and Teacher Forms)
The Conners Rating Scales measure adult perceptions of a child's AD/HD-type behaviour. The four scale scores are:

- Oppositional Behaviour – likely to break rules, have trouble with authority, easily annoyed and angered, etc. (five items)
- Cognitive Problems/Inattention (CP/I)-difficulty completing homework, trouble concentrating, learn more slowly (five items)
- Hyperactivity (HYP) – Always on the go, difficulty sitting still, more impulsive and restless than most individuals their age (seven items)
- AD/HD Risk (AD/HD)–identifies those at risk for AD/HD (twelve items)

Scores over 65 indicate significant concern. Parent and teacher ratings are charted below.

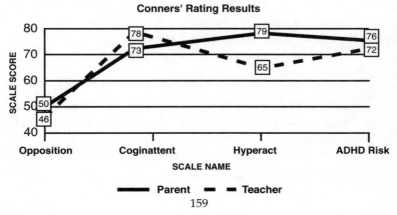

Conners' Rating Results

The most important result is that parent and teacher ratings greatly exceed the minimal cut-off score of 65 for the general AD/HD RISK scale. This means that in across both home and school settings, John displays a significant amount of behaviour characteristic of youngsters with AD/HD, namely inattentive, distracted, problems with concentration, off-task easily, etc.

Another noteworthy finding is that the component parts of AD/HD – inattention, impulsivity, and hyperactivity – are also significantly elevated for both parents and teachers. That is, parents and teachers observe significant levels of inattention, impulsiveness and excessive activity (e.g., restless, cannot sit still, etc.).

John is NOT perceived as Oppositional. This means that parents and teachers do not observe significant levels of negativity frequently associated with oppositional children (e.g., angry, resentful, irritable, etc.).

PIERS-HARRIS CHILDRENS SELF-CONCEPT SCALE (PHCSCS)
The PHCSCS yields an overall self-concept score, and six specific subscale scores, as given below:

- Total Score = Overall self-concept (total evaluation of self)
- Behaviour = Self appraisal of behaviour at home and school
- Intellectual/School Status = Self-view of cognitive skill
- Physical Appearance = Belief about physical attractiveness
- Anxiety = Degree of perceived worry, preoccupation
- Popularity = Perceived status with peers
- Happiness/Contentment = Self-perception of overall mood and satisfaction

John scored below invalidity requirements on three response scales. This means that he responded to the PHCSCS with accuracy and honesty.

John's Total Self-Concept score is slightly negative. However, he reports positive self views in four areas and negative self-perceptions

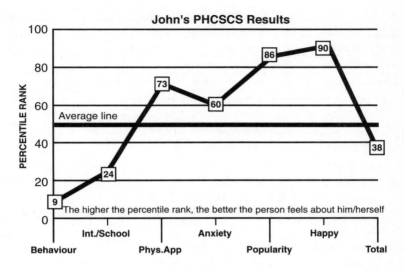

John's PHCSCS Results

The higher the percentile rank, the better the person feels about him/herself

in the other two domains – behaviour and school ability. His most negative self-concept areas are those typically reported by children with learning and behaviour difficulties.

SUMMARY AND INTERPRETATION

1. To identify John's learning and behaviour needs (see the following Table)

NEED	COMMENT
Learning Problems	None indicated.
Behaviour Needs	Consistent report regarding AD/HD. Indications are:
	• Developmental history and current concern.
	• Parent CPRS ratings.
	• Teacher CTRS ratings.
	• Difficulty with tests of attention (e.g., CPT, WISC-III SCAD).
	• Observations of inattention and lack of mental stamina

NEED	COMMENT	
Emotional Issues	No difficulties indicated.	
Social Adjustment	Adequate connection with same age peers.	
Physical Health	Within normal limits.	
Family Factors	None identified.	Diagnostic code: 3-1

2. To provide recommendations given the needs identified.

RECOMMENDATIONS

1. Statement of Special Educational Need:
* Attention Deficit/Hyperactivity Disorder (Mixed Type)

2. Suggestion for Educational Provision:
* Resource teacher allocation at 2.5 hours per week.

The focus of Resource assistance is provided in the following recommendation.

3. Suggestion for Areas of Resource Focus:
* Attention and concentration training.
* Behaviour programming.
* Liaise with class teacher and parents.

4. Handouts for Class/Resource Teacher (related to above areas of focus):
* Handout 4A – Random Beeper
* Handout 4B – Tips for Teaching Students with Attention and Learning Difficulties
* Handout 4C – Home-School Note System (Primary School version)

5. Ideas and Handouts for Parents:
* Handout 5A – Parent Tips
* Handout 5B – Programme to Improve Academic Productivity
* Read more about AD/HD and related problems:
  * Christopher Green (1995), *Understanding AD/HD...*
  * Thomas Phelan (1996), *All About Attention Deficit Disorder.* Available from Child Management, Inc. 800 Roosevelt Road, Glen Ellyn, Illinois, USA 60137.
  * Stephen Garber (1996), *Beyond Ritalin.* (available from

Harper Collins).

- Support and encourage John with hobbies and interests.
- Participate in the local AD/HD support group.

6. *Medical/Psychiatric Management:*
- Consider a Child Psychiatric Consult with Professor Joe Attuncion. Contact (000) 000-0000.

7. *Review:*
A review in March 2004 is suggested. Parents are encouraged to contact me at this time.

William K. Wilkinson, EdD
Reg. Psych., Psychological Society of Ireland

THE DIFFICULTY OF DIFFERENTIAL DIAGNOSIS

As you might realise by now, AD/HD is not an easy condition to diagnose. If AD/HD was the only learning, behaviour, emotional, and social problem known to affect children, then the situation would not be as complex. However, one needs only to review Chapter 2 to glean just a thumbnail sketch of other common problems which can be entangled with AD/HD. The skill in partitioning the presenting problem into the right classifications (and not using classifications that are not present), is technically referred to as differential diagnosis. Differential diagnoses are especially significant in situations of medical crises, where the doctor, faced with thousands of potentially relevant diagnoses, must make the correct decision in a limited time-frame.

In order to understand the notion of differential diagnoses as it relates to AD/HD, this psychologist continues to collect assessment and diagnostic information. Each case is given a diagnostic code, based on two interwoven coding systems. System one is a brief list of relevant 'problem' codes. It is provided below:

	Diagnostic Coding System
AD/HD Primary	Comment
1. Attention Deficit (AD) Only	AD pattern without HD
2. Hyperactivity Disorder (HD) only	HD pattern without AD
3. Mixed Type (both AD and HD)	Both patterns obtained
AD/HD Co-morbid or secondary	AD/HD may co-exist or be less important than the following
4. Oppositional Defiant Disorder (ODD), Conduct Disorder (CD)	Common co-occurring behaviour disorders (see Chapter 2).
5. Depression and/or anxiety Anxiety	Possible co-occurring emotional problems
6. Specific Learning Difficulty (Dyslexia) Mechanics > Comprehension/Reasoning General Learning Difficulty Speech and Language related Gifted and Talented	Learning/Cognitive Problems
7. Autistic-Type Asperger Syndrome	Pervasive Developmental Disorder; undifferentiated social-relational problems
8. Dyspraxia	Physical-Co-ordination Problems
9. Multiple Codes Apply	An example could be 1, 5, and 6.
10. AD/HD Insufficient	AD/HD pattern may or may not be present. If present, AD/HD-type behaviours are overshadowed by atypical health, family, or education factors.

Briefly, the Coding system closely follows the organisation of Chapter 2, with the notable addition of AD/HD relevant codes (as in Chapter 1). This psychologist uses specific 'decision rules' as to what constitutes the presence of any code. For example, the presence of SLD (dyslexia) is based on a specific WISC-III and WIAT score pattern. Likewise, the presence of another behaviour problem, like ODD, is based on rating scores and parent report.

The second coding system refers specifically to the rows in the previous Table which are banded by darker boundaries. This leads to a general decision about AD/HD, namely:

1. AD/HD Primary and No Other Relevant Problem (Codes 1-3 only)
2. AD/HD Co-Morbid (co-occurring with any of codes 4-9 and of equal importance)
3. AD/HD Secondary (less important than codes 4-9, but faintly or inconsistently present)
4. AD/HD, and all other codes, Insufficient (see note in previous Table)

The codes in these two tables were applied to 100 cases. The results are presented in the following charts:

Chart 1.

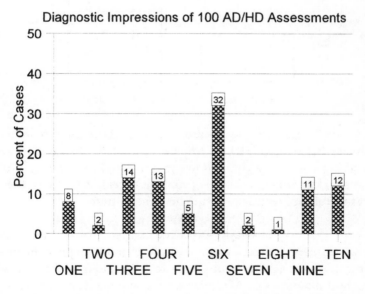

Chart 1 provides the frequency of each of the ten codes in the preceding Table. So, for example, the Table shows that in roughly one-third of the cases, children presented with some type of learning difficulty (code 6). On the other hand, the least occurring codes relate to dyspraxia (code 8) and autistic spectrum disorders (code 7).

Chart 2.

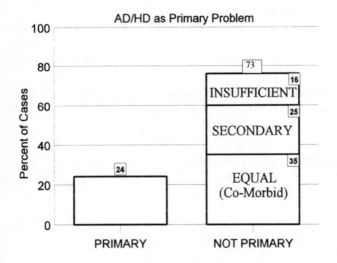

Chart 2 indicates the position of AD/HD relative to other problems (e.g., is AD/HD the foremost problem, or secondary to something else?). The chart shows that in roughly 75 per cent of cases AD/HD was not the sole problem, of less importance than another concern, or was of insufficient magnitude.

SUMMARY AND CONCLUSION

The assessment process, warts and all, is made explicit in this chapter. Several critical issues were raised regarding the assessment and diagnoses of AD/HD. A complete psychologist report was provided. The report particulars were fictitious, but the material is accurate in terms of structure and general content used by this psychologist. Finally data on the general outcomes of an assessment were provided using data this psychologist has collected for 100 cases.

There are two linking points to draw in preparation for the next chapter. One is the term 'multi-disciplinary': This means that a combination of professionals are involved in the assessment of AD/HD. In the next chapter, reference is made to 'Multi-Modal' treatment. The same principal applies – AD/HD is usually best treated from several different angles (e.g., education, family, medical, etc.).

Finally, realise that the treatment of AD/HD is complicated by the fact that in about 75 per cent of the children referred to this psychologist, AD/HD is not the only issue (if an issue at all). Thus, the relevant factors which emerge during an assessment each require a separate intervention programme.

Chapter 5

MULTI-MODAL TREATMENT

'What can we do to help?'
'What is the next step?'
'What do you suggest we do ... ?'

Adults frequently ask these types of questions when told a child meets guidelines for AD/HD. The issue of 'what to do' is probably the fourth and final one in a natural progression. The first question is, 'does my child have AD/HD?' The second is, 'are there any other problems which may explain the present difficulties? The third is, 'what are the causes of the problem?' And finally, the question which leads into the material for this chapter – 'what can be done to help?'

As you might expect the answer to the question of what can be done depends greatly on the answer to the previous questions. For example, two children may exhibit behaviour patterns which match that of AD/HD. However, child one may present behaviours typical of AD/HD and no other learning or behaviour problem. The treatment programme for this child would differ significantly from that of child two, who may present with the AD/HD-type behaviours, but also one or more of the other difficulties described in Chapter 2. The treating professional must consider each issue and design an intervention plan to meet the different needs of the child.

It would be unwieldy to discuss different treatment programmes for all of the previous problems noted in the earlier chapters. Thus, this chapter is de-limited to the discussion of multi-modal treatment of AD/HD. In other words, if one refers back to the charts at the end of the previous chapter, the ensuing discussion pertains mainly to the roughly 25 per cent of cases where AD/HD is apparent and no other problems are clinically significant. Of course, the discussion is also relevant to the 35 per cent of cases where AD/HD is as important (co-exists with) as another problem (e.g., dyslexia).

What is Multi-Modal Treatment?

If one peruses the material in many books on AD/HD, there does not appear to be a coherent, or overriding principle which unifies the various programmes suggested. For example, here is a list of some of the chapter titles which pertain to treatment:

- Counselling and Training Parents
- Top Tips for Better Behaviour
- Treatment in School Settings
- Stimulant Medication
- Teaching Children to Monitor their Behaviour
- Social Skills Training

It should become apparent that there are multiple 'modes' (aka formats, procedures, etc.) to intervene. Some modes require parent and/or family participation. Others require educational provisions. Other interventions focus on social skills and the larger groups in which AD/HD individuals interact. Alternatively, some professionals teach particular skills to children with AD/HD (e.g., self-control). Finally, there are medications and other medical interventions which obviously require medical management.

It should be additionally clear that no single professional could possibly manage all the various treatment formats suggested. This is why there is typically more than one individual assisting in the intervention process. Hence the reference to 'multi-modal' or 'multi-disciplinary' treatment of AD/HD. In this context, multi-modal refers to multiple professionals managing different treatment formats (Keen et al, 1997).

Who are these professionals and what are the formats? In Chapter 3, five different domains relevant to AD/HD were discussed – medical, family, educational, child, and cultural. Each of these domains can be re-phrased as a format in which treatment can be provided. For example, psychiatrists, neurologists, and paediatricians medically manage AD/HD. Psychologists, social workers, and family therapists may be in charge of family and/or individual child matters. The educational domain is cared for by teachers while cultural-social interventions may be the purview of any appropriately trained mental or medical health professional.

The remainder of this chapter outlines some of the most common treatment programmes grouped into the five aforementioned areas. The order each topic is presented is based on the principle that, whenever possible, non-medication treatment programmes should be tried before considering a medication trial. Thus, the medical management of AD/HD is the last domain to be discussed.

LEARNING ABOUT AD/HD

Learning more about AD/HD is a form of 'treatment'. It is often the case that an individual reads about the behaviours associated with AD/HD and this leads to a self-referral for professional consultation. It may also lead to further reading, which is always advisable, because increased knowledge allows one to get more out of professional consultation (e.g., know what questions to ask). The References section at the end of the book provides further reading.

Learning more about AD/HD can extend from articles/books to the internet and to local networks/support groups. Participating in a support group is one of the most valuable ways to learn about AD/HD. Only in this format can a newcomer to the topic find out about the characteristics of other children identified with AD/HD, and how other families have adjusted to the condition. Appendix 1 lists several support networks.

HELP FOR PARENTS

Most, if not all, basic reference books on AD/HD include 'tips' for parents in managing the difficult behaviours of children with AD/HD. In fact, some book titles suggest a 'parenting' focus, such as *Keys to Parenting a Child with Attention Deficit Disorder* (McNamara, 1993). In other similarly slanted books, the author appears motivated to eliminate medical management of AD/HD. *Ritalin is not the Answer* ... (Stein, 1999) is so classified.

It is important to remember that strategies to help parents manage difficult behaviour do not necessarily imply that parents are the cause of the behaviour. It is accepted that in 'true' cases of AD/HD, the most 'able' parents are severely tested. Recall from Chapter 3, that the leading causal factors in explaining AD/HD are genetic and bio-chemical. Hence, children are pre-wired to be inattentive, impulsive, and excessively active. Parents and other family members 'respond to' but do not create the problem.

Nevertheless, it is important to respond in the best possible way to AD/HD-type behaviour. Since parents interact early and often with the AD/HD child, negative interactions (e.g., responses) can intensify problems; positive interactions can reduce the stress and daily combat that tends to wear one down.

Let's put parent strategies into perspective. One of the most common parent responses is technically known as the 'verbal reprimand'. It comes in many forms, ranging from 'no', to 'don't do that', to 'how many times do I have to tell you not to do that, can't you see that you can't do that, when are you ever going to learn that it is not ok to ... (continue harangue)'. This happens in all families with all children. However, what if the child is temperamentally geared to want everything now, cannot wait for things, cannot concentrate for long enough to block out a desire, and other hallmarks of AD/HD. When these dispositions are present, then the number of verbal reprimands issued every few minutes can be startling. I have watched parents give verbal reprimands every 20/30 seconds – saying the same thing over and over – 'don't do that' – and with no effect whatsoever on the child. Eventually, over the course of the day, some requests will be granted because of the child's persistence and the parents' lack of behaviour management principles to combat the child's continued 'demanding' behaviour.

What if the child with AD/HD-type behaviour repeatedly requests something she cannot have (e.g., sweets)? Dad responds to the request with, 'no, you can have something sweet after dinner'. Child repeats request with long face and supplicating tone (e.g., 'just one sweet'). Dad repeats 'no'. Child continues to sulk and whispers, 'just one'. Finally Dad acquiesces ('OK, just one').

This may seem like much ado about nothing, but something quite powerful underlies this interaction. It is referred to as 'negative reinforcement'. Negative reinforcement means that one is highly motivated to remove a distressing (negative) situation (e.g., child's whiny voice). However, the child's negative behaviour (e.g., whiny/demanding) is inadvertently increased, which is why it is called reinforcement. Essentially, the child repeatedly presents a 'negative' behaviour (whine, moan, whimper, sulk). In turn, the parent is motivated to stop the behaviour by accommodating the request. This sequence has the unfortunate effect of 'reinforcing/increasing' the very behaviour parents wish to decrease. The goal is to help parents learn to modify children's behaviour rather than the other way around.

In addition to specific behaviour management techniques, there are other factors which can help parents respond more effectively to difficult behaviour. These factors are presented first. Subsequently, specific behaviour management tips are offered.

RECOGNISE INDICATIONS OF **AD/HD** IN YOURSELF

If AD/HD has a genetic basis, then a parent (or parents) is likely to have some AD/HD tendencies – restless, cannot stay on task, always on the go, inattentive and so on. It is essential to investigate this possibility, because 'impulsive' children may collide with an 'impulsive' parent (e.g., rash, harsh, inconsistent discipline). In addition, children observe and may try to emulate parent behaviour, so that a parent may unwittingly 'model' the type of behaviour they wish to discourage.

MARITAL DISCORD

Try to imagine the disruptive influences of a child's AD/HD-type behaviour on family harmony. Other children may be easy to discipline and there is relatively less friction. In contrast, parents may have little success in altering the behaviour challenges of children with AD/HD (even though the same methods are used). A general sense of frustration in the family will intensify with potentially divisive influence regarding family relationships. At principal risk is the relationship between mothers and fathers. It is this psychologist's experience that father's tend to underplay issues (e.g., understate, or deny problems) while mothers may do just the opposite – be 'over-involved'. These reactions become 'polarised' over time often leading to less communication. Both reactions may result from continually challenging child behaviour, which is invasive, disruptive and constant.

It also seems to be that if the marital relationship has any pre-existing issues (e.g., communication, values, expectations, needs, personality styles, etc.), these issues will be magnified in families where AD/HD is present. For example, assume that a father's personality is rule-governed, strict and there is a high need for order and control. Assume further that the mother's personality is more flexible, laid-back, casual, and where order and routine are not high priorities. One can imagine the difference of opinion each parent will note in the other when discipline problems occur.

Father will accuse mother of 'spoiling' the child; mother will counter that father is overly strict and does not understand the child. Anger and resentment may develop and this will adversely effect the family process.

Marital discord is commonplace in families with children who meet criteria for AD/HD. As a result, some of the most important interventions may be derived through marital therapy/counselling. If possible, parents can work through individual issues, and how these issues influence their relationship. If successful, then the therapist can begin to assist parents in providing a united front regarding child-rearing issues. Key skills would be communication, negotiation, support and encouragement. In addition, parents must learn to keep child-based problems in perspective (e.g., to not forget each other).

GENERAL FAMILY STRESS

In this category fall the countless factors that create general stress among families. Specific stressors may be caring for extended family members, financial worries, work-related stress (e.g., travel, temporary work, etc.), house disruptions (e.g., renovations, repair), relocation, health issues, sibling relationship issues, etc.

Parenting a child with AD/HD is stressful in and of itself; the obstacles and challenges are significant. Thus, the greater the general family stress, the less likely parents will be able to meet the specific challenges involved in managing AD/HD at home. For example, after this section, a number of behavioural management programmes are detailed. These programmes requires energy and commitment on parents' part. The greater the amount of family stress, the less likely parents can commit to home-based interventions.

While there is some degree of stress influencing all families, parents must make adjustments when it comes to parenting a child with AD/HD. For example, how can work-related travel be reduced? Can other family members share in child care? Can that grand scale renovation be down-sized?

BEHAVIOUR ANALYSIS FOR PARENTS

Behaviour analysis (sometimes known as Behaviour Modification, or Applied Behaviour Analysis) is the most frequently used and widely researched non-medical intervention. The general philosophy is to teach parents about the specific needs of children with AD/HD, how the behaviours associated with AD/HD present special and unique challenges to parenting, and outlining the types of child behaviour techniques that parents can use to increase appropriate behaviour and decrease inappropriate behaviour. Since the focus is teaching parents behaviour methods, this approach is sometimes referred to as Parent Training. An example programme is the one developed by Russell Barkley and associates (Anastopoulus and Barkley, 1989).

Behaviour analysis is often misunderstood and misrepresented by both parents and professionals. Although the methods used are based on scientifically proven learning principles, behaviour analysis is sometimes naïvely and incorrectly viewed as 'coercive' and 'controlling'. For example, one well-known learning principle fundamental to behaviour analysis is positive reinforcement. As previously stated positive reinforcement is defined as any consequence which increases the behaviour it follows. We receive and give positive reinforcement on a daily basis. As just one example, if you encounter a car on a narrow road, and the other car pulls to the side of the road to let you pass, and you wave in acknowledgement of their considerate action, you have just used positive reinforcement. That is, your wave was a consequence in reaction to the driver's behaviour of pulling over, and it is highly probable that the driver will engage in this action in the future (thus, with your wave, you increase/strengthen, the other driver's behaviour).

Behaviour analysis is misrepresented when the above example of positive reinforcement is viewed as 'bribery' or 'manipulation'. That is, positive reinforcement is automatically associated with 'reward' which is then degraded to 'bribe'. Personally, I am always grateful when another driver acknowledge's my co-operative behaviour (pull over to let a car pass). I am equally annoyed when this behaviour is not acknowledged (which is another behaviour consequence known as 'ignoring'; ignoring has the effect of decreasing the behaviour it follows).

Perhaps more than anything else, behaviour analysis requires one to take a deeper and more 'analytical' perspective to problem behaviour. To begin with, it is vital to stop and think about parent-child interactions. It is often suggested that parents observe and record certain problem situations (e.g., making requests, homework, etc.).

What is Behaviour Analysis? Simply put, behaviour analysis is the study of behaviour. One way to study behaviour is to observe and record it. There is much we can learn simply by stepping back, watching, and noting a behaviour, such as what exactly is the behaviour (this is much more difficult than you might realise), under what conditions is the behaviour most likely to occur, how often and for how long does the behaviour occur, and what are the reactions to the behaviour.

What exactly is meant by 'behaviour'? A behaviour is a specific act a person does which can be observed and measured. Take writing. The number of days per week that I sit down to write for at least 30 minutes could be recorded. Regarding AD/HD, one of many possible behaviours which define the condition could be 'not completing a task within a specified period'. The task may be a chore, homework, or other request. It is easy to measure this behaviour because the adult can issue a request once and if it not done, it can be noted as such.

OBSERVING AND RECORDING
Observing and recording your child's behaviour may seem trivial and the pay-off may not be immediately clear given the effort. However, the effort is well worth it. Why? First, observing and

recording a behaviour requires one to think about exactly what the problem is. This type of critical thinking can lead to insights as to how to rearrange the environment to reduce failure, to change the task, and to make other modifications which can greatly benefit you and your child. Second, unless a behaviour is observed and recorded, there is no way of revealing its significance. Parents tend to overestimate problems and underestimate 'good' behaviour. Thus, observing and recording may reveal less of a problem than originally perceived. Third, if one continues to observe and record, one can detect small improvements which may not otherwise be noticeable.

Observing and recording a behaviour requires one to set aside time to watch the behaviour and make some note about it. The recording is typically done in a diary, small notebook, or data sheet fashioned for a specific behaviour (several examples will be provided later). As you watch a behaviour, you learn more about it. For example, take the principle symptom of Attention Deficit – Inattention. A behaviour analyst would ask, 'what exact behaviours define inattention'. One could say, 'off-task often during academic work'. The behaviour analyst is not satisfied, 'what does off-task mean'? The respondent might say, 'leaves seat often during homework, looks out the window, stares into space, asks irrelevant questions during homework, etc'. Now the behaviour analyst is engaged because the behaviours just noted could be measured. For example, one could look at the child every 30 seconds for a five minute period and place a ✓ (which is referred to as a data point) if the child was in his/her seat working at the moment of observation. A five-minute recording period would result in ten observations. If the child received ten ✓s, one could say the child was attentive. If the child received no ✓s, one could say the child was inattentive, etc.

Thus, one critical principle regarding behaviour analysis is the use of precise language. Abstract concepts like 'inattention' must be defined by behaviours which can be easily measured.

Once this step is completed, then the behaviours listed need to be recorded to get some idea of the actual problem.

It is usually important to record not only the specific behaviour(s) but the conditions in which problem behaviour is likely to occur – a certain time, place, with certain people, etc. These conditions are known as 'antecedents'. Sometimes one can change the antecedent and the problem behaviour is reduced. For example, the 'homework' environment can be arranged in a place relatively free of distractions and enticing objects.

Finally, after the behaviour occurs it is important to note the consequences – how other people react to the behaviour. Sometimes, it is important to ask 'what is the function of inattention?' Does it lead to desired parent attention? For example, if a child makes anecdotal comments are passed, does this lead to discussions about particular events which occurred during the day? If so, homework might be the only time when the child can talk about important matters. Thus, inattention may serve to gain parent attention.

An example observation and recording form is given below. It is known as the A-B-C Recording Form (A = Antecedents; B = Behaviour; C = Consequences). A completed ABC form is also provided:

ABC OBSERVATION AND RECORDING FORM
Directions
Select a behaviour which you wish to record and write a clear definition of the behaviour. An example of a behaviour definition is:

'Self-injury = biting, hitting head, body, or hand on hard
    object, hitting self ...
'Verbal abuse = shouting, cursing, negative statements ...'
'Aggression = pushing, kicking, hitting another person ...'

If the above definitions are suitable then use them. If you wish to modify the behaviours to fit the person's particular needs, write the definition of the behaviour you wish to record below:

Behaviour Definition: _____

_____

_____

Use this form to observe and record the behaviour(s) defined above. An antecedent is what happened before the behaviour occurred, such as, 'gave the person correction', 'person given a request', etc. After each behaviour episode indicate the severity using a scale where 1 = Extremely Mild and 10 = Extremely Severe. A consequence is what you did after the person's behaviour such as, 'tried to talk with him/her', 'yelled at the person', 'left the room and ignored her', etc.

COMPLETED ABC FORM

Select a behaviour which you wish to record and write a clear definition of the behaviour. The behaviour observed and recorded is:

   'Tantrum = crying, running away, throwing self on floor ...'

Use this form to observe and record the behaviour defined above:

Date	Antecedent	Behaviour	Severity (1 to 10)	Consequence
12/2	Denied request for sweets in shop	Crying, running away, throwing self on floor	8	Tried to ignore; had to physically assist off floor, went home, didn't finish shopping
12/2	Given request to get ready for bed	Crying, running away, throwing self on floor	5	Ignored; denied reading together
13/2	Given request to	Crying, running away, throwing	4	Repeated request; had to help do task

Date	Antecedent	Behaviour	Severity (1 to 10)	Consequence
	put away toys	self on floor		
13/2	Denied request to go to neighbours house	Crying, running away, throwing self on floor	7	Tried to calm; eventually gave sweets to stop tantrum
13/2	Given request to get ready for bed	Crying, running away, throwing self on floor	6	Decided to play board game first; then bed

A final set of pointers about observing and recording. First, every time you observe make sure you record. A recording is the data entry (e.g., ☺, ✓, +, etc.) for the observation period. The type and number of data marks depends on the behaviour observed and recorded. If the behaviour occurs many times in a short period, a ✓ is best. If the behaviour is completing homework within a 30-minute period, a ☺ or + could be used each day homework is assigned. Make sure a written recording is made after each observation. If the behaviour is negative (e.g., physical aggression to brother in the form of hitting, pinching, kicking biting) and it didn't occur for day, then mark the observation/recording form '0'; do not leave the day blank.

Second, determine when and where to observe/record. Using the above examples, if the behaviour occurs often during the day, then a daily period can be set aside specifically for observation (e.g., ten minutes in the morning and evening). If the behaviour is supposed to occur once a day, it could be recorded after its presumed occurrence. It is sometimes useful to bring a small diary so behaviour outside of the home can be recorded (e.g., running away in a store, tantrum, etc.).

Third, while more than one person can observe/record, it is important that each observer understands what is to be observed (exact behaviour) and how it is recorded. It is also wise to keep the data sheets in a convenient location relative to its recording. For example, if the task is to put toys away after using them, then the recording form could be posted on the door of the room where toy play usually occurs.

Finally, the specific type of observation and recording required will be determined during professional consultation. As already noted, behaviour problems can have different definitions and it is the definition of the behaviour which determines how it is observed and recorded.

ANTECEDENT MODIFICATIONS

An antecedent is the event which occurs immediately before the target behaviour (the one that is being observed and recorded). The completed form indicates five examples of antecedents which preceded a tantrum. If you review these antecedents you will note that all five have to do with 'requests'. Specifically, the child was either told they could not have something desired, or given a task to perform. In this case, an antecedent modification could be changing the request. Perhaps the requests are too vague, or require the child to do too much. For example, 'get ready for bed' could be changed to 'put your pyjamas on' or 'brush your teeth'. The best way to word requests is discussed later. Further, the exact way in which the child's request is denied could be modified (e.g., 'you cannot have that chocolate now, but you can have one biscuit after dinner').

In general, antecedent modifications are very common and can be quite useful. In the classroom, the most common antecedent intervention is seating a child closer to the teacher's desk. Presumably, when one removes an antecedent reliably predicting misbehaviour (e.g., sitting next to a particular child, or in a particular place in the room), the child's behaviour will improve. Other common antecedent modifications are (a) changing the task to promote success (e.g., less homework), (b) changing the time of day when the task occurs (e.g., homework immediately when home from school rather than after an evening meal), and (c) the conditions in which the task is performed (e.g., homework in kitchen to homework in less distracting room).

In general, the number of antecedent modifications is as varied as the number of behaviours which follow them. However, the most important general rule is to programme for success. That is, after observing/recording, one can study the antecedents and make changes accordingly. These changes will reduce the risk of problems and increase the chance of success.

CONSEQUENCES

Consequences are the various reactions which occur in response to a behaviour. Again, the completed form shows various examples of parent response to tantrums. As you will see shortly, many of these examples are negative reinforcement. And negative reinforcement, by definition, increases the behaviour it follows. Thus, this particular parent may be inadvertently increasing tantrum behaviour when just the opposite is desired.

Consequences are the 'bread-and-butter' of behaviour analysis. The general philosophy is that people are motivated to gain positive reinforcement and avoid negative events. Stated differently, everyone seeks to maximise reward and minimise cost. Using this general principle, one can change consequences to increase a desired behaviour (by providing positive reinforcement after the positive behaviour occurs) and decrease inappropriate behaviour (by using punitive methods). Herein lies the bad press given behavioural methods, because terms like 'punishment' are highly connotative. I prefer to think of methods to increase and/or decrease behaviour.

Briefly, there are two general types of consequences, each with two different forms. The following diagram shows the basic consequences:

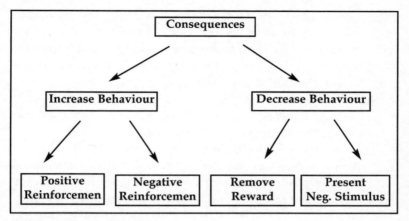

POSITIVE REINFORCEMENT

Positive reinforcement occurs when a behaviour is followed by a desired event. A positive reinforcer is the specific item used to increase a behaviour. Praise, hugs, high-fives, thumbs-up, food, activities, money, stickers, etc., are common examples of positive reinforcers.

When children present with AD/HD it is common for parents to focus on bad behaviour and de-emphasise good behaviour. This can have the unfortunate effect of increasing negative behaviour and decreasing positive behaviour. The programme below is designed to increase positive behaviour and decrease negative behaviour using the principle of positive reinforcement:

USING POSITIVE REINFORCEMENT: CATCHING THEM WHEN THEY'RE 'GOOD'

1. Rationale

When children have behavioural difficulties, parents spend a great deal of time reprimanding (e.g., 'Don't do that') and providing corrective feedback (e.g., 'You didn't pick up your clothes'). More and more time is spent in the negative cycle of 'problem behaviour-negative response'. Good behaviour is ignored because it is expected while difficult behaviour usually gets parent attention. This programme offers an alternative approach. Even the most disruptive child will behave appropriately at times and we must train ourselves to look and respond to good behaviour as well as problem behaviour. THIS PROGRAMME IS EASY TO READ BUT NOT SO EASY TO DO.

2. *Method*

- Consider the positive aspects of behaviour your child exhibits – what he/she enjoys (indoor and outdoor activities).
- Also, during 'high-risk' times (e.g., with brother/sister, meal, etc) make a concerted effort to re-train your attention to positive behaviour, even if it occurs for small periods. You may need to make reminder cards and post them in high profile areas of the house at first in order to make your awareness of positive behaviour more conscious.
- When your child is behaving appropriately (e.g not bothering you, playing appropriately, doing school work), stop what you are doing and provide POSITIVE FEEDBACK like: 'I really like the way you are playing so nicely', 'what a good boy/ girl for letting me talk on the phone without disturbing me'.
- Be positive, genuine and expressive when providing praise. Go to wherever the child is engaging in good behaviour (e.g., sitting room, outside, etc.).
- After providing positive feedback immediately return to what you are doing. For very difficult children you may need to focus on good behaviour every two or three minutes. You can gradually increase the time between positive reinforcement the following day and set a maximum time based on your child's needs.
- Sometimes parents may wish to purposely watch their child during play activity. Parents can engage in another activity in the same room, or in some cases, may wish to narrate the child's activities (as a commentator would). If you narrate, ASK NO QUESTIONS AND GIVE NO COMMANDS. Just describe what the child is doing at all times. Occasionally provide POSITIVE

FEEDBACK – what you like that the child is doing (e.g., 'I like it when you play quietly' or 'I like it when you don't throw toys').

- Whenever misbehaviour occurs in your presence or during times when you are undertaking this programme, try to IGNORE IT. For example, if you are playing with your child and he/ she throws a toy, turn away and attend to something else in the room. If misbehaviour escalates, leave the room and return later when the child is behaving more appropriately.
- Each parent should spend at least fifteen to twenty minutes with the child each day with this programme in mind.

Realise that while positive reinforcement is designed to increase appropriate behaviour, it is sometimes the case when one inadvertently and positively reinforces negative behaviour. Providing sweets to calm a child during a tantrum is essentially 'rewarding' the child for the tantrum and will have the effect of increasing tantrums in the future.

NEGATIVE REINFORCEMENT

Negative reinforcement also increases a behaviour but, as the name implies, through more negative means. Essentially, one can avoid or escape a negative event by engaging in a particular behaviour. For example, suppose a shopping centre finds that people park in their facility but walk to another shopping centre. To combat this, the centre metres cars in their lot and any car in the centre for more than two hours is clamped. It is likely that people will not engage in this type of car-park behaviour because they want to avoid the negative consequence of being clamped. Thus, consumer-only parking is increased through negative reinforcement.

Children will recognise negative reinforcement in the form of 'threats' (e.g., 'eat your peas or you won't get dessert'). 'Pea eating' is negatively reinforced because by doing so the child avoids a negative event (not getting dessert).

Negative reinforcement is an extremely important principle for parents to grasp because it can be a frequent mode of communication between parents and children. For example, children may use negative reinforcement more effectively than parents. If a child whines or continually demands something from a parent, and the parent eventually accedes, it is likely that the parent wishes to 'escape' from the negative situation of hearing uninterrupted whining (especially if the parent is trying to relax or complete a task and does not want to be disturbed).

While there are no specific programmes presented regarding negative reinforcement presented here, the concept is important simply to understand how parents modify child behaviour and vice versa. Negative reinforcement is different from methods used to decrease behaviour because, by virtue of the name 'reinforcement', it is used to increase those behaviours we wish to see more of (or children wish to see more of in parents).

Remove Reward. When children engage in negative behaviours, it is possible to reduce these behaviours by taking away privileges. Another way to look at this procedure is that the child's behaviour costs them something; some desired object, activity, or parent attention is lost after the behaviour. When children are not allowed out to play following a certain behaviour (e.g., aggression to sibling), a reward (playing) is taken away.

One effective technique parents can learn is to remove their attention following undesirable behaviour. That is, rather than lecture, nag, scold and engage in long harangues, it may be useful to engage in 'planned ignoring' – a deliberate attempt to remove your attention when a negative behaviour occurs. The reasoning is that your attention may be positively reinforcing the child's negative behaviour. The second example given earlier includes two types of reward removal – parent ignoring, followed by a loss of a desired activity.

Present Negative Event. These tactics usually meet with more controversy relative to the other consequences. This is so because, unlike any other consequence, the child's behaviour is suppressed by presenting an immediate and negative response. The most contentious negative event is corporal punishment (e.g., spanking). Sometimes Remove Reward consequences are confused with Punishment. After all, when a child loses a privilege, isn't this a form of punishment? Yes, in the general sense, but the logic of Remove Reward consequences are 'loss' (subtract) of desired activity/object whereas the logic of Punishment is presenting (adding) a negative stimulus (verbal reprimands, running laps, writing lines, isolation, etc.).

Verbal reprimands are the negative comments made in response to undesirable behaviour. They range from common statements, such as, 'stop that', 'don't do that', 'stop teasing', 'Quit whining', 'Be quiet', etc. Verbal reprimands are easy to use. Unfortunately, because reprimands are so common and frequent, it is often the case that negative comments lose their potency to change behaviour. Children become 'de-sensitised' to complaints. As a result, parents may increase the intensity of the comments (raise their voice, or use more negative terms).

USING VERBAL REPRIMANDS
Defined: verbal reprimands refer to verbally instructing children that a particular behaviour, verbal or physical, is inappropriate. The following are guidelines for parents in using verbal reprimands.

1. Make eye contact with child (get their attention).
2. State the undesirable behaviour (e.g., 'your feet are on the table'; 'you left your toys out'; 'you used bad language').
3. State the goal ('your feet belong on the floor'; 'you need to put

your toys in the toy basket'; 'ask nicely if you can _____')

4. When you speak, use a calm, matter-of-fact voice. Do NOT yell, nag, lecture or criticise. Be brief, level-headed, refer to the behaviour and what you expect.

5. When you speak, do not ask a question like 'could you put your toys away?')

6. As soon as the child complies with your request (the goal you give), praise with a comment like, 'I like the way you asked your brother for ...'; 'thank you for cleaning up'). If the request is completed quickly and properly, be extra supportive and appreciative.

7. 'Catch' your child spontaneously engaging in desired behaviour (e.g., 'I like the way you're playing with your sister'; 'That was really nice the way you brought your plate to the sink ...')

8. If the negative behaviour persists, consider its function – is the child engaging in a behaviour to get you to react? If so, how can you react to positive behaviour while minimising negative conduct? What are other consequences you can use? Be familiar with common behaviour suppression procedures such as 'time-out' and 'response cost'. Consider a reward system based on 'points' whereby the number of points earn various rewards. The more points the greater the reward. If appropriate behaviour occurs, award points. If it does not, remove points.

9. Ask 'does this child know how to engage in the behaviour requested?' (e.g., dressing self, chores, etc.) If not, teach the desired behaviour.

10. Behaviours such as social etiquette (saying 'thank you'; 'hello') can be practised and modelled. The child should then demonstrate the behaviour and if it occurs in a 'natural' situation, praise accordingly.

Another type of behaviour restriction technique is known as satiation. When using satiation, the child continually repeats the inappropriate behaviour (or some reference to it). The logic is that the child will get tired of the behaviour and the behaviour will come to have a negative association. As a result, the child will be less likely to engage in it. In school, children sometimes have to 'write lines' such as, 'I will not talk out of turn' twenty, 50 or even 100 times. This is a form of satiation. Having the child repeat a swear word is another example of satiation.

OTHER BEHAVIOUR METHODS

A true Behaviour Analyst would inform us that all discipline methods (in fact all behaviour) is based on the human desire to maximise reinforcement and minimise negative events. No wonder then that there are many methods, in different guises, which can be considered off-shoots of the core consequences just discussed. A sample of these programmes are covered next.

BEHAVIOUR CONTRACT

The behaviour contract is a method where a written agreement is developed between parent/teacher and child. The agreement specifies exactly what consequences will occur when specific behaviours occur. An example contract follows:

A BEHAVIOUR CONTRACT

I _____ agree to accept the following daily responsibilities
    (student)

- TO COMPLETE A SPECIFIC AND DAILY AMOUNT OF WORK in each subject area (exact amount of school work to be determined by student and teacher and checked at the end of the class).
- To remain on-task when in-class assignments are given. On-task means to stay in my seat and not talk to other students.

If both of the above daily goals are met, I receive the following daily privileges at school:

- Individual use of computer from 1.30 to 2.00.

I _____ agree to the above privilege in accordance with

(student)   this contract.
We have read and reviewed the terms if this contract and agree to
it. The contract will be evaluated on the _____

Signed:_____   _____
              (student)   (teacher)
Witness:_____   Date:_____

Natural Consequences. If a child forgets to do their homework,
what happens? Perhaps the child is required to make up the work
while the other children are outside on a break. Thus the natural
consequence of not completing homework is loss of a desired
activity (Remove Reward). If a child leaves a jacket at school and
must walk to school the next morning without the jacket, the natural consequence of being 'cold' may be aversive enough to
reduce 'forgetting' in the future. Thus, natural consequences are
the clear and direct link between behaviour and its outcome
(Dreikurs, 1987).

Parents may be adverse to the idea of natural consequences
because some natural consequences are difficult to accept. For
example, it may seem unduly punitive to parents to require a
child who forgets his jacket to go to school without one. The natural consequence of walking to school not properly clad has its
own natural consequence (the potential to get sick/ill).
Nonetheless, there probably are other examples where natural
consequence represent the best strategy and parents may need to
stop the impulse to immediately rectify a situation without the
child incurring any natural consequence. For example, if the child
breaks a favourite toy because of carelessness, it is probably wise
not to replace it immediately.

Limit Setting. The reader may be familiar with the concept of limit
setting which refers to the types of behaviour permitted and not
permitted. Limits are the rules parents and teachers use which

inform children what is desired and what is not.

Ideally, parents establish a core set of rules, perhaps five, which are clearly stated and unambiguous. Rules can be phrased in terms of behaviours which are encouraged/desired (e.g., 'use manners at the table – ask nicely for something, say thank you, eat nicely, don't talk with food in your mouth', etc.) and those not accepted (e.g., 'do not take your brothers toys without asking him first'). Other household rules may pertain to bedtime, sharing, eating, chores, homework, etc.

It is important to consider how parents can encourage children to follow household rules.

HELPING YOUR CHILD TO FOLLOW RULES

1. Get your child's attention before you issue a request.

2. Issue only one request at a time and keep it short and simple.

3. Be specific and clear.

4. Use 'do' requests – phrased positively. Avoid using words like 'stop' or 'don't'.

5. Avoid giving choices when they do not exist – 'would you please ...' 'will you pick up ...' Avoid questions and 'let's' requests.

6. Be patient. Don't nag. Use guided compliance (whereby if the request is not complied with on the first issue, you gently prompt the child towards the request).

7. Be matter-of-fact; use a firm, neutral tone of voice.

8. Make sure that the child comprehends the task (rule) and can actually perform it.

9. Reward all compliance enthusiastically ('I am really pleased you put your bike away').

10. Large tasks – such as cleaning the room – should be broken into smaller parts (e.g., 'put the toys on the floor in the basket').

11. Set up a standard routine.

12. Be sure that your child earns more of your attention for compliance than for non-compliance.

Develop Realistic Expectations. Point eight needs further elaboration, because a rule or task is sometimes beyond the child's ability and/or developmental level. For example, a tennis coach may expect young children (say seven to eight) to serve in a more adult style than the average child in this age group can actually perform. While a particularly talented individual might come closer than others, the coach may be frustrated by the children's difficulty in mastering the movements which comprise the 'serve'. However, with more experience and/or more knowledge of child development, the coach may realise that the initial expectations were unrealistic. Hence, it is important that our expectations about behaviour be individually suited to each child's age and ability level. This will avoid undue frustration when a child finds a particular behaviour difficult to master.

Task Analysis. Relatedly, it may be wise for parents to break larger tasks into smaller parts. There is a method known as 'task analysis' where parents and/or teachers can evaluate a task in terms of its parts, and expectations are based on completion of some of the task. For example, parents may ask a child to tidy their room. However, the room may be extremely messy and it might be better if just one aspect of the task is required of the child (e.g., 'put the lego in the lego box').

Goal Setting. Another behaviour method is goal-setting because a properly conceived goal indicates what, how, and when behaviour will occur. A clear goal can be a powerful force of self-motivation, because we use our attainment (or lack of) to judge ourselves, or believe that goal attainment is important in how others perceive us.

GOAL SETTING PROGRAMME
Go over this form with the student. Record responses to each item and review at the end of the week.

Planning
1. My specific learning goals for this week are (be as specific as possible):
2. I will know I have accomplished my goals by:
3. Actions or steps I will take to accomplish these goals:
4. Possible blocks that may interfere with my goals are:
5. If I need help I can go to:
Confidence
6. My confidence in reaching my goal is:
No confidence   Very confident
0   25

Evaluating
7. My satisfaction with goal attainment is:
Very unsatisfied   Very satisfied
0   25

8. Reasons for attaining or not attaining my goal (if not attained, review reasons and return to step 1 with new goals):

As noted earlier, AD/HD often co-exists with oppositional behaviour, and Russell Barkley (1998) has developed an approach for dealing with this. The gist of this approach is summarised below.

TIPS FOR DEALING WITH OPPOSITIONAL BEHAVIOUR
1. Side-step the child's attempts to engage in negative interactions. Do not respond as usual – look away, change the topic, provide another activity, use a calm voice.
2. Use a rational choice method – 'you have two choices. Either you can do X or you can do Y. It is your choice'.
3. Allow for expression of feelings but do not allow verbal abuse or shouting.
4. Think of a problem as one with a solution that you and your child can find. Discuss choices and the pros and cons of each. Decide on a plan and follow through on it.
5. Search for positives. Oppositional children look for negatives

and usually get them. Find a positive element and always point it out (e.g., remember how well you ...')

6. Oppositional behaviour is sometimes associated with harsh and inconsistent parent responses to defiant behaviour. Make every effort to avoid these parenting pitfalls.

7. Recognise that defiance, anger and demanding behaviour may be a young child's way of communicating their feelings. Thus, rather than responding to the surface behaviour, attempt to see your child's behaviour as a form of communication and a request for connection with you.

8. Participate in a structured self-help parenting programme to overcome defiance. The most scientifically validated programme is the one in Russell Barkley's book – *Your Defiant Child: Eight Steps to Better Behaviour*. Some features are:

- Know your priorities.
- Act, don't react.
- Act, don't yak.
- Try to see things the child's way.
- Stop blaming.
- Keep your distance.
- Make consequences (good or bad) immediate.
- Make consequences specific.
- Make consequences consistent.
- Establish incentive programmes before punishment.
- Anticipate and plan for misbehaviour.

Family Problem Solving. The family problem-solving emphasises communication and brainstorming. The communication aspect requires attentive listening and the conscious attempt to not respond with anger or defensiveness. Most parents know that when the child complains or makes a negative remark a similarly negative remark is made in return. This does not advance the situation. Instead, parents are asked to try 'reflective listening' which is trying to communicate what/how the child is feeling. So, for example, if the child makes a critical remark, 'you are always blaming me', the parent would not respond with, 'that's not true', or worse, 'that's because you're always making mistakes'. Instead, the parent tries to listen to the underlying feeling being expressed by the child, 'it sounds like you feel angry because you think I am always blaming you'. This interaction might sound contrived (it is), but if parents try to respond with a more empathic ear, it is amazing what children will reveal. So, for example, continuing with the preceding dialogue, the parent's reflective listening might lead the child to reveal his/her true feelings. 'Yeah, I am angry. I can't seem to do what I'm supposed to do in school, and then I come home and do things wrong again.' Notice the child is taking some responsibility and widening the problem to include school. New insights (problems) are noted and the fact that the child may be encouraged to take some ownership for them means that mutual problem solving can begin. The gist of this approach is related below.

FAMILY PROBLEM SOLVING

1. Rationale

Communicating and discussing difficulties when all family members are present can be an effective way to solve problems. Sometimes families have regularly scheduled 'family meetings' to discuss issues. Other times these discussions happen spontaneously. The ideas to follow are designed for these family encounters:

2. Method

- The most fundamental issue is for each family member to stop habitual patterns of behaving by 'STOPPING' a response talking about whatever the problem is.
- At this time the automatic reaction is to NAME and BLAME – 'you did', 'he said', etc. This is ineffective. Instead, try to get family members to look at the 'we did' – recognising that it

is the interaction of people which creates problems.

- Have everyone state the problem so it is agreed. The problem may involve several people.
- Discuss different plans. What are some different ways to interact? Do not criticise any view at this point.
- Discuss all the plans – what would happen if, which is most likely to succeed, etc. Reach an agreement on the best plan.
- Follow the plan and evaluate whether it worked. If so, is every one satisfied? If not, repeat the process.
- During problem solving, stay in the present and do not bring up past difficulties.
- Effective communication is the key – for example, do not give long angry reproaches. Be brief and use 'I' statements – 'I like it when ...' State the specific behaviours you want – be clear so that each family member knows exactly what they are supposed to do.

  Be an active listener – eye contact, nod. Sometimes it is useful to paraphrase what was said in order to ensure the comment is understood.

  Make impact statements – 'When you do ... I feel ...'
- Another idea is to help everyone recognise anger and realise when they are too angry for effective problems solving (e.g., loud voice, destructive communication). Agree to take a break. Each family member should cope with anger through relaxation and coping self-statements (e.g., 'Remain calm', 'How else can I get my feelings across', etc. Reunite and try to resolve conflict through the points above).

Modelling. There is another behaviour approach known as obser-vational theory which emphasises how others learn by observing and watching how other people act. Basically, children often take cues from their parents. They observe and may model their behaviour after their parents. Thus, it is important for parents to 'do as they wish others to do'. If parents wish their children to be organised and responsible, this same behaviour should be part of the parents repertoire.

Parenting Style. Finally, it is useful to assess your particular parenting style along the dimensions mentioned earlier – permissive versus authoritarian. Each parenting style will directly reflect on the types of consequences used, the clarity of rules, rule enforcement, etc. The ideal situation is a balance as defined by the 'authoritative' parent.

FINAL COMMENT

When all is said and done, the Behaviour Analysis (ABC) approach requires parents to act differently. This is not easy, and it may be the case that behaviour gets worse before it gets better. However, the principles previously discussed are proven effective in changing behaviour. To ensure effectiveness, consider these general pointers.

- Make sure that positive reinforcement is in fact positive. Make a list with your child and ask what material (CDs, card collections, toys, etc.) and activity reinforcers (e.g., toy play, walks, listening to music, etc.) your child desires. Realise that by definition, a reinforcer increases behaviour. If the reinforcer used does not increase behaviour, it is not a reinforcer. Other items of high value should be used instead.
- All behaviour change methods should emphasise the positive and use punishment techniques as sparingly as possible.
- The effectiveness of any consequence is based on two 'Cs' – consistency and contingency. Consistency refers to the consequence being implemented immediately after the behaviour and that the consequence is used the same way by different people, across the day, and in different settings. Contingency means that the consequence is provided only for the demonstration of the desired (or undesired) behaviour. For example, if a child receives material rewards from different

people for behaviours other than the target ones, the effectiveness of the behaviour plan will be greatly diminished.

- An effective behaviour management plan is usually co-ordinated by a mental health professional who specialises in 'behaviour therapy', 'behaviour analysis' or 'behaviour modification'. In the professional literature, reference is often made to 'Parent Training' which, in the case of AD/HD, means that parents are educated about AD/HD, how it disrupts family process, and subsequently parents are taught strategies for dealing with difficult behaviour. Parent-training programmes typically last around ten sessions, depending on the type of programme, the philosophy of the trainers, etc. There is usually an element of 'booster sessions' and follow-up consultation as needed. There is an enormous amount of research regarding the effectiveness of teaching parents behaviour management techniques and the subsequent reduction in particular problems. Several treatises devoted just to this topic are listed in the reference section.

- Finally, the behaviour approach to AD/HD represents the most viable non-medical alternative to the treatment of AD/HD. It is well researched and documented as an effective treatment strategy. Further, most experts suggest that behaviour methods be tried before considering medication (Hoza, et al, 1995).

HELPING AD/HD CHILDREN AT SCHOOL

AD/HD is to school as hot is to cold, heavy is to light, north is to south ... you get the idea: AD/HD and school are opposites. Consider it. The core characteristics of surviving at school are to listen, remain seated, pay attention, have all the learning materials you need before starting a task, finish what you start, pay attention to detail, wait and so on. Each one of these characteristics is the prime weakness of children with AD/HD. Teachers know fairly quickly which children exhibit the types of behaviours associated with AD/HD. And, in the regular classroom, with little support, and similar learning expectations to children without AD/HD, both the child and teacher are likely to experience ongoing frustration.

Topics relevant to helping children with AD/HD adjust to school were noted in Chapter 3. The following is a summary of the main points:

- Consideration of special education placement.
- Class size – all else being equal, the smaller the better.
- Use of special learning materials and specialised equipment (e.g., computers).
- Active, multi-media teaching.
- Emphasise oral relative to written work.
- Capitalise on strengths and interests.
- Modify classroom environment (e.g., seating arrangements, partitions, cue cards, etc.).
- Possible allocation of resource teacher time.

Of these topics the reader may be interested in the type of specialised equipment available for children with AD/HD. An example 'Attention Training' device is noted in the Figure overleaf.

The display box is placed on the child's desk. The teacher uses the remote to activate the warning light. This immediately informs the child he/she is 'off-task'. The child can return to the task and earn a 'reward point'. The teacher presses another button to add a point to the counter. If the child remains off-task, the remote is used to deduct a point.

Remote

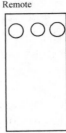

Buttons control points on box on child's

display. Also activate light on top of box

to indicate off-task behaviour

Child Display   Indicator Light

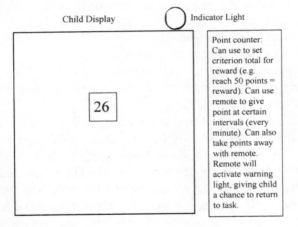

26

Point counter:
Can use to set
criterion total for
reward (e.g.
reach 50 points =
reward). Can use
remote to give
point at certain
intervals (every
minute). Can also
take points away
with remote.
Remote will
activate warning
light, giving child
a chance to return
to task.

Parent involvement

An example of a parent-teacher collaborative programme is given below:

HOME-SCHOOL NOTE SYSTEM – PRIMARY SCHOOL STUDENTS

1. Rationale

The Home-School Note System (HSNS) is an effective means to improve a student's academic and behavioural functioning. The HSNS involves a collaborative effort between parents, teachers and students. The basic principles are establishing daily goals and rewarding and encouraging progress towards these goals.

2. Procedure

Parents, teachers, and where relevant, students, specify the exact behaviour and/or learning goal. These goals are listed and a note sent to parents from teachers to indicate whether the goals were achieved. If a goal is attained, the teacher immediately praises the student and marks a 'yes' on the note card. If the goal is not attained, a 'no' is marked. Each goal should be clear and attainable. An example report card could look like the following.

Name of student:_____ Date:_____

Daily Goal	Yes +	No
Come to class with learning materials*		
Complete in-class English assignment		
Complete in-class Maths assignment		
Complete in-class Irish assignment		
Do not disrupt other students (e.g., leave seat, talk to other students, etc.)		
Comment ^ (overall day; specific goals, other ...)		

* = Daily goals noted here are arbitrary. Actual goals are individually determined, based on teacher concern. Each goal is listed in this column. Make sure the goal can be easily assessed as the end of the class session. The number of goals can vary from one to five. More than five becomes unwieldy.

+ = Can be '$1/2$ Yes' if goal partly met.

^ = The daily note can be reduced to a comment section only. However, some number/notation system is needed to determine the quality of the day, such as:

Excellent = 4;   Good = 3;   Fair = 2;   Needs improvement = 1

ADDITIONAL POINTERS ABOUT USING THE HSNS ARE:

- For students with AD/HD, the daily goals may be monitored for smaller and specific time periods (ten-minute part of class).
- The teacher may need to model for the student what certain goals mean (e.g., to participate). The student must clearly understand the difference between a 'yes' and a 'no' for each goal.
- The teacher can review the goal at the end of each period, comment, sign, and give to the student. A daily report can be reduced to once or twice a week later on.
- It is vital that teachers review goals immediately at the end of each class period. It is equally vital to be as positive and encouraging as possible. The idea is to draw attention to positive behaviour during each class session – this can be done in the comment section.
- Parents have the same mission – look for the positive. If the card has all 'Nos' do not lecture or reprimand; offer encouragement and reiterate your confidence that goals can be met. If the positive aspects are emphasised, the home-school note will be a success.
- Consider an incentive system based on 'yes' totals – the more 'Yes' the larger the incentive. 'Yes' totals can be tallied daily or weekly with a graded reward provided at this time (e.g., graded reward means a bigger incentive based on more 'yes' marks). As an example of a weekly graded reward system consider the following. If the note has five daily goals and the child meets each one every day of the week (assuming a five-day week) the maximum number of 'Yes' marks is 25. Of course no 'Yes' marks each day equates to 0 for the week (if this happens, review the system and determine if goals are realistic; consider reducing the time

202

period to a specific segment of the class, such as a ten-minute period). The graded reward could be:

0-7 = No reward (but encouragement for next week)
8-15 = Medium reward
16-25 = Large reward

- Talk with your child about the types of rewards he/she desires (social, food, toy, event, etc.) and put each one into the medium or large category. Do not provide the agreed upon rewardsfor anything other than the HSNS.
- This is a collaborative programme – everyone is working together to achieve success.

Finally, there are a number of specific objectives and teaching strategies which facilitate the successful education of children with AD/HD. The following 37 points are the ones this psychologist recommends the most:

1. Educate yourself about attention deficits. There are many good books on the topic written especially for classroom teachers. One reference is *Classroom Strategies for ADD* written by Clare Jones and available from ETC consult (see Reference section).

2. Identify local educators or mental health specialists (e.g., psychologists, social workers, psychiatrists) with knowledge of attention deficits. Look for people with have worked extensively with ADD children and families.

3. Build school support. Consult other teachers about students who present with attention weakness. Ask for help when you need it.

4. Examine your instructional techniques relative to procedures known to grab and maintain student interest and attention (e.g., novelty of lesson, level of enthusiasm, whole class participation, etc.). Consider adopting novel instructional techniques such as Co-operative Learning.

5. Alter the physical environment to accommodate learners with attention difficulties:

    a. Seat student near good role model or teacher.

    b. Reduce to minimum the number of naturally occurring classroom disruptions (e.g., students entering/exiting room, outside noise).

    c. Eliminate or hide 'seductive' objects (e.g., computers, games, etc.).

6. Maintain structure and routine; try to keep to same daily sequence. ADD students do better when they know what to expect. Provide a daily schedule to student. When you vary from schedule give student plenty of forewarning.

7. When giving directions, repeat them and provide them orally and in writing. Make sure the student makes eye contact with you. Simplify complex commands. Repeat directions as needed. Have the student repeat the instructions to make sure the command is understood.

8. Use feedback often. ADD students need frequent feedback. Check on them often, prompt them when needed, encourage and praise 'on-task' behaviour no matter how minimal. In this regard, re-train yourself to 'catch' the student engaged in work (even if for ten seconds) rather than reprimand for 'off-task' behaviour. Be supportive and encouraging whenever possible.

9. Break large tasks into manageable parts. For example, if other children are doing problems 1-10 in a maths workbook, shorten the assignment to the odd numbered problems only. Academic work can easily overwhelm ADD students. Thus, shorten the assignments and modify to adjust to the child's attention span. Also, by reducing and simplifying assignments, children realise they can do more than they think, which promotes academic self-esteem and a sense of personal mastery. Similarly, use the principle that 'quality' of work is more important than 'quantity'.

10. Ask the student what they think will help. Children with ADD can be very intuitive and tell you what they need if you ask them.

Use a structured self-questioning system such as:
* What is the problem? What is the best plan? Do the plan! Did the plan work?

11. Look for materials which help children with attention difficulties understand the nature of these difficulties. There are a number of books which are written for early primary school students that help explain attention weakness in a language they can understand.

12. Help the child become more self-observant. These children often do not know how their behaviour affects others. For example, if an ADD child distracts another child, you might ask, 'do you know what you did?' or 'how could you do that in a more positive way?'

13. Try to promote self-monitoring skills using a simple procedure: teach the child to internalise and self-question, such as: 'what do I want' (e.g., to borrow a pencil) 'what are some ways to get it (e.g., see if I have one in my bag ... if not, ask the teacher ...)

14. Try to watch (e.g., body language) and listen (e.g., hearing frustration behind a negative comment like 'this book is stupid') to the child's emotion (*Teacher*: you think the book isn't very good ...; *Child*: well, the book isn't stupid, it's just I don't understand some of the words; *Teacher*: I think I can help you with that. Why don't we try to ...) The point is not to respond to negative behaviour, but to recognise that this behaviour likely reflects underlying frustration and a low sense of self-esteem. By looking at the emotional components of learning, teachers can redirect negative interactions into more constructive and positive ones.

15. When disciplining, consider the following:

a. Have about five classroom rules clearly posted. Go over these rules and the consequences associated with following and not following them. Be very clear in your description of what is expected and what happens when rules are or are not followed.

b. Enforce rules as discussed clearly, without fuss, and consistently. Do not engage in long discussions of 'fairness' or redirection of blame ('it wasn't my fault, it was ...'). Simply do what you said you would do and do it quickly and without a lot of attention drawn to the situation. This will help the student recognise boundaries and limits.

c. If using correction do so without long lecturing or raising your voice. Soft reprimands work more effectively, and should be brief and said close to the student ('you need to get back to work'). Watch for excessive use of 'don't' requests ('don't bother Sean'); try to use as many 'do' requests as possible ('return to your seat').

d. Use a 'praise and ignore' approach. That is, ignore minor irritating behaviour (e.g., looking out the window, snickering with another student) and praise 'on-task' or 'co-operative' behaviour.

e. Consider using daily 'report cards'. Spend a minute or two at the end of each day (even each period) reviewing behaviour. Use a reward system for positive behaviours and a response cost programme (loss of access to reward) for negative behaviours.

f. Consider using a 'home-school' note system. This encourages liaise and frequent communication with parents.

g. Watch for transition times. ADD children are particularly vulnerable to 'not settling' after breaks and lunch periods. Set up a clear contract with the child that they are to be in their seat, with materials ready, and working three minutes after arriving. Place a 'happy' or 'sad' face on their desk depending on their compliance with this rule. Use a timer if necessary.

h. If AD/HD type behaviours arise during class, counteract by redirecting the child to the assignment. Provide minimal attention to disruptive behaviour.

i. Avoid using discipline techniques which bear any resemblance to academic activities (e.g., writing lines, giving extra homework). The problem is that children can develop conditioned aversion to the punitive activity and then generalise this aversion to academic activities of similar persuasion (e.g., from writing lines to any type of written work, even when the written work has no punitive undertones).

j. Consistency and firmness are vital to successful discipline of ADD students.

k. Stick with a co-ordinated discipline programme for a sufficient length of time.

16. Keep the child 'connected' with the rest of the group. Co-operative learning groups help ADD children work in a 'team'. Also, have the child give hand-outs to other children, or be 'line leader'. Look for ways to reduce detachment.

17. In many cases, ADD children are seen by other children as 'selfish' and 'self-centred'. Try to teach social skills which promote better relations with peers. Model and reward sharing, or asking other students for help. Teach them how to praise other children (e.g., 'wow, you really know how to do these maths problems').

18. In areas of academic weakness (e.g., reading) do not avoid having the student read out-loud, or spell words in an oral spelling test. Instead, have the child read a smaller amount and a passage well within their level of independent reading. Or make sure that the student will likely spell the word you give them correctly, based on previous knowledge. Skipping an area of weakness usually reinforces the student's notion that they are 'not good at it'. It may be better to engage them but at a different level. If other students tease the child about the easier reading/spelling they get, these students should be dealt with accordingly.

19. Review the general curriculum and look for ways to promote the child's strengths while minimising areas of weakness. If the child is adept at visual skills, then direct them to these activities (e.g., finding missing pieces in pictures, looking for differences in pictures, constructing models, etc.). Likewise, if the child is good at drawing, emphasise this as much as possible. If the child is particularly weak in an area (e.g., language skills) find ways to minimise language instruction (e.g., reduce Irish assignments).

20. Consider using a 'random beeper' method for encouraging the ADD student's self-awareness of their attention skill.

21. Always be on the look out for positive events. Almost all of the

day of an ADD child is spent in negative interactions – with peers and adults. In every day, look for one or two positive episodes and feed this back to the child – 'Today, I really liked the way you got back to work after the break', 'I like the way you asked for help'.

22. Identify an ADD child's personal interests (e.g., drawing, building, constructing models) and build their interests into curriculum.

23. Use computer-assisted instruction. Have available a multimedia PC and educational software which stimulate learning. Computers are very useful instructional tools for ADD children since they provide a rich visual environment as well as quick and immediate feedback.

24. Identify peers who have a positive and negative influence on the ADD child's behaviour. Increase the child's contact with positive peer influences through instructional grouping. Reduce the child's contact with negative peer influences.

25. Look for curriculum materials which are well presented. Dense, highly cluttered materials, such as the 'Busy at Maths' workbook are overwhelming for an ADD student. Consider presenting a small set of items/questions on a single page. Make the print large and provide ample space for the response.

26. Relax homework standards. This is perhaps the single most important modification. Instead of asking for 30 problems, have the child do all the odd numbered ones. There is no suggestion that the curriculum will be compromised; only that 'busy', 'repetitive' work will be reduced. For ADD students, this can make an enormous difference.

27. Recognise the general educational environments which are most successful for AD/HD children. These are:

- Small class sizes (ideally one to ten or fifteen)
- Individualised instruction and pace
- Personal contact between teacher and student – get to know pupil on an individual basis

- availability of computer technology and other learning tools

29. Help the child be organised – use homework diary or other homework form.

30. Keep lessons brief and to the point. Avoid extensive assignments which require prolonged concentration

31. Encourage self-esteem – use praise, be warm, have fun, inject humour.

32. Identify the child's interests (e.g., soccer, animals) and integrate interests into learning.

33. Make a concerted effort to get to know the student on a personal level.

34. Alter perceptions to recognise that attention deficits are a real disorder like any other disorder (e.g., dyslexia, autism). It is extremely difficult to realise that attention problems are not intentional – children do lack the fundamental 'hardware' to sustain attention and block out distractions. As a result, it is easy to expect the child to achieve more (especially since AD/HD children are typically intelligent and academically able). If we view AD/HD as a disorder in and of itself, we are more likely to set realistic goals, be more understanding, reduce frustration and promote success.

35. Wherever possible, relieve pressure by reducing workload, concentrating on strengths and eliminating class activities which may result in tension and worry (e.g., reading aloud to classmates, excessive written work).

36. Circulate often during independent seat-work to ensure that the child is 'on-task'.

37. Get in touch with a local AD/HD support group.

Child Focused Treatment

So far, interventions are aimed at giving parents and teachers increased awareness and/or effective strategies for dealing with AD/HD. The child directly benefits from these interventions because those adults who frequently interact with the child are now equipped with greater understanding of the condition, and hopefully, new skills to deal with it. However, the child is not an active participant in these programmes. Rather, the child benefits from changes directed to external forces, i.e., parents, school.

There are, however, non-medication interventions in which children with AD/HD are the primary players. The goal of these approaches is to help children understand AD/HD, learn more about the specific behaviours associated with it, and ultimately, teach them methods for dealing with difficulties like 'inattention', 'impulsivity' and 'over-activity'. This section covers several of these programmes.

Children can Read About AD/HD

This might sound like a contradiction in terms – reading is a sedate activity and children with AD/HD are over-active, impulsive, and their attention span is limited. However, parents may wish to purchase reading materials designed for children with different reading and attentional skills. Some of these books use metaphors, include colourful illustrations, and may help the child to develop greater insight and awareness. Several examples are provided in Appendix A.

Paying Attention to Attention

Obviously, the core fault in attention deficit is limited 'attention and concentration span'. However, it is difficult for children, let alone adolescents, to grasp a complex concept like 'attention'. Also, it is sometimes wise to use activities which help students understand the nature of attention as well as how they perform on attention related tasks.

The random beeper method described next is akin to giving someone feedback about the number of times they say 'uh' during a speech (the goal of which is to reduce the use of 'uh' as it is distracting). One way to do this is to tape the person's speech and play it back. The speaker, turned listener, may be dismayed at how many times 'uh' was said. This provides an impetus to be more aware of 'uh' saying come the next speech.

The Random Beeper method is similar in that children are asked to record the number of times they were paying attention when a random 'beep' sounds. Tapes with random beeps can be purchased or handmade.

RANDOM BEEPER METHOD

1. Introduction

This procedure is one way to increase self-awareness of attention skill. It can be used with a single student or an entire class. It is designed for resource teachers, although regular classroom teachers and parents can use the programme as necessary. It is best to use the programme in smaller groups (e.g., no more than fifteen or twenty).

2. Procedure

• Purchase or prepare an audio-cassette that contains beeps or tones about every 45 seconds, on average. Some beeps can occur at shorter intervals (e.g., fifteen seconds), some at longer intervals (90 seconds). On average, the interval should be 45 seconds. Prepared tapes are available (see Appendix 2).

• Prepare a recording sheet, like this one below:

Was I paying attention?

Yes	No

Explain to students what paying attention and concentrating mean. You might play the tape and demonstrate you are working by completing a writing task. You might also show the negative example – not paying attention (e.g., when the beep goes off, look out the window, or some other off-task behaviour). Tell the students that each time they hear a beep they are to ask themselves whether they were paying attention. If so, they mark 'yes', if not, they mark 'no'. For very young children, you can use happy and sad faces instead of yes/ no.

- Make sure students understand completely what they are to do. You might have them repeat the idea.
- Use the random beeper during independent seat-work, preferably a writing task.
- It is wise to closely supervise the programme to ensure students who are off-task are not marking 'yes'. It is also wise to set a goal (e.g., eight 'yes's) and provide a reward if students reach the goal.

Self-Control (or self-talk) Training

One of the most difficult behaviours exhibited by children with AD/HD is that their behaviour does not seem to have an internal monitor or editor. That is, actions occur without forethought, waiting is next to impossible, and there is a great amount of irre-sponsibility (careless behaviour). Essentially, children do not reflect, think, or consider the implications of their behaviour. As a result, some child-based treatments are designed to encourage self-control by teaching children a number of 'self' techniques, variously known as self-monitoring, self-talk, self-reinforcement, etc. For example, children can learn to self-record their behaviour (much like the Random Beeper method previously discussed).

Self-talk is another approach. Children are taught to 'exter-nalise' their thinking by 'talking aloud'. For example, this writer can be forgetful to a degree that is annoying to self and others. To combat 'forgetfulness' most people use 'external memory' (make lists). The type of self-talk I use is to 'talk aloud' when recall is needed (e.g., approaching my sons' school, I might say, 'I need to ask teacher A about, pick up child's hat, and talk to another parent about ...'). These comments are said aloud and help me to be organised and to recall what actions I need to take. The same approach can be used with children. Essentially, you show them how to do a task or recall information by modelling the strategy. In the case of recall, you might ask the child to state what they need for each subject before going to school. Or when performing a task with several parts, you can verbalise the procedure as you do it – 'first, I lift up the handle and push it through the slot; then I swing the gate back; then I lift up the other gate latch; then I pull this gate back.' The child then performs the task while talking aloud. After the task is repeatedly completed, it may no longer be necessary for the child to verbalise the actions while performing the task.

'Internal' self-talk is another type of self-control method. For example, children with AD/HD are at great risk for poor social interactions because of the impulsive nature of their behaviour. Hence, if a child with AD/HD is upset by another child, and would normally 'hit' back in return, the child with AD/HD can be taught to internalise his or her thinking as follows:

- Covertly yell 'stop' (before hitting another child).
- What is the problem? (I want something the child has).
- What are some other ideas? (What if I ask the child to share the toy with me when they are done? What if I ask my mom that I would like the toy? What if I hit the child and grab the toy?).
- Which plan is the best?
- Do the plan (ask the child to share when done).
- Did the plan work (child did share! Plan worked. Or, child didn't share, I'll tell my mom what I did but the other child isn't sharing).

- Do plan (and so on).

Another self-control method is to teach children to raise their hand before butting into a conversation. If the child demonstrates this behaviour, stop your conversation momentarily and praise this behaviour. Of course if any self-control strategy is used, the observer should lavish praise and reward.

The success of 'self-control' methods has been mixed. In some cases, especially more severe AD/HD, children will not be able to participate in these programmes because their behaviour is too excessive and self-control is too difficult. However, there are other situations where self-control training can be effective.

SOCIETAL AND CULTURAL CONSIDERATIONS IN THE TREATMENT OF AD/HD

There are four ways to approach this topic. One is to recognise that children's behaviour does not exist in a vacuum. There is an external response to it, beginning with other family members and spreading to peer groups and other individuals in the wider community. The response of these individuals to behaviour can be targeted for change, much like parents were the target of treatment earlier in this chapter.

A second perspective is to recognise cultural differences in the perception of behaviour and how this might influence children. In situations where cultural perceptions contribute to AD/HD-type problems, these perceptions could be altered in a more appropriate fashion.

A third view is that of cultural tempo, which is borne from the changes in society brought about by technology, family quality, work patterns, etc. The general notion is that the speeded up nature of today's culture is a contributing factor to 'speeding up' children; hence the need to discuss the association between cultural tempo and AD/HD.

Finally, there is a culture specific to AD/HD, and is in fact called the 'Culture of ADD'. This idea is well discussed in Lawrence Diller's *Running on Ritalin*. According to Diller, there is a 'victimisation' process once parents and children learn that a child 'has' AD/HD. The word 'has' is in quotation marks, because it is precisely this type of language which furthers the victimisation process. Essentially, AD/HD is viewed as a static, disease entity, which can be viewed as the cause of all difficulties – 'my AD/HD made me do it', 'I have AD/HD', 'our son's AD/HD ruined our marriage', etc.

What follows is a brief discussion of each of the above topics with suggestions for imparting a more useful view of AD/HD. The primary goal of this discussion is focusing on positive changes those in the wider community can make to improve the behaviour difficulties associated with AD/HD.

Family and Classrooms as 'Communities'

In the section on behaviour analysis for parents, the focus was parents. In families with two or more children, the family becomes a small network of behaviour influences. It is accepted that siblings of a child with AD/HD need support, especially since much family time is spent coping with the difficult behaviour associated with AD/HD. In this regard, the non-AD/HD child may feel neglected, or questioning why his/her brother or sister has a different set of rules. The non-AD/HD child is likely to harbour negative emotions towards the child with difficult behaviour because this behaviour is a source of constant tension – lack of respect for privacy, domineering, rough, destructive, interferes with play, etc.

Parents may need to explain to other children about AD/HD, and what methods they are using to help the child. It is useful to understand the concerns and needs of non-AD/HD children. For example, if the child complains that her brother frequently intrudes on her privacy, or takes things without asking, parents need to establish clear consistent rules regarding this type of behaviour. For example, a 'personal space' time could be used to enforce this rule. Likewise, it is reasonable to provide a lock box for a child's special/treasured belongings, so these belongings do not mysteriously disappear. Obviously, observations of positive peer interaction, ir following the rules, would be the target of positive reqards. .

Another, more controversial approach to treating families is known as family counselling or family therapy. In this format, the entire family is seen as a unit – siblings, parents, and the child who meets the criteria for AD/HD. The value of this approach is increased if the therapist has experience working with families in which one or more children present with AD/HD. In addition, active and directive approaches (e.g., instructional) tend to be more effective than those which require longer periods of 'talk' and more passive listening (one can imagine how boring the AD/HD child would find this process).

SOCIAL SKILLS TRAINING

One of the common problems associated with AD/HD is social skills difficulties. Social skills include the various interpersonal processes which build harmony with others–sharing, complimenting, dealing with conflict, etc. In this regard, AD/HD children have significant difficulties. Hence, these children may have fewer friends, less closeness with friends, and may be at risk for social exclusion (e.g., not invited to birthday parties). Some of the more common complaints this psychologist hears are (a) domineering – gets along fine with others if everyone does what the child wants, (b) does not share, and (c) tends to grab and take possessions from other children without asking or without their permission. In regards to (a) one outcome of this social deficit is that the child with AD/HD gravitates to playing with younger children because these children are more likely to submit to domineering behaviour.

If one reviews the symptoms of AD/HD it is easy to understand why social skills are lacking. Take impulsivity for example.

The child may intrude on other children, or make negative comments without first thinking of how these comments might make other children feel. A lack of attention span means the child will flit from one activity to another, and this can be annoying for other children who are trying to persist and complete a task. Essentially, most of the behaviours associated with AD/HD are at odds with social harmony.

The suggested form of treatment is to help other children understand AD/HD and be able to accept and make some allowances for negative social behaviour. At home, parents need to be frequent observers/listeners to social interactions. For example, if a parent observes positive interactions, this should be noted and enthusiastically praised/rewarded. In cases where a negative event occurs, this needs to be corrected by explaining the proper action, teaching this action if need be, and looking for it in the future. Further ideas to assist in social development are provided below.

HELPING CHILDREN WITH SOCIAL SKILLS

- Supervise and monitor your child's behaviour. Intervene when necessary to teach social skills, like giving a compliment, initiating a conversation, or sharing. Monitor peer exclusion or teasing and correct immediately.
- Clarify social involvement at school and, if a concern is noted, problem solve with the classroom teacher (e.g., what are ways to improve difficulties – what can teacher do, parents do; when and how will progress be checked?).
- Have your child participate in clubs or after school lessons in areas of interest – sports, drama, music, or other hobbies.
- Get involved with other parents. Parent connection is a good way to improve child connection.
- Realise your value as a model; if you expect your child to behave towards others in positive ways, do likewise.
- Learn about the different types of social skills so you can be

a better instructor – there are numerous categories and specific skills. A sample follows:

* eye contact
* recognising non-verbal expressions (e.g., sad, anger, etc.)
* maintaining appropriate physical distance
* sharing
* negotiating
* express an interest in another person's activities
* offer to help
* recognise negative emotions in self (e.g., anger, sadness) and know how to deal with these feelings

---

In some cases, children with AD/HD may benefit from specialist intervention in the form of 'social skills training'. Some therapists work with children in small groups, and where they are taught a variety of social skills. There are a number of social skills training packages.

The classroom has a natural social ecology or dynamic. In this regard, teachers are well positioned to modify the classroom community to help a child with AD/HD. Like parents, teachers are encouraged to observe and rectify any social difficulties witnessed in the classroom or on the playground. Some common problems are:

* 'loner', does not interact with peers, prefers solitary play, etc.
* specific social skills deficits, such as bossiness, difficulty sharing or taking turns, demanding, argumentativeness, etc.
* few companions, tends to be left out of games, social events.
* relates better with adults, or smaller children but not same-age peers.

Teachers can clarify the nature of the problem through observation and discussion with children. There are specific interventions for classroom teachers designed to promote social welfare, such as:

- emphasising social and emotional materials in the curriculum (materials which help children learn about themselves, emotions, perceptions, interpersonal skills, etc.
- Place a priority on social harmony by closely watching children's social behaviour and group dynamics. Have a zero-tolerance regarding peer exclusion, bullying, and other social problems.
- facilitate social connection through co-operative learning.
- Alter the physical environment of the classroom to increase contact with positive models and decrease contact more negative peer groups.

Cultural Differences in Perception of Behaviour

This topic was covered earlier. The conclusion was that there is insufficient knowledge of how cultural beliefs and behaviour either encourage or discourage AD/HD. One gets the general feeling that some cultures may view AD/HD not as a disorder but as a sign of a healthy and strong personality. If this is so, it is not surprising that the incidence of AD/HD would be lower in countries which have a similar attitude about children's behaviour. At present, there are no clear implications related to the treatment of AD/HD.

Cultural Tempo

There is little argument that the nature of families and child rearing has changed greatly in the past twenty years. These changes are a response to enormous social forces, such as changes in work patterns, with more dual income families and the subsequent need for childcare facilities. Children may be transported from school to an after-school care provider, collected in the evening, with meals, homework, recreational pursuits, etc., all crammed into a small period of time.

There is no doubt that the quality of family life has changed as a consequence of busy schedules, long commutes, etc. Parents and children spend less time together and there are fewer family occasions, such as drives in the country, picnics, walks, play time, and other casual and enjoyable events.

There is also the shadow of technology and the advent of the 'video' technologies – play stations, computer games, game boys, etc. In addition, the internet and the commonplace use of mobile phones does more to separate people rather than unite them in face to face conversation.

While the prospect that changes in society are responsible for child stress and ultimately, behaviours characteristic of AD/HD, this link is difficult to objectively prove. One could argue that the prevalence of AD/HD should be rising, since 'cultural tempo' is a phenomenon of the past twenty years. Apparently, this is not the case.

Perhaps the best advice is to ask readers to consider the notion of cultural tempo as it may be adversely influencing their parenting, their relationships with other family members, their level of stress, etc. There is no substitute for 'quality' time with children, and this time should be budgeted in on a regular basis. Every attempt should be made to reduce the interference of technologies or job demands on family process. Some of the 'old-style' forms of entertainment should be re-introduced, such as mutual hobbies (e.g., sports, collecting objects of interest, nature, board games, etc.), visiting places of interest on a regular basis, picnics, meals out, travel, etc.

The AD/HD Culture

The last form of 'culture' discussed is that specific to AD/HD. The problem, which is well articulated by Lawrence Diller, is the 'club' mentality sometimes attached to AD/HD.

The idea goes something like this. Assume that a child is 'diagnosed' as having AD/HD. The diagnosis is a turning point, because much of the child's difficult and challenging behaviour is explained by the condition known as AD/HD. There is a great sense of relief and satisfaction in knowing that a child is not behaving in a difficult way on purpose, or with the expressed intent of annoying and irritating all those who relate to the child. Instead, the problematic behaviour has a cause, and that cause is beyond the child's control – it's all to do with biochemistry. Thus, the child behaved a certain way because of his 'AD/HD'.

From this point, assume further that the child's parents learn more about AD/HD by joining support groups, reading, attending conferences, logging onto internet sites, etc. Parents come to understand that there are other parents in similar predicaments. Along the way, and probably without notice, there is a subtle change in attitude. People learn to believe in the medical model, and adopt the view that AD/HD is akin to more physical and tangible types of ailments (e.g., cancer, diabetes, etc.). Further, as a tried and true medical disorder, it is believed that the single most effective cure is medication.

And, to some degree, there is truth in every point just made. Recall from earlier that most experts accept a biological basis for AD/HD, and, as you will see shortly, medication is the single most effective treatment for it.

The danger, as Diller (1998) points out, is that people come to gradually lose any degree of empowerment. People may think that there is really very little they, or anybody else, can do to help the child. Behavioural change is impossible. Responsibility for making personal changes is forsaken and everything depends on a 'pill'. When this point is reached, Diller contends that one may now be a member of the 'AD/HD' club.

To some degree this 'clubbish' attitude is relevant to all types of medical and mental health diagnoses. It certainly is not unique to AD/HD. However, one glaring difference which makes the 'culture of AD/HD' potentially more dangerous is that the diagnosis of AD/HD is one of the most common given in child guidance clinics (at least in the United States) and it is one which centres on children. In addition, medications relevant to AD/HD are controversial. Thus, the implications for society are immense.

Perhaps, if anything is to emerge from this dialogue, it is to guard against a similar process of over-dependency on a 'label' and all the dangers which lie therein. One of the prime problems is that medication does indeed change behaviour and does so immediately. Thus, the use of medication strengthens the medical model approach and parents may be further enticed by its efficacy. It is with respect to medication that the next section is introduced.

MEDICAL MANAGEMENT OF AD/HD

We learned earlier that AD/HD has a strong biological association. As a result, there is an obvious need for medical management. Further, before AD/HD can be properly treated, it needs to be medically diagnosed. And any of a number of medical problems which can mimic AD/HD need to be ruled out. This is why medical management is vital to effective treatment. What follows is a practical guide to consider in the medical treatment of AD/HD.

ASSESS SENSORY PROCESSES

Although it may be easy to overlook, a basic hearing or vision problem could explain some of the symptoms common to AD/HD. For example, a child may be inattentive and have problems listening due to hearing loss. Likewise a child with a visual acuity problem may lose interest and become disruptive when asked to copy from the chalkboard. It is wise to have a child's hearing and vision assessed in order to rule out sensory processing deficits.

Even if the child's hearing and vision are within normal limits, their learning style may emphasise either the visual or auditory modes so that more inattention is noted when the least preferred mode is the source of input. Tests like the WISC-III noted in the previous chapter will identify such learning styles.

GENERAL MEDICAL EXAMINATION AND SPECIALIST CONSULTATIONS

A general medical examination is required in order to rule out medical problems which may lead to problems similar to AD/HD. Thyroid functioning, diabetes, hypoglycemia and asthma are several of the more common medical problems which can mimic AD/HD.

More specialised consultations may be useful regarding allergies. Although Barkley (1997) concludes that the association between allergies and AD/HD is unclear, it is common for parents to note such a link. This is especially true in the case of food allergy and food intolerance. For example, parents may note that after eating chocolate, or drinking coca-cola, their child becomes 'hyper'. These items are high in food chemicals such as amines and salicylates and these substances may need to be eliminated or greatly reduced, depending on the severity of the reaction. A qualified specialist in this area will be able to assess and recommend an appropriate dietary strategy.

Regarding diet, it was long ago speculated that food additives caused some AD/HD-type behaviours. In 1975 Dr Benjamin Feingold claimed that much of the behaviour associated with AD/HD could be reduced through a special diet, known as the Feingold diet (a diet excluding all food additives, artificial flavourings, food colourings and food preservatives). The diet was initially said to have positive and dramatic effects on children's behaviour. However, the accumulated research now shows a less consistent and positive association between the Feingold diet and AD/HD-type behaviours (reviewed in Conners, 1980).

Most experts now agree that unless a child's diet is very atypical, there is no reason to alter it. The most sensible approach is to make sure the child has a balanced diet and one that does not rely heavily on foods high in artificial flavourings or colours. If parents are concerned about their child's diet, then consultation with a nutritionist or related specialist is strongly recommended.

Finally, it is sometimes wise to consider neurological consultation, especially if there is any significant neurological condition which may mimic AD/HD. One of the most common is epilepsy, especially petit mal seizures where the person momentarily loses consciousness (e.g., staring into space, not listening when spoken to, etc.). These episodes resemble some of the characteristics of attention deficit but have a different cause and treatment regime.

By far the most common and scientifically validated form of medical management for AD/HD is medication therapies. There are different medications available but the most common group are referred to as psycho-stimulant medications. These medications are discussed next.

PSYCHO-STIMULANT MEDICATION
This particular topic is one of the most controversial aspects of AD/HD. Consider a sample of some of the books and popular press titles in the past few years:

- *Ritalin made my son a Demon*
- *Running from Ritalin*
- *Ritalin is not the Answer*
- *Ritalin Nation*
- *Beyond Ritalin*
- *Drugging our Schoolkids*

These titles make reference to the most commonly used medication for AD/HD, namely Ritalin. Ritalin is not the only psycho-stimulant medication used to treat children with AD/HD. Other common medications are dexedrine and Cylert. Before discussing the controversy surrounding Ritalin (and psycho-stimulant medications), it is important to have some background knowledge about psycho-stimulant medication and how this type of medication came to the fore in the treatment of AD/HD.

The use of stimulant medication to treat children with AD/HD began at least 60 years ago, when a physician reported success in treating a child with many of the symptoms of AD/HD using Benzedrine (a stimulant medication). One must realise that it does not make intuitive sense to treat children who already have elevated activity levels with a stimulant medication. Would this not worsen the very behaviours one is treating?

In fact, just the opposite happened. And similar improvements were noted with other children using different stimulant medications. Since this time, several different explanations have been offered as to why stimulant medications worked with AD/HD children. At one time, an 'under-arousal' theory was postulated such that inattentive and hyperactive behaviours were the person's attempt to 'jump start' a 'low battery'. By providing stimulant medication, the battery was jump started thereby reducing the child's behaviour attempts to rejuvenate the malfunctioning system.

More recent explanations stress the neurotransmitters discussed earlier and the transfer of these chemicals between nerve cells. Generally, it is believed that stimulant medication increases key neurochemicals (e.g., dopamine, serotonin) and/or creates a more efficient passage of neurochemicals between synapses.

To be clear, stimulant medications are designed to do just that – stimulate the central nervous system. Most of us certainly know of naturally occurring stimulants, such as caffeine in coffee or tea. Interestingly, scientific study has shown that caffeine has no discernible effect on children with AD/HD (Greenberg and Horn, 1991). Thus, while Ritalin and other stimulant medications are grouped in the same category as any other stimulant, do not think that coffee or tea will provide a suitable substitute for psychostimulant medication – it won't.

Since there is much to discuss about medication and AD/HD, the remainder of this section is divided into the following parts: (a) what behaviours medication does and does not effect, (b) when medication may be indicated, (c) possible side effects and their control, and (d) central issues in the use of medication.

The Effect of Psycho-Stimulant Medication. The influence of Ritalin and similar acting medications is immediate. One can usually notice an effect after 20 minutes and the effect remains for about 3 to 4 hours. Of course, the influence of any medication depends on the dose, the characteristics of the child, etc., so realise that the above time estimates are generalisations. Typically, Psycho-stimulant medications have the following effects:

- increase in time on-task (e.g., child will complete more tasks and will be less inclined to leave work incomplete, etc.).
- increase in concentration and attention; less distracted.
- reduction in careless, sloppy work; more attention to detail.
- the child is less demanding – there is less flitting from one activity to another, less need for parent attention, less need for constant stimulation, etc.
- the child is more relaxed and able to wait.
- home atmosphere is more calm and relationships may be perceived more positively.
- less restlessness and activity.

It is equally important to know that medication is not a cure. For example:

- pills do not teach skills; rather they provide temporary calm and allow the child to learn more effectively. However, there is no substitute for quality teaching.
- medications do not provide long-term solutions. Rather, medications like Ritalin improve receptiveness to learn and thus can assist in long-term behaviour change.
- It is generally accepted that medications like Ritalin are effective in about 75 per cent of the cases. The range in

medication effectiveness is about 60 to 90 per cent.

In a minority of cases, no improvement is noted, and, in some cases, a disimprovement is reported.

When Medication May be Needed. This really depends on the outcomes of an assessment. In many cases, AD/HD may not be the primary problem, or it may not be relevant at all. Other learning and behavioural issues may be of greater importance and relevant treatment for these needs take precedence.

However, if a child has been comprehensively assessed and the prevailing theme is suggestive of AD/HD, a new tier of questions come to bear. First, how severe is the AD/HD? Obviously, the more severe the presenting problem, the more likely medication may be required. The second, and perhaps more important issue, is the degree non-medication treatments were tried. Are education and family interventions in place? What direct assistance is provided to the child? If different interventions are tried and do not succeed then medication becomes a more significant consideration.

It is this psychologist's experience that most parents would rather their children remain unmedicated. This view makes sense in the context of the negative associations related to all medications, the most important of which are potential side-effects. In addition, Ritalin and related medications are the subject of great myth and misconception.

Side Effects. Different side effects are associated with each psychostimulant medication. For example, potential side effects associated with Ritalin are:
• loss of appetite.
• difficulty falling asleep, or staying asleep.
Less common side effects are:
• stomach aches.
• headaches.
• dizziness.

- significant increase in blood pressure and heart rate.

In retrospect, the above side effects are very much in keeping with the idea of stimulants in general (including coffee). Anyone who drinks coffee before going to bed will testify to the difficulty falling asleep. Further, if one were to measure blood pressure after a cup of coffee, one would see a rise in this pressure. The same is true with stimulant medications.

It is also important to note that all side effects can be controlled by monitoring dose levels and through regular visits to the prescribing Physician. It must be stressed that the consultant in charge will be able to advise about dose levels and side effects.

Issues in the Use of Medication. The use of medication to control AD/HD is one of the most controversial aspects regarding this disorder. The issue is highly emotive, and many people may seriously question both professionals who prescribe psycho-stimulant medications and the families who receive this assistance. However, those who are doubtful probably do not have children who have the condition and thus are unaware of the personal stress associated with coping with AD/HD.

In any case, it is most sensible to be prudent, realistic, and data-based in making decisions about medication. The following guidelines are suggested.

- obtain a thorough medical and psychological assessment (not just one or the other – both). In cases where the assessments point predominately to AD/HD, consider medication as one viable treatment plan.
- Understand the severity level of AD/HD. Does the information suggest isolated characteristics of AD/HD, or the full-blown clinical syndrome? One relatively simple litmus test is assessing the general degree of upheaval at home and school. The greater the behavioural difficulty, the more severe the AD/HD, and the more likely medication may be considered.

- Review the suggestions from professionals regarding non-medication interventions. Employ these recommendations – education, family, child, and cultural. If a significant and positive effect is noted, then medication is not necessary. On the other hand, if little or no effect is witnessed, medication may be considered.
- If medication is undertaken, it is important that the attending physician be experienced in the medical management of AD/HD. There is a very thorough protocol which is recommended regarding medication. It requires the use of a placebo (e.g., a 'pill' which looks exactly like medication but is neutral, a sugar pill), alternating medication and placebo without parent/teacher knowing which is which, taking daily logs of behaviour, and reviewing the information after a sufficient period. The medication is only continued when the data show that behaviour is improved on medication days and not placebo days.
- In addition, side-effects should be monitored carefully and regular health check-ups made part of the medical management.

Finally, it is necessary to dispel some of the myths which have grown as the use of psycho-stimulant medication becomes more commonplace. A sample of myths and misconceptions follow:

- 'Taking Ritalin is likely to lead to drug addiction.' In some popular press articles, there is the suggestion that long-term use of Ritalin places children at risk for later drug addiction. It is difficult to understand this view, because it is the absence of treatment for children with AD/HD which results in greater risk for drug dependency. That is, children with AD/HD who are not treated with medication would be at considerably higher risk to 'self-medicate' with drugs relative to children who are properly treated. One would expect that 'self-medication' would be stimulant-type drugs, such as amphetamines, cocaine, etc. However, knowing that teenagers with AD/HD would be 'risk-takers' there is no limit as to the type of drug which may be used or the amount of it. In any case, here are a sample of quotes from two leading authorities regarding AD/HD treatment with stimulant medication and drug addiction:

- 'The results suggest that there is no increased risk for drug abuse associated with treatment, although more research is needed to rule this out conclusively.'
- 'Properly treated ADHD children or adults do not become dependent on or addicted to stimulants.'
- 'Long term use of psycho-stimulant medication leads to permanent emotional or personality problems.' Absolutely untrue, although children who are erroneously prescribed the medication and for whom the medication is poorly managed, may be at risk for negative long-term consequences. However, poor assessment/diagnosis coupled with faulty medical management would not be confined to AD/HD and Ritalin, but would apply to all medical/psychiatric difficulties.
- 'Ritalin "cures" AD/HD.' While effects may be quick and positive, Ritalin does not cure AD/HD. It creates a greater receptivity to learn, but the actual learning is dependent on child and teacher/parent.
- 'Ritalin is being over-prescribed.' Media reports of the misuse of Ritalin are now common in the popular press. Certainly, there is confusion between the increased recognition of AD/HD and prescriptions for it. Naturally, as the recognition of a condition increases, so to will its most common treatment. There is also great variation in professional practice, within a country and across countries. But these variations, while interesting, detract from the best practice, which is multi-disciplinary assessment, use of non-medical interventions before trying medication, careful

monitoring of medications, etc.

SUMMARY

What is now clear is that simple, one-channel treatment approaches are unlikely to succeed. Paul Cooper in his aptly titled paper 'Biology, Behaviour, and Education; ADHD and the Bio-Psycho-Social perspective', emphasises that AD/HD is a multi-factored problem, not just for the child, but for society in general.

The preceding information provides examples of interventions across the five modalities this psychologist sees as critical to AD/HD: Child Interventions, Family Interventions, School Interventions, Societal/Cultural Interventions, and last, but not least – Medical Interventions. It is hoped that readers will remember these five categories as the areas in which treatments can be applied.

Finally, in my graduate studies, professors freely gave hand-outs regarding the topic of discussion. In one class, 'Child Counselling' I saved the following note. The sentiment seems an appropriate way to conclude this chapter.

The child's voice ...

Don't spoil me. I know well all I ought not to have. I'm just testing you.

Don't be afraid to be firm with me. I prefer it. It lets me know where I stand.

Don't use force with me. It teaches me that power is all that counts. I prefer to be led.

Don't be inconsistent. That confuses me and makes me try harder to get everything I can.

Don't make promises you can't keep. I will lose trust in you.

Don't fall for my provocations when I say or do things to upset you. I'll only try harder for more 'victories'.

Don't be too upset when I say I hate you. I don't mean it but I want you to feel sorry for what you have done to me.

Don't do things for me that I can do for myself. It makes me feel like a baby and I will continue to put you in my service.

Don't let my 'bad habits' get me a lot of your attention. It only encourages me to continue them.

Don't correct me in front of people. I'll take more notice if you talk with me in private.

Don't try to preach to me. You'd be surprised how well I know right from wrong.

Don't nag. If you do, I will protect myself by appearing deaf.

Don't demand explanations for my wrong behaviour. Sometimes I don't know why I did it.

Don't protect me from consequences. I need to learn from my experience.

Don't put me off when I ask HONEST questions. If you do, I will stop asking and find my information elsewhere.

Don't ever think it is beneath your dignity to apologise to me. An honest apology makes me feel warm towards you.

Don't worry about the amount of time we spend together. It is how we spend it that counts.

Besides, I love you so much, please love me in return.

Chapter 6

STRAIGHT TALK – ANSWERS TO TWENTY COMMONLY-ASKED QUESTIONS

In the course of meeting children, families, teachers and other concerned parties, certain questions repeat time and time again. I've found that the number of questions is not remarkably high. Rather, there are a certain set of 'core' queries which seem to repeatedly surface. Therefore, it makes sense to address these queries in 'question-and-answer' format.

1. How do I know if my child should be assessed for AD/HD?
Basically, by the amount of distress caused at home and/ or school. The more distress the more an assessment is warranted. Let's be clear. If it is truly AD/HD, the child will have problems coping with school, getting along with others, and completing basic tasks that other children typically have little or no difficulty doing. The child's difficulties usually result in considerable stress to family members and teachers. In cases of legitimate AD/HD, the difficulties observed are apparent early in the child's life and persist through the life span in one form or another.

There is no 'line-in-the-sand' regarding how much distress is required. Each family will have different ways of coping, different resources, and there will be differences in tolerance. In some families, where a child may show significant indications of AD/HD, the child will never be assessed. In this family it may be the case that professional assessment is viewed in a negative light, that the family has sufficient resources to handle the problem, and/or has a higher tolerance for difficult behaviour.

However, I would argue that in this case, the family will endure unnecessary suffering. Further, the child will be treated as if no special need is present (when it is). In the absence of knowledge about the condition, the child will incur tremendous frustration ('why can't I do this?'), with frustration turning to anger, anxiety, and/or complete lack of self-confidence. In turn, adults will compound the error by feeling the same frustration and expressing these feelings to the child. In fact, just the opposite is required – understanding, patience and compassion. Given this scenario, the long-range implications are obviously bleak.

If you suspect someone has AD/HD-type tendencies, review the list of behaviours noted in Chapter 1. And, as indicated in Chapter 5, it is useful to read further about the subject. It is very important that parents express concerns to teachers (and vice versa) because one fundamental requirement about AD/HD is that the behaviours associated with it are not confined to one context or the other (e.g., a child does not truly meet basic criteria for AD/HD unless the behaviours are noted at home and school). If there is unanimity in perception, an assessment may be required.

2. Where can I go for help?

A list of support groups are listed in Appendix 1.

3. Who should I go to for help?

One must understand that the most likely basis for AD/HD is biological. As such, the foremost and most successful treatment is psycho-stimulant medication. Thus, in cases where AD/HD is clinically significant, medical management is required.

The most important aspect of medical consultation is that parents feel comfortable discussing child behaviour difficulties with the doctor, be it general practitioner or specialist (e.g., child psychiatrist, neurologist, paediatrician, etc.). Rapport is critical. So too is an 'open-mind' on the part of the doctor. This psychologist has learned that some parents are disappointed when, upon first contact with the medical profession, the consulting physician advises the parents to read about behaviour management methods, to examine their marriage, and/or to take medication to calm down (that is for the parents to calm down), etc. These recommendations often prove ineffective.

At least two different professionals will be required in the complete assessment of AD/HD. One professional will be able to complete the type of assessment outlined in Chapter 4. This is most commonly a psychologist, and it is not of great relevance whether the psychologist is an educational or a clinical one. What is more important is that the individual has experience working with AD/HD children and families. The second professional is a medically trained doctor. Subsequent to a general practitioner referral, this individual is most likely to be a child psychiatrist or paediatric neurologist (although these medical specialists are not the only ones to treat AD/HD, they are probably more likely to manage AD/HS than other medical consultants).

4. Besides psychologists and medical doctors, are there other individuals who should be contacted?
The answer to this question depends on the outcomes of the assessment. If the assessing professional feels the family can benefit from additional input (e.g., from specially trained individuals), this will be suggested.

Teachers play an invaluable role in an assessment. Their involvement in the AD/HD evaluation is not optional; it is fundamental and actually required. This is so because behaviour difficulties resembling AD/HD must be exhibited in the home and school context. Obviously the only way to find out about school behaviour is from classroom teachers. A complete psychologist assessment will require input from classroom teacher(s)and any difference in perceptions will be quantified (e.g., see Conners' Rating Scales, Chapter 4).

As for individuals with 'specialised' training (e.g., dieticians, homeopathy, hypnosis, biofeedback, etc.), many 'therapies' for AD/HD have been advocated, but few yield scientifically proven results. Although parents may provide personal testimonials, one can never be sure if these testimonials are due to post-decisional dissonance (e.g., 'I'm spending money and travelling long distance to see _____,therefore it must be working').

However, while I am sceptical of alternative treatments for AD/HD (a view supported by anyone who reads the AD/HD literature and can judge research methods), I realise that people may seek such services because of (a) dissatisfaction with medical/mental health advice, and (b) the lack of ongoing treatment for AD/HD. Alternative methods can fill this void. The quality of the information shared during an assessment should lead to accurate recommendations about who should be involved in ongoing treatment. For example, if parents have significant marital difficulties, or are overly punitive in their management, it is critical that this information be shared with the assessing clinician. If it is not, then the assessor will be unaware of the 'real' issues and the quality of the assessment will be compromised. In addition, the entire diagnostic-treatment process is jeopardised (the evaluating professional may make an incorrect diagnosis and incorrectly recommend a treatment approach that is not warranted). Ultimately, the child's welfare is compromised.

5. How should I approach my child's school about an assessment?

In the majority of cases, this will not be an issue, as the classroom teacher is likely to suggest an assessment to parents. If a teacher (or teachers) have not approached parents, but parent concern is significant, there is no reason to delay with an assessment. The vast majority of teachers are aware of a child's need for an assessment and are supportive of it. If there are differences in parent and teacher perceptions about a child's behaviour or learning, such differences are not surprising. There are substantial differences in the home and school environments, and it is not unusual when behaviour difficulties are more prominent in one situation relative to the other. There are different expectations at school and home, different relationships, different activities, different social structures, etc.

However, there are core activities which must be done at home and school – usually a child must stay seated for some period (e.g., meals), there is the expectation that the child can engage in mental work (most children typically do some homework), being organised, getting along with others, etc. If AD/HD is genuinely present, then both parents and teachers will observe the same problems, such as avoiding mental work, not able to stay on task for any significant period, unable to complete work, flitting from activity to activity, having trouble remaining still, not able to relax or be quiet, and so on.

6. What are the implications of an assessment for my child's education?

The implications of an assessment for a child's educational programming are immense. There are educational provisions for children with AD/HD, namely resource teacher allocation. Other provisions may apply depending on the severity of the problem, the child's learning profile, and the degree to which other problems co-exist with AD/HD.

In addition, a psychologist's report may outline general teaching programmes and tips for teachers in order to assist the child with AD/HD.

7. Is there any conclusive way of determining whether a child has AD/HD?

No! There is no diagnostic device, such as a blood test, X-Ray, MRI or other medical procedure that unequivocally detects AD/HD. AD/HD is not like more medically exact health problems, such as cancer, heart problems, eye/ear disease, etc. Thus, any diagnosis of AD/HD will be tentative. This caveat must be fully understood, because it introduces error into the process – diagnosticians can make incorrect conclusions. Ultimately, the best that professionals can do is conduct a comprehensive assessment, using as many evaluation procedures as possible, and selecting the most valid measures available.

8. As a parent, how should I participate in the assessment?

The assessing professional will gather information from parents, as was discussed in Chapter 4. While Chapter 4 discussed what types of information will be requested, what is more important is how parents approach the parent meeting. If parents approach the discussion in a guarded, 'edit-mode' manner, then valuable information will not be shared and the quality of the assessment is necessarily compromised. For example, if parents are 'hiding' a volatile relationship, if they are embarrassed about sharing their feelings about their teenagers sexual orientation, etc., these omitted details will hinder an accurate assessment. The point is that parents should openly and honestly discuss any area that they feel may be related to their child's presenting problem.

Let me continue this discussion, because it is so central to 'straight-talk'. One problem that parents may be remiss to discuss is the amount of quality time spent with the child. For example, parents may both work late and have very little interaction with their children on a day-to-day basis. After school, children may be with minders until the evening. At that point all the night-time routines set in so there is little time for enjoyment, casual conversation, fun/games, etc. Some children may adapt to this situation better than others, and the children who do not adapt so well may act out. This acting out behaviour (perhaps reflecting the child's frustration, anger, etc.) is then misinterpreted as AD/HD

This situation came to my attention recently, when a parent informed that he had noticed an improvement in his son's behaviour as a function of altering his work schedule. His work schedule was adjusted because of ongoing school problems which eventually led to expulsion. Without school, the teenager needed supervision, and parents adjusted their busy schedules to provide more frequent contact. As a result, behaviour improved.

Parents may not be able to see the connection between lack of quality time and children's behaviour, because the gradual increase in work responsibilities is insidious and almost imperceptible. Nonetheless, it is important for parents to consider the possibility that a decrease in time at home may be relevant and to share this concern with the assessing clinician.

Another issue is that children with AD/HD relate differently to their mothers and fathers. It is well known that children with AD/HD are less difficult for their dads relative to their moms. Barkley cites a number of reasons for this but the following two are of specific interest. One is the different way in which mothers and fathers react to negative behaviour. In general, mothers tend to reason with the child while fathers are more inclined to act (e.g., discipline). A second factor is that mothers tend to spend more time managing homework, making requests of the child, etc., relative to fathers. Thus, mothers are more likely to witness behavioural difficulties relative to fathers. If parents are aware of these types of differences in contact and behavioural management, these differences should be noted during an assessment. By providing this information, the assessor will be able to make more useful recommendations.

Then there are relational issues which parents do not communicate, perhaps because they do not recognise them. These are the more subtle, long-standing patterns in parent-child affection relative to parent-child detachment. Day-to-day interactions may speak of rejection and hostility, even though the assessing clinician may never know this.

For example, many years ago, when I lived in the USA, I can think of one case where a child was referred for difficult behaviour, namely teasing and disrupting other children. My conclusion was that the child showed some indications of AD/HD but these behaviours were not of significant breadth or severity to warrant a formal diagnosis of same.

Several years later, I made acquaintance with people who

lived near the child in question (in fact, their children were often teased by the child in question). These acquaintances provided an interesting account of the family's day-to-day lifestyle (never knowing I had assessed the child being discussed). The gist of their observations were that the parents tended to be aloof and distant from their children. If this was true, then this parent-child relational pattern could account for the type of behavioural difficulty leading to the child's assessment (e.g., child's negative behaviour reinterpreted as a way to get parental attention). However, it is unlikely that parents would have insight into this type of negative relationship pattern. And, not having this information, the evaluator would draw conclusions that would not be entirely accurate

9. Is there a known cause of AD/HD?

There in no unequivocally known cause of AD/HD. However, there is a large and ever-expanding scientific data base which points to genetic and biological determinants of AD/HD (refer to Chapter 3). The genetic link refers to the heritability of AD/HD while the biological roots of AD/HD refers to the most likely neuro-chemicals and brain sites associated with the disorder. What does this all mean in practical terms?

Regarding genetics, it is essential that parents (most likely dads), evaluate their history in light of AD/HD. Can parents recognise an AD/HD pattern as children, and perhaps with some residual effects continuing to present? What is the current status of these same behaviours – do you consider yourself restless, unable to concentrate for long, have a disdain for sustained mental work (e.g., reading), find it difficult to complete projects, make rash and impulsive decisions, etc.?

For adults, it is often the case that AD/HD was never detected because the problem was heretofore unrecognised. I often hear parents, especially fathers, relate a similar pattern in their history when discussing their child's present difficulties. It is also interesting to note that many of these adult males are self-employed, or

employed in positions which are active, outdoor and involve frequent moving around (e.g., travel). There continues to be a dislike
for sedentary activities (e.g., reading, doing paperwork, sitting for
extended periods, etc.) and a corollary joy of being on the go, out-
doors and involved in physical labour. For example, in some cases,
a mother will report that her husband could not attend a two-hour
meeting because he would find it difficult to sit and concentrate
for that period of time. Similarly, it is rare that an adult with
AD/HD will be able to assist with his child's homework.
Relationships can also be difficult in that the adult (usually men)
is frequently impulsive (e.g., makes rash decisions regarding
money), may be unable to complete projects (e.g., try to do many-
things at once and leave most jobs incomplete), and does not pay-
attention to details or/mundane tasks (e.g., domestic jobs).

If fathers (and sometimes mothers) can identify with the brief
pattern just outlined, this identification is important in two ways.
First, it assists in identifying children with the same pattern.
Second, and overlaying the genetic component, is the learned
aspect of AD/HD. A child's most valuable model is her/her parents. As a model, parents, through their behaviour, reveal what
behaviours they desire and what behaviours they do not. If the
valued behaviours include some of those associated with AD/HD
(e.g., restless, always on the go, difficulty participating in mental
work, leave projects incomplete, etc.) then children may get the
message that these are acceptable ways of being. And, to further
complicate matters, it is sometimes the case that the behaviours
associated with AD/HD are the ones which can lead to financial
success (e.g., always working/can't relax, etc.). Therefore, children may see that to earn a lot of money, one must behave like an
individual with AD/HD.

The message is for families to consider what behaviours are
being modelled for their children and whether these behaviours
fit the AD/HD rubric. However difficult it may be, it is wise for
fathers to act in the exact opposite to their natural proclivities. For

example, allot a small time per week to help with homework, finish the job(s) that is (are) incomplete by not taking on any new projects until the previous ones are done. Do not enter into any new proposals when you already have too many irons on the fire. Take on a few domestic duties that were previously the responsibility of your spouse. A few, but concerted changes can re-dress the message to the child that AD/HD-behaviours are valued.

Finally, the biological/neurological perspective provides a strong rationale for psycho-stimulant medication (or alternative preparations which are scientifically proven to enhance the particular areas/chemicals related to AD/HD). In the case of genuine and significant AD/HD, behaviour programmes, parenting, teaching modifications, etc., would be secondary (albeit important interventions) relative to medication.

Although a diagnosis of AD/HD does not presume cause, it is certainly suggestive of one. One can diagnose AD/HD based on the amount of 'surface' behaviours which resemble an AD/HD-pattern. While it does not necessarily imply that the behaviours thus classified are due to genetic/biological factors, there is a clear suggestion that medical factors are relevant. Why?

Think of the logic. Obviously, when researchers study AD/HD, they use samples of children who are identified as having AD/HD. If researchers find that samples of AD/HD children have specific neurological deficits, it follows that children identified with AD/HD will be at similar risk.

Finally, it is equally important to understand what factors may be associated with AD/HD, but not necessarily the cause of it. For example, genuine AD/HD-type behaviour is not caused by stressful environmental factors; however, children who fit the AD/HD pattern cope poorly with stress (e.g., extreme negative behaviour) compared with children who do not have AD/HD. It is a mistake to think that environmental factors like marital discord, death of a family member, moving house/school, etc., cause AD/HD. Rather, children with AD/HD are at greater risk for maladjustment to major life changes relative to children who do not have the condition.

One of the most important questions regarding the cause of AD/HD (or any behavioural difficulty for that matter) is the degree of behavioural change following a stressful event. For example, consider the following two situations.

In situation one, the child is noted to have dispositions (long-standing traits, noted in early infancy, even prenatally) towards excessive activity, restlessness, difficulty persisting on-tasks, short attention span and other hallmarks of AD/HD. Assume that the child is then exposed to some stressful event and behaviour dis-improves. In this case, it seems most accurate to say that an ingrained behaviour disposition towards AD/HD is aggravated by some event. There is nothing to rule out AD/HD.

In situation two, assume a child does not exhibit the characteristics of AD/HD. This child is then exposed to a stressful event (e.g., abuse, parental separation, etc.) and behaviour deteriorates, perhaps mimicking AD/HD. In this situation, one might see behaviours descriptive of AD/HD, and the child may even meet the basic requirements for AD/HD (as per professional diagnostic guidelines). However, this psychologist would have great difficulty seeing situation two as a 'genuine' example of AD/HD.

When I encounter situation two, my personal explanation to parents is that the child meets basic guidelines for AD/HD. I further add that AD/HD is a 'descriptive' category which unifies a particular set of behaviours occurring with a certain prevalence in the population. The term 'descriptive' is necessary because, as said earlier, AD/HD does not presume a cause. Yet it seems indiscriminate to simply rephrase a set of behaviours into a diagnostic category and then pass this information back to individuals who already know the answer. How is a family's situation forwarded by simply re-packaging information, giving it a title and then suggesting remedies?

Rather, it is this psychologist's view that AD/HD is best

viewed as an innate predisposition to behave as children with AD/HD do. The disposition is typically noted early in the child's life. The current 'age of onset' between four and seven years is a convention related to the initiation of formal schooling. After all, it is typically between these ages that children enter formal education. It is at this time that the first real demands of the child are made regarding sitting still, paying attention, completing academic work, etc. As one might expect, this is the time when problems associated with AD/HD may first be revealed. Also, that behaviour difficulties are not noted in early educational environments (e.g., play school, Montessori, etc.) is not surprising as these environments tend to involve smaller groups, allow more self-selection regarding learning, allow more activity, are of shorter duration, and usually child-directed (e.g., independent play).

10. How can I tell if my child really has AD/HD or instead, displays a lack of motivation?

There is a classic theory about the psychology of learning that simply states:

Behaviour = Ability x Motivation

In the case of AD/HD, this formula could be translated to:

On-task/complete work = Attention/Concentration x

Interest in Subject

It is important to consider attention and concentration as a specific ability, as one would consider reading or playing golf. To get better, one has to practice. However, one is less likely to practice if disinterested in the activity. Thus, to increase the desired goal of staying on task and completing work, we must stimulate interest. If a child is interested in the task, there is less risk for the difficult behaviours which accompany AD/HD. In the case of children with AD/HD, interest in a task will reduce excessive behaviours (e.g., distracted, ability to stay-on task, fidgety, etc.) but not eliminate them.

Stimulating an interest in school-work requires a revision of traditional instruction and homework. This is easier said than done, partly because the standard curriculum, with its emphasis on writing, drill/practice, and homework, may under-stimulate children, especially children who have pre-existing problems with their attention/concentration spans. Every attempt needs to be made to make learning meaningful by linking basic academic subjects with an interest the child has (e.g., construction, farming, animals, sports, etc.). Reading materials in areas of interest are essential, as are parent behaviours which demonstrate the value of reading and other sedentary-type mental activities.

11. If my child had AD/HD, but was never assessed/treated, what would be the long-term outcome?
This query is derived from a parallel question which is: How did society cope with AD/HD before the present level of public awareness? For example, what was life like for a child with AD/HD in the years 1850, 1900, 1950, 1970, etc.

Children throughout history have probably displayed the clinical features of AD/HD – short attention span, easily distracted, dislike for sustained mental work, restless, always on the go, unable to wait, etc. In fact, some of the qualities were probably admired and perhaps were associated with success (e.g., inventors, entrepreneurs, etc.). My guess is that throughout history, the majority of children with AD/HD continued to display its core characteristics into their adult life. During the journey, one would predict early school leaving (or at the least, great difficulty coping with the standard school curriculum), lower levels of basic academic skills (e.g., reading, writing, maths), higher incidence of drug use, more delinquent behaviour, semi-skilled work, frequent job changes, problems managing adult responsibilities, difficulties with relationships, and so on.

And, these same risks would probably apply to the present generation as they did previously. For example, assume a family exists at the moment with a child who meets stringent and conservative criteria for AD/HD. The child is not formally assessed/treated? What will happen?

As touched on in Chapter 1, the answer to this question depends on the type and severity of AD/HD, how individuals respond to problem behaviours associated with AD/HD, and the fact that AD/HD may co-occur with other learning, behaviour or developmental disabilities. For the sake of discussion, if we de-limit the child in question to presenting only with AD/HD and of significant severity, and with well-intentioned parents/teachers, this hypothetical child will likely have greater risk for school adjustment problems (e.g., homework problems, issues with teachers, possible disciplinary action, missing school, reluctance to attend, etc.), relationship difficulties (e.g., more volatile inter-actions, anger, frustration, hostility, frequent changes in signifi-cant others, etc.), problems with self-management (e.g., food, money, clothing, appearance), and difficulties in the world of work (e.g., frequent job changes, part-time work, semi-skilled work even though the person may be of average to above average ability, problems with supervisors, not meeting job responsibili-ties, etc.). There is also the greater chance for contact with the legal system, increased risk for substance abuse, and the possibil-ity of depression and anxiety. These problems can spin out of con-trol until the teenage/young adult becomes suicidal.

The fictitious child used for this discussion would be at greater risk for all of the above compared to the child without AD/HD. Since AD/HD has serious and chronic implications, it is wise to have children identified as soon as possible. Early identification leads to early intervention, and although the course of AD/HD is said to be chronic, the long-term outlook is brighter if one is aware, allowances are made, and validated treatment programmes are used at home and school.

12. What are some basic tips for parents of children with AD/HD?
There are six basic tips which this psychologist refers to as STICKS.

- Sensible: Use a common sense, healthy approach to basic life activities such as diet, recreation and school. Make sure that the food the child eats is more nutritious than non-nutritious, and that academic work is balanced with recreation.

- Time: Make time for your child in a way which limits negative interaction (e.g., questions, comments, critique) and promotes positive relations. Making time may mean adjusting work schedules.
- Immediate feedback: children with AD/HD require immediate feedback about how they are doing. Try to be available with positive comments and corrective feedback, when necessary.
- Change your thinking from anger, impatience, and expectation to patience, tolerance, and understanding. Recognise that the AD/HD-type behaviours your child demonstrates (e.g., difficulty waiting, unable to sustain concentration, etc.) are not intentional and that there is no malice in the problem behaviour associated with AD/HD. Rather, difficult behaviour reflects a genuine 'condition'.
- Know the behaviours which are not directly due to AD/HD (e.g., refusing to follow requests, aggression, etc.) and be firm/consistent in approach to same.
- Strengths – emphasise the positive qualities your child exhibits.

13. Can children with AD/HD manage a mainstream school curriculum?

Maybe, depending on the severity of the condition and any other difficulties which may be entangled with it. It also depends on certain qualities of the school, such as class size, knowledge of staff about AD/HD, availability of resource teacher, parent-teacher collaboration, etc.

The transition from primary to secondary school may prove difficult. Secondary school puts a premium on organisation, time management, ability to work independently, ability to engage in 'passive' learning (e.g., listening to lecturer), etc. These skills are the antithesis of AD/HD.

It is often wise to approach the secondary school staff and mention any learning or attention problems. Relevant provisions and training can be instituted to increase the chance that secondary school will be completed.

14. Does professional opinion differ about the validity of AD/HD?

Yes! Parents sometimes report that a particular professional has informed them that there is 'no such thing as AD/HD' or 'AD/HD is just an excuse for difficult behaviour'. In the worst case scenario, a young adult is referred for an AD/HD assessment. In reviewing the case, one might find that the individual was assessed by medical doctors, psychiatrists, psychologists, or other mental health professional. The reports provided to parents may mention AD/HD-type problems and a variety of explanations, but never use the term AD/HD. For example, in one case, I recall that the assessing psychologist pinpointed the parents' discipline style as the area of concern (e.g., father 'laid back', mother 'too strict'). A parent recently told me that upon visiting a psychologist, she was told that her lack of sleep (because of her child's sleep difficulties) was aggravating the child's negative behaviours. The recommendation was for the mother to get more sleep (she was prescribed sleeping tablets).

In addition, AD/HD is occasionally discredited and downgraded by mental health professionals who regularly write about such matters. For example, one often reads that AD/HD is 'conjecture', it is an overused diagnosis, it is caused by 'poor parenting/lack of love' and that parents are 'drugging their children'. No wonder people are confused about AD/HD.

When I hear of the above rebuttals, my first response is that to deny AD/HD is to deny the entire notion of child psychology/psychiatry. AD/HD is really the 'common cold' of childhood behavioural difficulties, similar to the frequency of 'depression' with adults. It is one of the most common reasons why parents and teachers seek guidance about children. As you might recall, AD/HD has a history dating back at least 100 years and is as 'real' as any other mental health issue.

It is unfortunate that professional opinion is not more standardised regarding AD/HD. The consequences of not catching AD/HD early in life can have potentially disastrous outcomes.

Disagreement about the status of AD/HD is based mainly on the different theoretical perspectives adopted by professionals. For example, AD/HD follows the medical model – there are symptoms, these symptoms have a course, and medical doctors are in the primary position regarding management. If one disavows the medical model perspective, then AD/HD will not be recognised, or perhaps recognised but only in name (not for the purposes of treatment). For example, some of the most critical of AD/HD are from the 'Behaviour Analysis' school. They take great issue with AD/HD and ask such questions as 'how many fidgets are too many fidgets', etc. They prefer to focus on a particular problem behaviour and teach people how to analyse and change the selected behaviour.

Alternative health practitioners may have different opinions and different 'remedies'. These remedies can be quite attractive against the backdrop of medications such as Ritalin.

Religion is also a factor in that most faiths hold well established and indoctrinated views about such matters as child behaviour, parenting, etc. For example, the saying 'spare the rod and spoil the child' comes to mind. A clinical diagnosis such as AD/HD may not be accepted because it simply provides an excuse for a child who is 'lazy', 'can do better', 'needs to try harder', 'can do it with more effort', etc. Parents may be advised to turn to 'prayer' and 'God' for answers.

I find it very difficult to understand how people who are not specialists in child psychiatry/psychology advise people NOT TO have a particular child assessed for a condition they may know little, if anything, about. It is one thing to advise people in what one believes in, but to dissuade individuals from medical/psychological assessment is dangerous.

15. Is AD/HD just another name for a 'Bold', 'Brat', 'Spoiled Child'?

No! No! and No! When we do not know of technical terms, or are uncomfortable using diagnostic labels (e.g., AD/HD), it is natural to resort to terminology which is in our everyday lexicon. In place of AD/HD, I have heard countless descriptive terms. The following is a sample list:

* Bold
* Giddy
* Class clown
* Strong-willed
* Stubborn
* Eager
* Young pup
* Away with the fairies
* Headstrong
* Difficult
* Disruptive
* Never Stops

The inevitable comments on school reports are:

* Needs to try harder
* Needs to apply self more
* Could get better results if tried harder
* Not achieving up to potential
* Must concentrate more

All of the above terms are often used to 'describe' a child who may meet the guidelines for AD/HD. Yet the term 'AD/HD' is not necessarily stated. As such, the possible basis for any of the above descriptive comments may never be explored. One can imagine the frustration for a child who is continually told to 'work harder', 'apply self', 'stop acting so wild' yet not be able to do so because of an underlying disorder. The child's sense of frustration, anger, and gradual despondency must be immense.

The main message is this: commonplace terms should not be viewed as a substitute for AD/HD. To say a child is 'bold' but to discard 'AD/HD' is naive, negligent, and potentially dangerous.

Finally, the 'spoiled', 'indulged' child may be true. However, in cases of genuine AD/HD, this less than ideal parenting approach may be a reaction to the innate tendencies of the child to be demanding.

Take for example, one of the most common symptoms of AD/HD – impulsivity. An impulsive child, by definition, has difficulty waiting for things. Thus, the child may ask a parent for something, the parent says 'no,' the child ask again, parent say 'no' and this sequence repeat 'ad nauseam'. After time, parents may simply give in to the child's demands to put an end to them. If this is done often, we have the beginning of a 'spoiled' child. Thus, while it may be accurate to say the child is 'spoiled' this view may miss the point. The more important question is: 'why is the child spoiled?' One answer could be AD/HD.

16. Are there other medications or non-toxic remedies that are used to treat children with AD/HD?

Yes. There are many alternative preparations. In some cases, there are 'white pills' which are 'natural' and claim to improve attention and concentration. Other remedies are tonics, flower remedies, herbs, etc. To be honest, most 'remedies' have little or no scientific validity. Yet, the power of the 'placebo' remedy is sometimes enough to assist to some degree (e.g., if one takes a 'neutral white pill' and believes it will help, the belief alone can result in improvements).

17. Does a poor diet cause AD/HD?

In general, no. However, this topic does not lend itself to a simple 'yes'/'no' verdict. Parents sometimes note that a child becomes very agitated, restless and 'hyper' after ingesting chocolate, coke or other substances. In this case, if behaviour is very much linked to a particular food item, then (a) the child probably does not meet criteria for AD/HD because the behaviour is de-limited to a reaction to a food chemical, and (b) the child may have a food allergy or intolerance. If the food allergy/intolerance is treated, then the behaviour should improve. This would not happen in the case of genuine AD/HD.

It is important for parents to have specific food allergies/intolerance addressed by medical specialists in this area. The same is true for other potentially harmful environment toxins (e.g., lead). It is equally important to differentiate true AD/HD from environmental reactions.

My general advice regarding diet is to be sensible and ensure that the child's diet is balanced and healthy. For some parents this can be difficult, especially since mealtime is a potential area of difficulty for a child with AD/HD – demanding non-nutritious food, leaving the table often, finicky, etc. Other factors come to the fore, such as how parents manage mealtime and difficult behaviour regarding same.

Since hunger is a basic biological drive, the child will, by necessity, eat what is provided them. If they do not, then there is always the next meal. In the end, the choice is this – the child can choose to eat good food, or not eat at all. It is very easy for bad eating habits to develop, but it is important that such habits are not be allowed (or reversed if already the case). To do this:

- try to schedule family meals.
- encourage the child to take an active interest in food (help select/prepare it).
- try not to make separate meals for children; expose them to the same foods adults eat (with exceptions for exotic, or overly spicy food).
- while it is important not to force children to eat everything on their plate, encourage the child to try new foods.
- model good eating habits – eat like you would want your child to eat.
- buy healthy food items.

- if a child refuses to eat something, do not substitute what is not eaten for something less nutritional (e.g., child gets more dessert because of not eating vegetables)
- use the 'Premack Principle' – 'if you don't eat your peas, you can't have dessert'.
- A more radical approach is known as 'paradoxical intention', 'that's okay that you are not eating your peas. Only mature, older boys eat their peas'.

18. Do children with AD/HD have sleep problems?
Yes. Barkley cites research showing that some estimates of difficulty falling asleep is as high as 56 per cent in samples of children with AD/HD (compared to 23 per cent in children without the condition). Frequent night waking and difficulty arising are other common sleep problems. It is also clear that these problems are evident early in the child's life (e.g., infancy). Because of the association between sleep difficulties and AD/HD, the following Bedtime protocol may be useful.

BEDTIME PROTOCOL
1. Introduction:
Bedtime difficulties are a frequent complaint made by parents of children with AD/HD. The programme to follow is designed to reduce and eliminate these problems.
2. Method:
- For children less than thirteen, set a bedtime consistent with their age. One source suggests three to four years of age then 7:00; five to seven = 7:30; eight to ten = 8:00, eleven to twelve = 8:30; and thirteen = 9:00. The first issue is maintaining these times regardless of time of year (long days in summer), holidays, special TV programmes, relatives visiting, etc. In my opinion, flexibility is needed in the summer where the times can be set at a later date to accommodate you and child (e.g., perhaps 30 minutes/one hour later). Once seasonal adjustments are made, stick with

the times and do not permit later bedtimes because of other occurrences (e.g., desired programme on later, if its on late, its not for children). Once bedtime set, put child to bed at this time every night. If you choose to let a child have a later bedtime, do so as a treat (e.g., relative staying). If child complains about the bedtime set, do not allow a later time as this defeats the purpose and will lead to further problems.

- Alter conditions to improve chance of meeting bedtime guidelines. For example, use blinds that do not allow in light in the summer. Reduce noise and respect child's need to get to sleep (e.g., do not make too much noise). Also, model good bedtime routines. Do not fall asleep on the couch or go to bed at very irregular hours.

- About 30 to 45 minutes before bedtime start 'quiet-time'. Quiet-time consists of sedate activities such as non-rough house games (e.g., puzzles), TV, reading. Do not allow loud, boisterous play or games.

- Develop a bedtime routine – the activities needed to do before going to bed – getting into pajamas, brushing teeth, getting a drink of water, etc. It also includes relaxing activities you do with your child before bedtime-story, singing, etc. The bedtime routine becomes a powerful signal to your child that it is time for sleep. CAUTION – do not make routine too long so you will not be able to spend the amount of time needed (e.g., child requests another story, play another game, etc.). Prior to bedtime let child go to bathroom and get a drink (if they wish) but do not let these activities last for more than two or three minutes.

- At the established bedtime tell your child it is time to go to bed. Praise the child for getting into bed independently. Tell your child goodnight and leave the room, turning off the light (or leaving on a soft light for younger children). Alternatively, put the child in bed around fifteen to 30 minutes before the agreed bedtime and let him/her amuse themselves quietly (e.g., reading, playing with a toy, etc.). Then turn off the light at the agreed bedtime.

- Do not respond to child's crying or tantrums after you leave the room, or to any further requests. DO NOT go back into the room. Do not answer calls for you (unless the child is sick), and do not remind the child to get to bed once you leave the room. Crying may persist for the first few nights, but it will reduce afterwards. Supervise bedtime closely the first few nights.

- If children get out of bed, make them stop what they are doing and have them go back to bed. If they are asleep somewhere other than bed, carry them back to bed. Return the child to bed every time you see (or hear) him/her up. Do not give into requests. Be firm, but not angry. Do not be discouraged if settling for bed gets WORSE RATHER THAN BETTER. Children usually test the first few nights to see if you mean it.

- If the child gets out of bed during the night, follow the previous point.

- Set up a reward you will deliver the next day provided that the child went to bed on time and stayed in bed throughout the night. Praise the child for doing so well and then deliver on the reward as promised. You can do this on a daily basis or at longer intervals depending on the reward.

- Discuss the programme with your child. Say you want to develop a better system for bedtime and that you will do the steps above (e.g., tell the child the exact bedtime you select, the routine, 'quiet-time', lights out at, and the reward). Have the child repeat the procedure to check understanding.

19. Do Professionals have to witness AD/HD in their clinic/office before a diagnosis of AD/HD can be made?

No. In fact, it is this psychologist's experience that AD/HD is rarely evident in the clinic setting. Why? When you think of it, the conditions of an 'assessment' are built in prevention plans against AD/HD-type behaviour. For example, the child attends an assessment in which there is typically high 'demand characteristics' – child may be unclear as to the exact reason for the assessment, child may be highly motivated to perform well, etc. In addition, the child attends in a novel setting, meets a new adult, performs various and typically novel tasks (which change often in terms of materials and difficulty level), works in a one-to-one setting with the novel adult, and typically performs in an environment which is relatively free of distractions. All of these conditions would be ideal in the 'real' world. Unfortunately, these same conditions can only be approximated outside the 'clinic'. As a result, it is rare to witness AD/HD in the clinic/office.

If professionals use their observations of no AD/HD in the assessment environment as a factor negating AD/HD, then a critical mistake is made. A similar mistake is made when people erroneously assume that because a child can play for long periods on the 'Play Station' or watch movies for a continuous period then how can this same child be AD/HD? Easy – the real world is not like a 'Play Station' with thousands of colourful computer images generated in a few seconds. If it takes this type of stimulation to keep a child engaged, this is more proof of AD/HD than negation.

Parents and teachers are in the best position to evaluate the child on a day-to-day basis. As noted in Chapter 4, both perceptions are essential in a comprehensive assessment of AD/HD.

20. What is your success rate?

I do not know. The question is not as relevant in regards to my practice, as the service provided is primarily assessment/diagnostic. Often, the information shared during an assessment is 'therapeutic' because it illuminates strengths and weaknesses. People gain insights, may change expectations, behaviour, attitude, etc. In addition, a number of 'treatment' programmes are provided to parents, teachers and sometimes the child. If these programmes and the other recommendations outlined in the report are implemented, the effects can be positive.

From a 'pseudo-scientific' perspective, it is necessary to define what is meant by success rate. For example, success can be quantitatively defined as the degree of positive change in parent and teacher perceptions of the child. Recall from Chapter 4 the Conners' Rating Scales which were described as one way of getting a numerical index of parent and teacher perceptions of specific behaviour problems.

This psychologist has reviewed six children after an initial assessment for AD/HD. The following Table provides parent rating results for these six children:

PARENT RATING RESULTS DURING AND AFTER INITIAL ASSESSMENT							
Initial Ratings				**Ratings at Review**			
Child #	Oppos.+	Inattent.	Hyper.	AD/HD	Oppos.	Inattent.	Hyper.	AD/HD
1	44*	97	60	74	59	71	53	63
2	62	95	77	71	49	59	44	50
3	61	79	73	78	50	54	59	56
4	64	90	90	88	44	59	69	55
5	45	68	66	75	53	63	76	71
6	69	44	90	61	64	62	81	61
Average	58	79	76	75	53	61	64	60

* = average score = 50 ('normal'); scores > 65 indicate a significantly elevated scale score.
+ = name of four Connors Scales (e.g., Oppositional, Inattentive, Hyperactive, general AD/HD).

If one looks at the averages along the bottom row, all scale scores drop (less perception of a problem), especially the three AD/HD scales – Inattention, Hyperactivity, and General AD/HD RISK. These results are encouraging, although the exact agent for the positive change is unclear (e.g., change in parent attitude, learning support at school, medical management, etc.).

Similar data is available for teacher perceptions and this data is provided in the next Table:

| TEACHER RATING RESULTS DURING AND AFTER INITIAL ASSESSMENT | | | | | | | |
| Initial Ratings | | | | Ratings at Review | | | |
Child #	Oppos.	Inattent.	Hyper.	AD/HD	Oppos.	Inattent.	Hyper.	AD/HD
1	48	79	61	68	45	67	56	67
2	66	66	66	76	48	61	47	53
3	79	56	78	89	47	59	74	71
4	45	64	66	76	45	49	60	54
5	90	47	74	54	76	46	60	54
Average	66	62	69	73	52	56	60	60

Teacher rating results also show an encouraging decrease in all scale scores, including oppositional behaviour. Score decreases are less notable for the Inattention/Cognitive Problem scale, which is understandable since the Teacher form emphasises cognitive difficulties (e.g., reading, writing, math delays). On the other hand, the parent form emphasises inattention (e.g., easily distracted, short attention span, etc.).

One of the cases included in the above tables is unique in that it involves some of the cultural/societal aspects noted in the previous chapter. The details of this child's background are presented in the following case study (while some details are altered/disguised to protect confidentiality, the basic theme is consistent):

JULIE'S CASE HISTORY

Julie was ten years old when referred for assessment. Her parents adopted her at around the age of two, from her country of origin (in Eastern Europe). At the time of her adoption, Julie was in ill-health and was not well cared for. As Julie's health improved, and she settled into her new home/country, parents noted many of the characteristics of AD/HD – constant need for stimulation, always on the go, difficulty settling for mental work, not listening to parents, etc.

This psychologist assessed Julie with an eye towards determining 'Special Educational Need'. A standard AD/HD evaluation was conducted (using the procedures mentioned in Chapter 4). The results from the evaluation showed clear indications of AD/HD and a specific reading difficulty. Subsequently, a report was forwared to the parents, with instructions to provide a copy to the school (which the parents did). Approximately eighteen months later, Julie was re-assessed, and these were the following points of change:

- Julie received one hour per day of resource teacher support for behavioural needs relating to AD/HD.
- Significant modifications were made in her curriculum.
- Parents made a number of interventions to reduce the adverse influence of 'cultural tempo' such as reducing television viewing, time engaged with video-technologies, etc. In place of these activities, a concerted effort was made to increase family 'quality-time' (e.g., discussions, games, etc.).
- Negative influence on behaviour by certain members of Julie's social group was monitored and altered in a positive direction.
- Finally, Julie was introduced to her birth mother through photographs and a 'family album'.
- A brief period of psycho-stimulant medication was started but abandoned in the long-term, with the efforts just noted.

Parents noted that the above modifications were not easy to implement, requiring significant time and patience. However, the gains were worth the effort. Julie is reported to be less aggressive, less restless, and more easy to manage. In addition, Julie made significant learning progress, namely a dramatic improvement in reading skill.

FINAL COMMENT

There is no doubt that AD/HD is a genuine and common behavioural problem in children. Despite the controversy that surrounds it, AD/HD does exist, and has for many years. Children with AD/HD were formally recognised as early as 1900, although a 'clinical' name did not exist at this time to classify the behaviour pattern frequently observed. AD/HD cannot be ignored, denied, or 'prayed-away'. It is a real problem and one which requires education and understanding.

This said, several key enigmas remain and will likely remain for some time to come. Like most child and adult mental health disorders, there is no exact biological or psychological marker of AD/HD (you cannot see it on an 'X-Ray', or find traces of it in a urine analysis). While the diagnosis will likely remain subjective for the short-term, medical consultants and mental health professionals can combine to evaluate the most central aspects of learning and behaviour. Once this information is obtained, the picture will be clarified regarding AD/HD and the problems which frequently co-occur with it, or eclipse it.

There are two final take home points regarding AD/HD. One is that AD/HD can be diagnosed without knowing the exact cause. In other words, a child (or adult) can present with a significant degree of the behaviours necessary to suggest AD/HD, but the diagnosing clinician can never be 100 per cent sure of the reasons for the behaviour. Certainly, the vast majority of research suggests biological/genetic components, but these components are still speculative. For the moment, we must live with the uncertainty between the problem and its cause.

Finally, this psychologist increasingly recognises the importance of situational variations in AD/HD-type behaviour as the main ingredient in determining the severity level. For example, consider the broad group of situational variables in people (mom, dad, teacher, grandparent, brother, sister, classmate, etc.), places (home, school, shopping centre, etc.), and time (morning, afternoon, evening, bedtime, etc.). In cases of true and severe AD/HD, a child's behaviour WILL NOT reliably change according to any situational variable; that is, the child displays AD/HD-type behaviour across different people, places and time. However, as a child's behaviour becomes situation specific (e.g., only at home, not at school; only in the evening, not during the day; only with mother; not with father, etc.) the diagnosis of AD/HD can be more difficult. Certainly, if a child's behavioural difficulties occur only in school but not at home (or vice versa) then a diagnosis of AD/HD is not justified.

The point is that children with AD/HD are not able to turn their behaviour on and off whenever, wherever and with whomever they please. Instead, the behaviours are involuntary and the child cannot control their AD/HD-type actions (even if he/she is distressed about behaviour). It is with regard to this point that one hears the most distressing comments from parents and teachers, which go something like: 'He really wants to do the right thing, but there is something that he is aware of; something that stops him from doing it'. That something may be AD/HD.

APPENDIX 1

Contacts for Organisations

As this writer resides in Ireland, the majority of these contacts are for the Irish readership. Some general contacts in England and America are also provided.

1. The Irish National Council of AD/HD Support Groups. Specific contacts:

- Hyperactive/Attention Deficit Disorder (HADD) in Dublin at 01-8748349.
- Attention Deficit Disorder Adult and Family Support Group in Dublin. Public information on request.
- In Cavan: 2 Tullach Mongan, Cavan, Co. Cavan. 049-4371637.
- In Cork: Kildarra, Bandon, Co. Cork. 021-4775488.
- In Galway: Cloon, Claregalway, Co. Galway. 091-798266.
- In Limerick: Social Services Centre, Henry Street, Limerick. 061-357085.
- In Kerry: 18 Shanakill, Monavalley, Tralee, Co. Kerry. 066-7128789.
- In Kilkenny: Jerpoint Abbey, Thomastown, Co. Kilkenny. 056-54954.
- In Monaghan: 12 Glencove Manor, Latlurcan, Co. Monaghan. 047-71098.
- Northern Ireland ADHD: 2 Dundella Avenue, Belfast BT4 3BQ, N.I. 04890-282371.
- In Tipperary: 68 Griffith Avenue, Clonmel, Co. Tipperary. 052-27057.

- In Waterford: 74 Farran Park, Upper Grange, Waterford. 051-872184.

2. Contacts for other 'special needs'
- Dyslexia Association Ireland (in Dublin): 01- 6790276. A number of local 'workshops' operate in various counties in Ireland.
- Irish Autistic Society (in Dublin): 01-8744684.
- Asperger's Syndrome (in Dublin): 01-2871122.
- Dyspraxia Association (in Dublin): 01-4946117. .

3. AD/HD Organisations in England and the U.S.A.:
- LADDER (National Learning and Attention Deficit Disorders Association): Contact in Wolverhampton, England. 01902-336232.
- International Psychology Services. Contact in West Sussex, England. 01273-832181.
- National Attention Deficit Disorder Association (in the USA) at (313) 769-6729.
- CHADD (Children/Adults with Attention Deficit Disorders). (800) 233-4050.
- Neurology, Learning, and Behaviour Centre (in Utah, USA) at 801-532-1484.

APPENDIX 2

Resource Material

1. Books for Children:
- Nadeau, Kathleen & Ellen, B. Dixon (1993), *Learning to Slow Down and Pay Attention.*
- Quinn, Patricia & Stein, Judith, *Putting on the Brakes: Young People's Guide to Understanding Attention Deficit Hyperactivity Disorder (ADHD).* Available from ADD Warehouse (Florida, USA) at 001-800-233-9273.

2. Books for Parents: (key selections from reference section)
- Barkley, R. (1998), *Your defiant child: 8 steps to better behaviour.* New York: Guilford Press.
- Diller, L (1998) *Running on Ritalin: A physician reflects on children, society, and performance on a pill.* New York: Bantam Books.
- Garber, S.W., Daniels-Garber, M., & Freedman-Spizman, R. (1996), *Beyond Ritalin,* New York: Harper Collins.
- Greenberg G.S. & Horn, W.F. (1991). *Attention Deficit Hyperactivity Disorder: Questions and answers for parents.* Champaign, Ill: Research Press.
- Kewley, G.D. (1999), *ADHD – A guide for parents and professionals,* London: LAC Press.
- McEwan, E.K. (1995), *Attention deficit disorder: Helpful, practical information,* Wheaton, Ill.: Harold Shaw Publishers.
- Phelan, T. (1996), *All About Attention Deficit Disorder,* Glen Ellyn, Ill.: Child Management, Inc., 1996.

3. Books for Teachers:

- Jones, C.B. (1994), *Attention deficit disorder: Strategies for school age children,* Tuscon, AZ: Communication Skill Builders.
- Lerner, J.W., Lowenthal, B., & Lerner, S.R. (1995), *Attention Deficit Disorder: Assessment and Teaching,* Monterey, California: Brooks-Cole.
- Rief, Sandra. *How to Reach and Teach ADD/ADHD Children.* Available from ADD Warehouse (Florida, USA) at 001-800 -233-9273.

4. Books about Adults with AD/HD:

- Wender, P. H. (1995), *Attention Deficit Hyperactivity Disorder in Adults,* New York: Oxford University Press.
- Weiss, L. (1994). *The Attention Deficit Disorder in Adults Workbook,* Dallas, Texas: Taylor Publishing Comp.

5. Training/Teaching Materials:

- Vernon, Ann, 'Thinking, Feeling, Behaving: An Emotional Educational Curriculum for Children', 1989 (available from ETC Consult in Dublin).
- The attention training equipment mentioned in Chapter 5 is available from the ADD Warehouse (Florida, USA) at 001 -800-233-9273.
- 'AD/HD – What do we Know?': 35-minute video programme presented by Dr Russell Barkley. Available from the ADD Warehouse (Florida, USA) at 001-800-233-9273.
- Why won't my Child Pay Attention: 76-minute video programme presented by Dr Sam Goldstein. Available from the ADD Warehouse (Florida, USA) at 001-800-233-9273.

REFERENCES

Anastopoulus, A. D. & Barkley, R. A, (1989), 'A training program for parents of children with Attention Deficit Hyperactivity Disorder. In C.E. Schaefer & J. M. Briemeister (Eds.), *Handbook of parent training: Parents as co-therapists for children's behaviour problems*. New York: Wiley.

Arbiter, E., Sato-Tanaka, Kolvin, I., & Leitch, I. (1999). 'Differences in behaviour and temperament between Japanese and British toddlers living in London: A pilot study.' *Child Psychology & Psychiatry*, 4 (3), 117 - 125.

Barkley, R. (1998). *Attention Deficit Hyperactivity Disorder: A handbook for diagnosis and treatment*. New York: Guilford Press.

Barkley, R. (1998). *Your defiant child: 8 steps to better behaviour*. New York: Guilford Press.

Cantwell, D.P. (1996), Attention deficit disorder: A review of the past ten years. *Journal of the American Academy of Child and Adolescent Psychiatry*, 35 (8), 978-987.

Cherkes-Julkowski, M., Sharp, S., & Stolzenberg, J. (1997). *Rethinking attention deficit disorders*. Cambridge, Mass: Brookline Books.

Claude, D. & Firestone, P. (1995). 'The development of ADHD boys: A twelve-year follow-up.' *Canadian Journal of Behavioural Science*, 27, 1-18.

Cooper, Paul (1997). 'Biology, behaviour, and education: ADHD and the bio-psycho-social perspective.' *Journal of Educational and Child Psychology*, 14(1), 31-38.

Conner, M.J. (1997). 'Making judgements about attention and concentration levels: How can we know what to expect.' *Emotional and Beahvioural Difficulties*, 2 (2), 14-20.

Conners, K.C. (1980). *Food additives and hyperactive behaviour.* New York: Plenum Press.

Diller, L. (1998). *Running on Ritalin: A physician reflects on children, society, and performance on a pill.* New York: Bantam Books.

DSM-IV, *The Diagnostic and Statistical Manual of Mental Disorders* (4th ed.) Washington, DC. American Psychiatric Association, 1994.

Driekurs, R. (1987). *Children: The challenge.* Harmondsworth, Middlesex, England: Penguin Books Ltd.

Elkind, D. (1981). *The Hurried Child: Growing up too fast too soon.* Reading, MASS: Addision-Wesley.

Fischer, B.C & Beckley, R.A. (1999). *Attention deficit disorder: Practical coping methods,* Boca Raton, FL.: CRC Press.

Garber, S.W., Daniels-Garber, M., & Freedman-Spizman, R. (1996). *Beyond Ritalin.* New York: Harper Collins.

Green, C., & Chee, K. (1995). *Understanding ADHD: A Parent's Guide to Attention Deficit Hyperactivity Disorder in Children.* London: Vermillion.

Greenberg G.S. & Horn, W.F. (1991), *Attention Deficit Hyperactivity Disorder: Questions and answers for parents.* Champaign, Ill.: Research Press.

Horacek, H.J. (1998). *Brainstorms: Understanding and treating the emotional storms of Attention Deficit Hyperactivity Disorder from childhood through adulthood.* New Jersey: Jason Aronson, Inc.

Hoza, B., Vallano, G, & Pellham, W.E. (1995). 'Attention deficit/hyperactivity disorder', in R.T Ammerman & M. Hersen (Eds.), *Handbook of child behaviour therapy in the psychiatric setting.* New York: Wiley.

Jones, C.B. (1994), *Attention deficit disorder: Strategies for school age children.* Tuscon, AZ.: Communication Skill Builders.

Kaldenbach, H. (1997), *Act normal! 99 tips for dealing with the*

Dutch. Amsterdam: Prometheus.

Keen, V.D., Olurin-Lynch, J., and Venables, K. (1997), 'Getting it all together: Developing a forum for a multi-agency approach to assessing and treating ADHD', *Educational and Child Psychology*, 14 (1), 82-90.

Kewley, G.D. (1999). *ADHD:– A guide for parents and professionals.* London: LAC Press.

McEwan, E.K. (1995). *Attention deficit disorder: Helpful, practical information.* Wheaton, ILL.: Harold Shaw Publishers.

McNamara, B.E., & McNamara, F.E. (1993). *Keys to parenting a child with attention deficit disorder.* Hauppauge, New York: Barron's Educational Series, Inc.

Phelan, T. (1996). *All About Attention Deficit Disorder.* Glen Ellyn, ILL.: Child Management, Inc.

Pollack, W. (1998), *Real Boys.* New York. Holt and Company.

Reid, R., Maag, J.W. (1997). 'Attention deficit hyperactivity disorder: over here and over there.' *Educational and Child Psychology*, 14 (1), 10-20.

Robertson, B.P (1997). Children and hyperactivity', in A. Thomas & J. Grimes (Eds.), *Children's needs: Psychological perspectives.* Washington, D.C.: National Association of School Psychologists.

Schwartz, S. & Johnson, H. J. (1985). *Psychopathology: A clinical - experimental approach.* Elmsford, N.Y.: Pergamon Press.

Squire, M. (1994). 'Introduction', in C. Alexander-Roberts, *The ADHD parenting handbook.* Dallas, Tex: Taylor Publishing Company.

Stein, D. (1999), *Ritalin is not the Answer: A Drug-free, practical program for children diagnosed with ADD or AD/HD.* San Francisco, CAL.: Jossey-Bass.

Tannock, R. (1998). Attention deficit hyperactivity disorder: Advances in cognitive, neurobiological, and genetic research', *Journal of Child Psychology and Psychiatry*, 39(1), 65-99.

OTHER TITLES FROM THIS PRESS

For Our Own Good
Childcare Issues in Ireland
Bernie Purcell

This book explores childcare issues in Ireland today and the impact on children's lives of both parents pursuing careers alongside parenting. Written by a parent and psychotherapist with first-hand experience of childcare problems, it is the ideal guide for parents who wish to make informed decisions about their children and their lives.

1-898256-81-0   PB   €11.95   2001

Reiki at Hand
Teresa Collins

Reiki is an ancient healing system using the universal life energy. It works at both a physical and an emotional level. This si the first instruction book to cover all three levels of Reiki, with step-by-step instructions and workshop programmes.

1-898256-40-3   PB   €16.95   1998